Kanga in the Breeze

The true story of an unusual sisterhood

Virginia Allen with Rosie Ndongu

authorHOUSE

AuthorHouse™ UK
1663 Liberty Drive
Bloomington, IN 47403 USA
www.authorhouse.co.uk
Phone: UK TFN: 0800 0148641 (Toll Free inside the UK)
*   UK Local: (02) 0369 56322 (+44 20 3695 6322 from outside the UK)*

Published by AuthorHouse 11/03/2022

ISBN: 978-1-7283-7579-3 (sc)
ISBN: 978-1-7283-7580-9 (e)

Print information available on the last page.

This book is printed on acid-free paper.

Contents

List of Illustrations

About the Authors

Virginia Allen is a social scientist with a doctorate in public health who has spent much of her life working in rural Africa, helping women to prevent most common diseases. Together with her husband, she co-founded a charity organisation, called Africa AHEAD which, in the past 30 years, has reached over 2 million people through starting Community Health Clubs across Africa. She received an AMCOW award for this contribution in 2010. Although she has published extensively on her work, these memoirs using reflections from her personal experience are her first non-academic writing. She and her husband live in Cape Town, South Africa where she continues to provide training online to start Community Health Clubs.

    Rosie Ndongu is a Kikuyu farmer turned housekeeper who, with only primary school education, has penned her thoughts in these genuine letters to Virginia enabling this story to be published. As she now lives alone in Kenya with few resources, all profits from the sale of this book will be used to support her retirement.

For all the strong mothers of Africa
as they struggle to ensure that their children
not only survive but prosper.

The Kanga

*'Once slavery was abolished you could dress
like a lady. No one could stop you.'*

Adija Bakari, a descendant of a slave woman

When slavery was abolished in East Africa in 1897, freed slave women would indicate their liberation by dressing more modestly, adopting the Muslim custom of hiding their hair, as their former Omani mistresses had done.

Instead of using an abaya and a veil to cover themselves, as in the Middle East, indigenous women took to covering their heads and shoulders demurely with a length of cheap calico cotton. A second cloth was wrapped around their body which indicated they had the right to dress themselves modestly, being no longer slaves.

At first, the white cotton was crudely block-printed black patterns on white: the effect was that of the plumage of a guinea fowl called a kanga in Kiswahili.

Kangas became standard dress all along the East African coast. Later, as literacy spread, proverbs were printed on kanga borders and women began to choose kangas, not only for their designs, but for their wise sayings.

Admirers chose kangas as bridal gifts, matching the riddles to fit a particular situation. In this way, the kanga has become a powerful medium to preserve Swahili oral culture and is also a symbol of feminine liberty and self-expression.

In this story we use proverbs composed by anonymous wise people over the years which have been passed down orally, as a theme for each chapter in order to help preserve these traditional Swahili values.

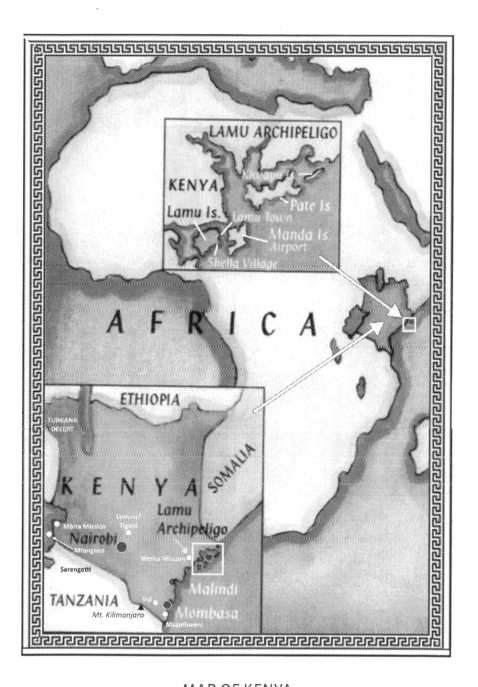

MAP OF KENYA
showing project areas and Lamu archipelago

Prologue

The Soggy Isle

'Kama Mama na kasirika, wote wata kasirika'
'If Mama ain't happy, ain't no one happy.'

Virginia: April 1986.

In Africa, the sun will be blazing down from another predictably blue sky. Here it is still pitch black. I lie awake in bed, clinging to the few last moments of calm, listening to the tedious plonking of rain drops on the windowsill. It has been dripping grey skies each day for the entire year as Anthony ploughs through his master's degree.

I shed the warmth of the duvet and go to the bathroom thinking of how to escape to the sun. Staring into the mirror as I brush my teeth, I hardly recognise myself: a discontented young woman with tired green eyes, red-rimmed from lack of sleep, my skin turned sallow from lack of light. The children are already up, rampaging around their cots, squawking for me like mad parrots.

Today Anthony meets the Big Mama. Perhaps today is the day of liberation from this soggy isle with its low skies and saddened people. I long to sweat out all the English toxins that have accumulated in my pores. In Kenya Anthony must be getting up about now. I close my eyes and beam him a tsunami of positivity, willing him to succeed for all our sakes.

Hauling up a heavy bucket of nappies, I tip the stinking liquid into the bath, wring out the coarse white cotton by hand. The acrid smell of stale bleach stings my nostrils, burns my hands. Heaving the bucket down the stairs into the dreary kitchen, I slop the nappies into the washing machine. Outside it is still dark in the little cement backyard. The detritus from last night's supper clutters the sink. I boil the kettle and ignore the pandemonium upstairs. For a few precious moments I drink my tea, clasping the mug to warm my hands, gathering energy to cope, hunched in front of the washing machine, mesmerised by the clonk and drone while the nappies slosh first one way and then the other. I cross off another square of the calendar on the door of the fridge and recount the days.

I know I will never get used to living here. I am from another planet. It was so easy in Zimbabwe when I had a nanny to help me. I used to enjoy having kids; it was fun watching their antics. I had three children under three, and I wasn't worn out like I am now. Here I am on permanent duty, and it is wearing me down. I am so deprived of sleep that I have lost my sense of humour completely. I don't want Anthony's help: all he has to do is to study and pass his exams, so we can get out of here as soon as possible.

'Almost a year since we arrived,' I remind myself aloud, 'how much longer can I last?'

Tristan slides down the stairs on the railings calling out 'Mum, Wendy's done a poo.'

I take another sip of tea, and hand him a biscuit, pretending not to hear him. The 'hob nob' breaks as he bites it, and I wait for him to howl as he always does when he can't keep a biscuit in one piece until the last mouthful.

'Broken bickie,' he yells, chucking it on the floor and reaching for another.

'No, you don't,' I snap. 'Just eat it.'

He turns up the howling, knowing this will get on my nerves. I relent and give him another biscuit. Anything to keep him quiet.

I climb the stairs to the twin's room to face the chaos. Charlie has thrown all his toys on the floor and is rattling the bars of his cot like a demented chimp in the zoo. Wendy is watching him, giggling as she rearranges her fluffy mound of animals, sucking on her fingers. The twins hug me with delight as I set them free. I pull off the stinking 'Babygro's' and their sodden cotton nappies. The little cherubs run around squealing with naked pleasure. Getting the three of them organised every morning in time for school is a nightmare, and my patience in the morning is minimal. If we were back at home, I would have help.

I have counted between myself and the three children there are 44 items of clothing every day to be found and put on before we go out - vests, pants or nappies, shirts and trousers, overcoats, socks, gloves and shoes for each child. At home there would only be three items: a t-shirt, knickers and a pair of shorts and they would be running around barefoot all day. I play a game of rhyming numbers with them to get all of them ready at the same time.

'Forty-two, get your shoes'

'Forty-three, time for tea,' shouts Tristan and the twins mimic him.

They tumble down the stairs for breakfast, full of fun, and I wish I could be more responsive. I mix them each a healthy bowl of 'Pro-Nutro' loathing the sweet smell. There is a temporary silence as they guzzle the cereal like contented horses with a nosebag. Within minutes they have flicked it all over the walls and are smearing the goo round their faces in glee. I wipe a sponge over each of their faces and release them from their highchairs.

'Forty – four, go to the door,' I shout like a sergeant major, as they line up and hold out their hands to put on their gloves. I get the bulky double wheelchair down the steps and struggle with the complicated mechanism for opening it. I don't have enough hands to pull the two knobs on each side of the chair and twist the handle at the same time. A male design which annoys me each morning. Tristan, meanwhile, is making a big show of sniffing his brother like a dog. He announces mischievously, 'Charlie's done a poo-oo! Charlie's done a poo-oo,' delighted with the effect it has on me, 'Bloody hell, Charlie not another one.'

Back we all go inside to change Charlie. I threaten Tristan and Wendy with no TV if they move from the hallway and haul Charlie upstairs to repackage him whilst he giggles in delight at the attention that an extra crap elicits from me.

Finally, I get both twins to climb into their chariot at the same time. They settle back comfortably in their bubbly waterproof outfits like miniature spacemen as I battle along the bumpy pavement, panting spume in the crisp autumn air. I curse as the cheap wheels stick in every rut. I picked this up at a second-hand shop as every penny counts this year. How I wish I had brought a new one built for bundu-bashing, rotating wheels with thick tyres.

Tristan runs ahead along the frozen path to the play school, practising his whistling, kicking fir cones. As they wobble along the bumpy pavement, I have a few moments of peace: Charlie is in a daze, happily sucking his thumb watching the cars go past, whilst Wendy is concentrating on wiping the silk on the edge of her comfort blanket around her nose, with her two little fingers halfway down her throat. For the next five blocks I can string my thoughts together. I am thinking of Anthony trying to achieve his mission on the other side of the world.

We reach the school as the bell rings. The usual bevy of chaotic mothers are racing to get their kids through the gate at the last minute.

Amanda Button, with her shock of orange hair and her little red nub of a nose is clinging onto her mum's legs sobbing dramatically, as she does every morning.

'Come on Amanda. Look here is Tristan. Go in with him,' begs her mum.

'She is in love with Tristan. The only way we can get her to come to school is so she can see him,' she confides in me giggling with pride.

'Young love. Isn't it cute?' I joke wryly. She is not sure if I mean it.

Tristan ignores his little admirer and runs off to join the band of bigger boys, desperate to get in with Tommy, impressive in his batman outfit. The thug-to-be has taken up his usual position on the top of the slide and is pushing everyone else away, as they try to climb the steps. Charlie follows Tristan like a shadow, hoping to be allowed to use the slide if his big brother is there.

Wendy looks at Amanda screaming and kindly tries to take her hand to lead her into the playground.

'No, won't go,' yells the pretty little strawberry blond as she opens her mouth to bellow again.

Her mother rolls her eyes at us and pushes her roughly into the playground after Wendy.

'This child is driving me crazy. I have only one kid and I am at my wit's end', she admits, 'I don't know how you cope with three, Virginia.'

'With difficulty,' I admit. With Anthony away in Kenya, this routine morning moan is my only chance of adult interaction for the day, so I lead them on, trying to make conversation but they don't often understand me.

'I'm going under for the third time. I think I have Mad Cow disease.'

She looks at me confused. 'What do you mean?'

I remind myself again to stop making unexpected remarks to Yorkshire mums and stick to the weather.

'You know,' I explain gloomily, 'being a mum has turned me into a mad old cow,' I put on my most miserable face and hang my head down. Now they get it. My face alone sends her into gales of jolly laughter.

'Perhaps coming from Africa, you have got S.A.D. — Seasonal Affective Disorder. I read recently you can get severely depressed because of a lack of vitamins found in sunlight.'

'Now there is a good excuse for the blues.'

'It's not usually this bad. It is getting worse every year,' says Tommy's mum as her little tyke pushes Charlie off the steps. He bounces amiably away in his Michelin man suit.

His mother yells out, 'Tommy, you be nice to Charlie now, you little blighter, or you know what's coming for you when you get home. No TV.'

'I don't know what I would do without TV. It's the only thing that keeps them quiet. I just can't imagine how I am going to cope if Anthony doesn't get this job in Kenya.'

'Well, lucky you to be able to escape to the sun in Africa. Us lot are here to stay,' says Ashley's Mum, as she jogs on the spot in her pink designer tracksuit. 'You know, I counted only two days this whole year that have been warm enough for me to wear a cotton dress.'

'This F-ing weather bloody well gets to you,' mutters Tommy's Mum, popping a boiled sweet into her mouth, and chucking the wrapping on the ground. I watch the paper blow off but don't dare say anything.

'I thought you guys would be used to the gloom, having grown up here,' I tease them. I have to admit that it is some compensation to know I am not the only one battling with this miserable climate. I am hating myself for being so short tempered, but these mums are just as demented, and they only have one child

'You never get used to this bloody weather. Just have to learn to get on with it,' says Ashley's Mum brightly before sprinting back home like a barbie doll.

❀ ❀ ❀

I climb the small flight of wet stairs to the front door thinking once again how I loathe living in this house, with its standard layout, differentiated from millions of other terrace homes only by the choice of wallpaper. Five layers of wallpaper I tore off on arrival. The history of each woman attempting to make this dreary place her home: chintz florals of the fifties, psychedelic whorls of the sixties, stripes of the seventies. I scraped off all this history and painted the bare walls sunflower yellow.

I pick up the clothes littering the bathroom and come down with another armful for the next wash. The nappies are now plastered round the edge of the washing machine tub. I pull them out and stuff them into the drier. Now there are two machines whirring away: the tinnitus of the dryer hums high above the rhythmic clonking of the washer. I retreat to the top floor where Anthony is usually crouched under the eaves, out of reach for hours while he quietly studies.

Peace at last for a few precious hours. I sit at his desk and take out my sociology textbook, my mental stimulation for the day. The only course I could find to do in one year was Sociology 'A' level, which together with my English and History might help me get into a proper university at some stage. Meanwhile I am stuck with a Diploma in Fine Art from an Art School that believed painting was dead. Not exactly a dazzling future ahead of me career wise. With my newly acquired interest in how the world works, I am looking forward to a few hours of intellectual arousal in 'The Protestant work ethic'. At last, I have found a plausible explanation for my desperate need to achieve something each day. It appears that I have inherited a sort of cultural predisposition to work hard by being non-Catholic.

The phone rings. I lift the heavy black receiver of the telephone on the desk and hold my breath, dreading to be disappointed.

'Virginia. Can you hear me?'

'Yes, yes. Hi, love. How are you? How did it go?'

'Well, it's a long story … but I think it went well. Mama Gola was so understanding.'

'What is she like?'

'She's an amazing woman. Really so strong and warm. You'll love her. The only thing is, she dug out the truth. I couldn't hide it from her.'

'What do you mean?'

'She'd worked out there was something fishy about my CV. She asked where I got my first building degree. I had to come clean—she's so intuitive. So, I gave her the whole story about us wanting to leave South Africa.'

'How did that go down?'

'Well, she looked at me for ages, sizing me up, and I just held her stare, really connecting. Then she smiled and said, "Well, that is very good, you are a proper African so I think you will understand us well." It's the first time I've ever been called an 'African', let alone a 'proper' one.'

'Brilliant. So, if she approves of you, then it should be okay with Aqua Aid, is that right?'

'Exactly. She'll apply for my work permit from Kenya. She wanted to be sure you'd also be moving here permanently. She doesn't want a bachelor. Turns out that is because the guy before me shacked up with a Danish volunteer. Mama Gola was scandalised and refused to renew his contract.'

'Well, no problem there. I will be around to make sure you don't get up to anything like that! I can't wait!'

'The funny thing is, last night, the same girl tried it on me. She was staying in the same hotel.'

'Did she try to seduce you?' I laughed imagining how flattered he would be.

'I could tell she was very available. Then the next day Mama Gola asked me if I'd met Agnetha. It was quite funny: when I told her I'd avoided having supper with her, it seemed to clinch her resolve to give me a job. It was like I had passed the seduction test. Anyway, whatever it was, I think it's on. Can you imagine? Our gamble for me to get a master's degree in the UK has worked. This dreadful time has not been in vain.'

'Incredible. God, what a coup. You did it!'

'One year, almost to the day, we'll be out of the soggy isle. All we have to do is pretend we are from England. Can't be too hard.'

'Unless someone asks us about our schooling.'

'Don't worry, we'll manage. Just put on your posh English accent, talk like our parents.'

'Well, we seem to have a classier accent than most of the people in Yorkshire, so it shouldn't be too hard.'

'You know what also helped? The fact that we have twins. She's a twin herself and considers it a great blessing to be the mother of twins. She's very keen to meet you and she hinted she might even give you a job as well. At any rate, you'll have your dream to explore Kenya. It is incredible here.'

As I replace the heavy black receiver, I am reeling with a sense of reprieve. I look out of the attic window, at the low grey sky, and tears of relief well up in my eyes.

PART 1

INTO REAL AFRICA

Chapter 1

Tea with Memsahib

'*Kuku mgeni hakosi kamba mguuni.*'
'You can spot a new hen as it has a string on its leg.'

Virginia: April 1986.

The road hugs the contours of the ridges up to Banana Hill, a scruffy trading post where smallholders sell their produce from a patchwork of rainbow-coloured fruit stalls. The mad minibuses known as '*matatu*' dart into the muddy bus stop, honking their brash horns. Loud-mouthed touts hang out of the doors, cajoling pedestrians to climb on board. Bananas grow everywhere like monster weeds along the roadside, their broad leaves fanning the earth. The women all have cotton *kangas* wrapped around them and draped over their heads creating an effect of a constantly moving kaleidoscope of brilliant colours. Many are trudging uphill along the rutted road like green porcupines, bent double under boughs of spiky bananas balanced across their backs. Men, by contrast, have no such burden but load the heavy branches of bananas onto bicycles and wheel their produce to market.

Above Banana Hill village, the tar road first cuts through neat lines of coffee bushes dangling their bitter beans. Higher up the escarpment, through the clouds, the roadside beverage changes to tea—rolling plantations of African Ceylon. The denuded earth is now clothed in a green school uniform, with acres of neatly clipped bushes stretching over the rolling hills. Wrapped in the mists of time, this was one of the areas of prime real estate, settled in the early 1900's by the original colonials. Only one or two giant forest trees have survived in these vast plantations. From the dizzy height of their branches, monkey vines trail to the ground like the mishmash of broken electricity cables that hang loosely along all the roadsides of Nairobi. An hour north of the capital city lies the little trading station of Limuru, where we plan to live.

Anthony turns into an untarred drive which leads to the farmhouse of the Hunter-Price Tea Estate. A low veranda opens onto a spongy lawn of dense *Kikuyu* grass. The garden is immaculately groomed, with islands of deep red azaleas and sky-blue hydrangeas, all in bloom. Little birds flit back and forth in nectar ecstasy, metallic green and scarlet breasts fluorescent in the sunlight.

We line up the three children outside the front door and warn them to behave properly. I press the brass button, then hear the clatter of short-stepping heels. After a short wait, the door is opened by a sprightly elderly woman, exquisitely dressed like a flapper from the 1920s, in a straight shift, with strings of pearls dangling to her waist. Her little blue eyes blink up at us. I nudge Anthony forward as he is better than I am at small talk.

'Mrs. Hunter-Price? How do you do? Anthony and Virginia, about your cottage.'

'Do come in.' She hops energetically ahead to open the sitting room door.

The decor meets all my expectations. 'Just like 'Out of Africa,' I whisper excitedly to Anthony.

Ethiopian camel-hair rugs are strewn across the red, polished cement floor. Faded photographs show hunting exploits from the thirties. Priceless Victorian antique furniture and a dresser filled with sterling silver ornaments give the room an air of faded aristocracy, hinting at better times.

Mrs. H-P leans forward sweetly to the children, who are squirming coyly behind my legs. 'Now, who have we here?'

'This is Tristan, the oldest, and the twins are Charlie and Wendy.'

'Oh, my dear, what lovely children. Do sit down.'

She circles the room, appraising us with her bright button eyes.

I steer the children around the zebra skin stretched out like a crucifixion on the floor and perch with them on the edge of a large squashy sofa. Anthony settles into an antique wingback chair, enthusing about the view.

'Oh yes, isn't it wonderful? On a clear day you can see all the way down to Nairobi and beyond to Kili.' From the other side of the estate, we see Mount Kenya. Our family chose this land for the view above the rift valley. Will you have some tea?' she asks in a refined little voice.

We nod and smile politely, then jump with fright when she shrills out, '*Mpishi. Kuja hapa!* Cook! Come here!' like a demented bird of prey.

In shuffles a wizened old manservant, in white uniform, complete with gloves and fez.

'Yes, *Memsahib*,' he says, trying to straighten up.

'Some tea and scones for the *visitors please.*'

'Yes, *Memsahib*,' he bows and shuffles out.

She turns back to us and, once again simpers in the voice she clearly reserves for visitors, 'Now, are you all ready to move into the cottage? We lived there when we were first married, and I must say it is very comfortable. Small but charming. *Mpishi* will take you across and open up for you when you have had some tea.'

Then she leans forward inquisitively towards me and squeezes my hand fondly. 'So! How nice to have some new blood. Now, do tell me all about yourselves.'

Her curiosity bores into my brain, which snaps shut like the muscle of a clam when poked. I shoot a glance to where Tristan is nosing around a display of butterflies in a cabinet. Charlie is on tiptoe trying to touch the faded Garden Inspectors lying, wings outstretched, pinned in neat rows and labelled with methodical detail.

I leap up to restrain them. She is so like my parents. Adults were not to be interrupted when I grew up. Children were to be 'seen but not heard'.

She calls out imperiously 'Now, don't touch the butterflies, boys. They are very rare and rather fragile. Why don't you go and explore the garden and see if you can find the aviary?'

The two boys make their escape, skidding on the gleaming floor as far as they can. Wendy opts to stay sitting on the floor, whispering sympathetically to the zebra skin, stroking its bristling mane.

Mrs. H-P hoots again, '*Mpishi*, where *is* the tea?' She spins her head around, like a little Scops owl.

Mpishi comes trundling back, manoeuvring his tea trolley into the room like a Zimmer frame, and judders to a halt with a rattle of cups in front of the grand dame. She lifts the fly net over the biscuits and flaps her hand irritably as if to shoo away flies.

'*Mpishi*, where are the scones? *Haraka*, quickly! *Sasa*, now!'

The old man shuffles off again, muttering to himself under his breath.

'Old Josiah, he's getting so forgetful. Been with the family since he was a boy. Never changes. We have to watch the sugar. He gets his hands on the booze too, if I don't mark the bottle. But what can one do? The young ones are even worse.' I am about to get the giggles as she reminds me of my own grandmother, a stereotype from a past era.

The silver teapot glints. I catch a whiff of the Earl Grey, tinkling into tiny porcelain cups too fragile for normal service. She hands each of us a cup and saucer, then settles bossily into her chair to wait for the scones. In comes *Mpishi* once more, this time bearing a silver salver with an elaborate display of large scones with thick cream and dripping in strawberry jam. Unused to such delights, Wendy's eyes widen as she takes her first hug bite, spreading crumbs over the sofa.

'Now, now dear,' tuts Mrs. H-P. She leans towards Wendy with a white napkin and wipes the cream off her cheek. 'I suggest you take some to your brothers. You can give the crumbs to the birds.'

Wendy carries the plate of scones from the room, carefully skirting the zebra. Having expertly dispatched the children, the little owl ruffles her feathers and settles back in her chair.

'Now do tell me your story. I gather you are from South Africa. So nice to have colonials in the cottage, my dear. The last people were expats from Europe. We have *absolutely* nothing in common with them, you know. Two-year wonders. They imagine they can make a difference in Kenya within a couple of years. Huh!' We both stiffen, too polite to argue with her. 'Hardly any of our type left now, you know. We're just the fossil remains of a dying breed,' she muses sadly. 'My grandfather started the tea plantations in Limuru over a hundred years ago. Since independence, all the land has been taken over by the Kikuyu. We old *wazungu* are clinging to the wreckage of this country. The Africans are just waiting for us to die out. Still, we can't complain while it lasts, can we, dear? It's not a bad life in the tropics.'

I stare into my teacup, trying not to get visibly annoyed. Anthony, for once, is also at a loss for small talk. Ever the expert hostess, she tries another tack, determined to find common ground with me.

'Now, tell me Virginia, where does your family originally hail from? Your parents, I mean.'

'They're both English. I was born in London,' I told her, knowing that would impress.

The classic question was not long in coming. 'And what did your father *do*, dear?'

'When my father retired from the Royal Navy, he requalified as a lawyer and emigrated to Zimbabwe.'

'Rhodesia, you mean?'

21

'Well, yes, at that time the country was called Rhodesia. Actually, I consider myself a Zimbabwean,' I said to make it clear where I stood on the issue of identity. 'When the government stopped allowing dual citizenship, I actually made the decision to surrender my British passport and become a Zimbabwean citizen.'

'Oh, my dear, how *could* you? Never give up your British passport. You never know when you will need it. My family has been here for generations, but I would never surrender my British nationality. Who knows how long Kenya will last? Our generation had the best of it. Now it is all gone. No more "Happy Valley" days for us. But - there will always be an England.'

I start warming up to the argument. 'Well, actually, contrary to expectations, Zimbabwe is doing quite well five years after independence. In fact, it must be one of the few truly non-racial states in Africa, where whites can fully belong.'

Her neck feathers visibly stiffen. She purses her lips, and looks sideways at me, saying, 'You wait, dear. In twenty years, the country will be bled dry.'

Realising it is pointless to aggravate our landlady, Anthony cuts in, 'Well, whatever happens, it is wonderful to be back in the sun.'

She turns back to him with relief, smoothing a crumb off her skirt.

'Well, you know, dear, if you are going to have a brood of children, so much better to have them in Africa, where you can get some proper help, whatever the politics.'

We can all agree on that point.

'Oh, my dear. I would not want to be bringing up children now. Thank God my children are grown up and married, and right out of this blighted continent.'

The conversation is becoming a minefield. I look at my dear husband, hoping he will help in his usual chatty way.

'How is Moi as President?' Anthony asks, enjoying leading her on.

She throws up her hands and rolls her eyes to the ceiling in disdain.

'Moi! He is no better than Kenyatta. Already feathering his own nest. The government is rife with tribal factions.'

'Which are the main ones? I ask, interested to learn all I can.

'The Kikuyu and the Luo are the two big tribes. Do you know that we have forty-four different tribes in Kenya?'

'Which tribe is Moi?'

'He is a Kalenjin, one of the smaller tribes, who traditionally dislike both the Kikuyu and the Luo, so he balances one against another.'

Her cynicism is intolerable. I rise to place my cup on the table, hoping to signal that it's time we were off. But Mrs. H-P is on a roll clearly and nothing will deflect her from the subject of local incompetence.

'Eventually they will pull each other down. It's just a question of time before one or other will get rid of him. You mark my words. They should thank us Brits. When we ran the country, we stopped them going at each other for years. Now, only twenty years after so-called independence, the country is a complete mess. In my view, democracy doesn't suit the African mentality. It's the cult of the big man here. The winner takes all for as long as he can.' There is another awkward silence. She shakes her feathery head, a determined little raptor with a snake in its beak.

'But who am I to give you advice? You have had a fair bit of experience coming from the south, haven't you? Of course, we Brits in Kenya were never quite as extreme as the good old *Boers*, but we had our ways of protecting ourselves against the *Mau Mau*.' She stares ahead into the middle distance, seeming to picture the ghosts of the Kikuyu uprising.

Then dropping the snake, she transforms again, and turning politely to Anthony, she twinkles, 'Now, what do you do, Anthony?'

Anthony falters, clearly wishing he didn't have to explain. 'Well water projects actually. I've been seconded by a British charity to a local organisation to help them with the technical supply of water for the rural areas.'

She pats his knee, shaking her head sadly. 'You'll never change the dear old 'Af'— simply can't be done, dear. We have been trying to help them progress for years. They are just not able to *take* any more improvement. Reached their level of incompetence, you might say.'

She taps her temple and raises her eyes to heaven again. Seeing our blank response, she adds, 'Still, I do admire you for trying. Just don't be disappointed if you hit a brick wall. And you be careful running round the bush, trying to help these people. They won't thank you, Anthony.'

'I'm sure we'll be fine.'

'Well, being colonials, you probably understand the great unwashed or the *watu* as we call them.'

'You mean the local Kenyans?'

'Exactly. Now, Virginia do take my advice. Don't get yourself bogged down with those children, dear. Before you know it, you will be old like me. Have some fun while you can.' She smacks my knee and winks in a conspiratorial way. 'We must get you an *ayah*.'

'Well, actually, we've inherited a nanny from Anthony's predecessor, but I'm not that happy with her. She's been terrifying our children with stories of bogeymen waiting to pounce. I'm looking for a kindly rural woman like I had when I was a child. I would be grateful if you could spread the word for me.'

'Difficult to find good help these days, mind you. The old type of nanny is vanishing. There are a lot of bad types around. Whatever you do, don't take one from the bush. You can't trust a soul. And...' She leans forward intimately, blinking her cornflower blue eyes at me, 'The one thing to remember is *never* to trust a Kikuyu, dear. Never! I can tell you; they are too smart by half.'

'I will bear it in mind,' I say stiffly.

'Thank you so much for the tea.' says Anthony standing up to go.

'Well, I hope you will be comfortable in the cottage. As for shopping, Virginia, you will be pleased to know we have "Harrods" around the corner,' she says with a twinkle in her eye, waiting for me to react. I don't get the joke.

'That is what we like to call our little Indian *duka* in the village. Not quite as grand as the one in Knightsbridge, mind you, but we can't have everything, can we? Mr Vishnam is a gem. He can get any luxury you might possibly want. Olives, feta, camembert, you name it. He has his connections. What would we do without the Indians? I do advise you, dear, to get on good terms with him as most of the luxuries are sold under the counter.'

Anthony looks at his watch. 'Oh dear, look at the time. I'm afraid we must be going if we are to get settled into the cottage, if you don't mind.'

She shrieks for the old man, who enters backstage deferentially, waiting for the next command.

'Mpishi. Here are the keys. Go over to the cottage with *Bwana* and *Memsahib*.'

'Now, one more thing, Virginia, do you sing? I do hope you'll join the choir. We need a bit of fresh blood,' she twitters, still valiantly trying to find something we can share.

'No, not really, I'm afraid. I'm very tied up with the children most of the time.'

'Well, anytime you need anything, let me know. Hope to see you at church on Sunday. My father built the church, you know.'

I go out to the garden and call the children who come panting up to us, faces flushed with spent energy. 'What do you say?' I prompt, hoping they will perform.

'Thank you for having me,' they all say automatically.

'So beautifully brought up, dear. Do come again soon. The *askari* will turn up at sunset. I don't want to alarm you but be sure to lock up well at night. We have had a nasty gang of thugs roaming around recently.'

'How ghastly,' I say, suitably frightened.

'Don't worry. This area is mainly a Kikuyu area, so we all use the Maasai as watchmen. They are the traditional enemies of the Kikuyu. Less likely to be bribed to stay asleep whilst a robbery takes place. Divide and rule, is the way it works best. You must know who-is-who in Kenya, dear, if you are going to survive here.'

Chapter 2

Finding an Ayah

'*Kipya kinyemi, kingawa kidonda.*'
'Novelty attracts, even if it is not beneficial.'

Virginia: April 1986.

The highlands of Kenya are a delight after the confined year in England, where the children were cooped up like hot-house plants. Now the pungent tea scent wakes us each morning as the dew evaporates into the rising mist, and the children spend their days playing outside, tumbling around barefoot on the lawn of thick, springy *kikuyu* grass, their feet becoming tough like those of African children. Instead of wading through the soggy moorland of Yorkshire, they are running through the long avenues between the tea bushes with the huge African sky arching above us. My soul is soaring in the sunshine.

We are out for our daily walk, exploring the endless plantations which surround our lovely new home. The kids are bombing around, shrieking as they hide from Teddy, the large Alsatian dog, who seeks them out down the lanes between the waist-high tea bushes. The occasional flash of blond curls catches the sunlight as the top of their heads bob above the bushes. Nervous of the snakes that may lurk unseen, I call them all onto the path and, holding hands, we stomp along in a line, chanting a Zulu song I learnt in my own childhood,

'Izika zumba, zumba, zumba
Izika, zumba, zumba, zay
Hold him down, you Zulu warrior
Hold him down, you Zulu chief, chief, chief.'

In that moment of high exuberance, two local women tread past us, each bent double under a stack of freshly cut elephant grass. The loads are fastened to their backs by leather straps clasped around their foreheads. Their faces are hidden under the grass mounds, necks straining forward to take the load. As they overtake us, one of the women looks up through the green fringe of grass hanging over her eyes and smiles at our singing. She has a beautiful, calm face. Our eyes meet. I smile back. The woman stops, still bent double under her load, looks at the children curiously. I sense she wants to engage with us. Smiling at the children, she says, *'Jambo, Watoto.'*

'Jambo, jambo,' reply the kids using their only word of Kiswahili.

She grabs at them playfully, pretending she wants to catch them, then joins in the marching with us uninhibitedly, stamping in time to the beat. The other woman, uninterested in us, has already disappeared into the distance, a walking haystack, silhouetted on the brow of the hill.

I am immediately transfixed by the straightforward love that shines through this woman's eyes. How different from the normal response in southern Africa - a servile deference which has always made me feel uncomfortable in my white skin. I have been longing to get into the villages, wanting to see inside the mud huts. Inspired by Gauguin, I want to illustrate their way of life. I am wondering if I could see where she lives.

'Can I help you take the grass home in the car?' I suggest, excited at my own daring.

She looks at me carefully and then at the twins and then laughingly nods, *'Asante sana,* thank you very much.' Her eyes shining at the opportunity. She is also taking a chance with me.

'How far is it to your home?' I ask, wondering what I am letting myself in for.

'It is near here, just the next village. Please, you are most welcome to my home.' She says gracefully.

'Are you Kikuyu?' I ask shyly, thinking of Mrs. H-P's rule, 'Never trust a Kikuyu.'

'Yes, I am Kikuyu. My name is Rosie. I live nearby with my husband's family. He is also Kikuyu.'

Despite the fact she is a Kikuyu, I trust her instinctively. I can't believe that she could be a threat in any way, and her English is surprisingly good for a simple farmer.

The children pile into the car, oblivious of the fact that this home visit will be a ground-breaking experience for me. She swings her huge load of grass off her back onto the ground and together we bundle it in the boot. I open the front door for her and she laughs, delighted at the privilege.

'What will my husband say when he sees me in a big car like this?' she asks the children.

This is a good woman, I know it. In fact, she is the kind of nanny that I have in mind to look after the children. She hasn't been cowed into submissive behaviour by previous memsahibs. I think of the way my mother used to bully her servants. I don't want to be like her. I want to start with someone who is uncontaminated by that colonial mindset. I wonder if I am the first white woman she has ever met.

How do I ask her to work for me? I say casually, 'I am looking for an *ayah* for these children. Do you know anyone who would like to work in my house and look after the children? I need someone with good English. Someone I can really trust to bring them up as if they were her own children?'

She looks at me slowly, eyes shining with excitement, 'But that person is me. I like to work so much for you, and I can look after the children so well. I have six children and I can do that work.' She has spoken without thinking. Then she stops realising she may have been too forward. 'But my English is not good enough, I think,' she corrects herself, giving me the chance to turn her down, but it is her spontaneity and lack of restraint that captivates me.

'Don't worry about your English. It's good enough. Anyway…' I stop myself. Perhaps I too am being too impulsive.

'Anyway, if you want to think about it and check with your husband that is okay.'

Mrs. H-P's advice from only a few days ago surfaces. I try to be more business-like.

'Do you maybe have any references from another job?'

'I don't know what that is? A reference?'

'It's like a letter from an employer to say if you can do a certain kind of job.'

'I don't have anything like that. You know, I haven't ever been inside a *mzungu* house, a white person's *house* before.'

She looked crestfallen, 'I don't know if I can do this job.'

I can't bear to see her disappointment and quickly reassure her.

'Don't worry. The job is very easy. With six children yourself you have lots of experience.'

'Well, I can try. I can learn if you can show me.'

As we drive off, I realise we can't take our huge hound to her place as it would frighten her children.

'I will just drop our dog off first at home. Then you will know where we live.'

'Do you want to see my little house?' she asks the kids. 'You can play with my children. You can feed my donkey with this grass. Is that nice for you?'

In response, they jump up and down with excitement. I can see that they, like me, have instinctively taken to her.

We draw up outside high gates and the Alsatian leaps out of the back of the car and romps up the long drive.

'Can I come and see you again?' she says to the children.

'Yes, yes, yes,' they pipe, making her laugh with their enthusiasm.

'I think your house is like a palace.'

I look at the lush green lawn leading to the cottage through her eyes and realise the vast distance between our worlds.

She directs me along one of the ridges of the undulating farmland, then off the tar road and down a rutted lane. We slosh through the pasty red mud, past small fields called *shambas* each side of the lane. Every inch of the land is ploughed, planted, or put to pasture. She points to a turn-off by a wooden kiosk at the side of the road, which is selling roasted maize cobs and tea. It is a small pedestrian track, but in our four-wheel drive vehicle, we bump along the path until it peters out next to a field of potatoes. The kids are bouncing around in the back, waving and squeaking.

As we stop, the car is surrounded by a cluster of children fanning out like iron filings around a magnet. They peer in at us without embarrassment. Our hitchhiker cannot fathom how to open the door. Charlie pulls the handle open for her, and she gives him a pat on the head. 'You see, I don't know about cars,' she tells him naïvely. She jumps down from the car, laughing at herself.

Like a returning conqueror Rosie calls out, 'See who has come. We have *wazungu* to visit us.' I am embarrassed to be called *wazungu*, but I soon realise that 'being called 'white person' in Kenya is a statement of fact, not a racial slander as it was at home.

'Wa-zun-gu, Wa-zun-gu,' the little crowd of children chant. They jump up and down, pointing at us rather rudely. Our children are not put off at all and stare back at the black children with equal curiosity, pulling funny faces.

'Shoo, shoo,' goes our hostess, sweeping the neighbours' children away.

'These are my children,' she proclaims, sorting her own children from the raggle-taggle pack of urchins, most of which wear muddy clothes and are without shoes. Rosie is not ashamed. She is proud of her family.

The cheeky kids switch the chant to, *'Jambo! Jambo!* Hello, hello!'

She shouts remarks to the neighbouring women, who come out of their huts, wiping their hands on their colourful *kangas* to see who has come.

She walks me towards her home. 'Can you have some tea?' our hostess offers graciously.

I nod excitedly. 'I would love to, thank you.' At last, the chance to get into a hut.

The bundle of grass is offloaded. The children seize the fodder and run off with her boys to feed the donkey. Her oldest daughter seizes my handbag to alleviate my burden, a pupil helping the teacher with her books. I have a moment of anxiety as I see it disappear ahead of me but try to ditch the reflexive distrust of our tribe. Allowing myself to be swept along on a warm tide of smiles, I duck through an orchard of gnarled plum trees into a clearing of red earth to a little square shack.

'Karibu. Karibu sana. Welcome to my house,'

'Asante sana, thank you,' I reply, using my few words of Kiswahili.

We squeeze in past a low table jammed up against a large painted dresser. The walls consist of old planks, the cracks between them plastered with mud. It must be freezing in winter. The ceiling sags just above my head. A homemade chair is pulled out for me to take my seat. Her kids sit around my feet, eyeing me shyly and giggling. I feel like a shining trophy in a dark cupboard. Little hands reach out timidly to touch Wendy's silky blonde hair. She giggles and hides behind my legs to avoid their attention.

'*Jino lako nani?*' What is your name? I ask the girls wanting to communicate. They hide their mouths behind cupped hands and hunch their shoulders shyly.

Rosie comes back into the room, pushing her husband before her. He removes his shoes before entering the shack.

'Okay, Mama, this is my husband, Kimendi.'

He leans forward respectfully and shakes my hand. I note the feel of tough skin, the thickness of fingers used to manual work. He is a good-looking man with regular features.

'Good afternoon, *Memsahib*,' he says in English, addressing me respectfully.

'Hello. My name is Virginia,' I say, deliberately, ignoring the elevation he has given me.

'Welcome. *Karibu sana.*'

Rosie comes back with our two boys to sit next to me at the table. Kimendi lines up his six children according to their age and introduces them to me formally, calling out their names. The oldest boy is a stocky teenager of about sixteen, called Ezekiah, rather like his father. Two slender girls, Faith and Mabel, who resemble Rosie, are introduced next, followed by three smaller boys, Joseph, Tomas, and Kariuki. I notice the smallest boy, Kariuki, is the most bright-eyed with his mother's winning smile.

'What a lovely family.' I say, hoping this is the start of many times with them.

Kimendi laughs charmingly, the embodiment of a happy husband. He too is very relaxed with me, and I warm to him immediately as I am inclined to take people at face value. He tells me he is a carpenter and works at the factory nearby. Outside, a cloud of smoke billows from the open fire where Rosie is boiling some water in a large black pot. I am absorbing every moment of this rare time, already thinking of Rosie as an *ayah*, our children getting to know each other. She will be my guide to local ways.

Tristan, his mischievous dark eyes alive with fun, picks up a battered guitar in the corner and starts fiddling with the strings.

'Can you play a song?' Tristan asks Kimendi.

African children would not dare address their elders so directly, but the kindly man takes it in good heart. He reaches for the guitar, tunes it, then strums a jive rhythm, humming quietly while his kids clap in unison. From outside, Rosie starts singing along. She appears through the smoky haze in the doorway, beating a long log of a drum, combining gaiety with a shy amusement at her own audacity. Lit up in an aura of smoky light, her head is thrown back in delight as she sings, showing a set of regular white teeth. Her two daughters catch her mood. In an instant, they switch from inhibited adolescents to mystic sprites. They begin to invoke God in a high-pitched rhythmic church song of praise. I try to join in, clapping my hands self-consciously with stiff Anglo-Saxon movements. When the water boils, Rosie disappears outside to make tea.

Then the traditional hand-washing ritual begins. The two girls squeeze round the tiny room, now filled to capacity. One girl pours water over my hands into a large plastic bowl. The other, like a well-trained sacristan serving a priest, passes me a folded towel to dry my hands. Each child in turn cups their dirty little hands for a small dribble of the precious liquid. Ever conscious of the shortage of water in Kenya, I ask Kimendi, 'Do you have a tap for running water in this village?'

'Oh no. The water is far. Mama carries it here every day from the river in the valley,' he says proudly. 'She goes three times each day to get water.'

'Three times a day? But it's a very steep path to the valley.'

'It is hard work for the ladies, yes. Especially when it rains, as the path is very slippery. But what can I do?'

He sighs as if he himself has to carry the heavy burden of a 20-litre bucket of water on his own head.

I mentally calculate that the amount we have just consumed with tea and handwashing represents at least an hour's walk to the water source and back. Her load of elephant grass was easy by comparison.

On the table are immaculate white cotton mats which match the antimacassars on the backs of the chairs. Two plates of cheap biscuits are placed on the table mats. An enamel mug of steaming hot, sweet, milky tea is passed to me. Glasses of juice are given to the children. There is an awkward pause as no one touches the food, except our children who have helped themselves and are munching unconcerned, delighted to have the food.

Rosie says, 'I think, um ... Can I thank God for the food?'

Unaccustomed to saying grace before meals, I put my hands together, pretending to be religious, but the children know what is expected as they say their prayers with Anthony. All heads bow and small eyes are squeezed tightly shut as Rosie takes a deep breath. She raises her hands and intones in ever-increasing urgency and volume:

'Dear Lord God, we thank you for our new friends who have come today to share our food and we tell you, Jesus, we are happy they are here and, Jesus, please make them to be with us always and for the children to know each other and grow old together,' she grabs a breath, 'because we praise you, Lord God, and we thank you for this food you give us because it is only you who can save us, Lord.'

'Amen,' I mutter, stunned by such genuine devotion, humbled by her loving words.

Conversation is suspended. All are preoccupied with the luxury of the biscuits.

'Who made the mats?' I ask to break the silence.

'It is my work,' says Rosie. She pushes open the door into the communal bedroom to show the frames for weaving the mats.

'What do you think, Kimendi? Can your wife work for us as an *ayah*?'

Without giving it a second thought, he smiles generously and says, 'It is okay. She can work at your house. It is good. Then she will learn to bring up our children better, so they are like yours.'

'But she is so busy, what with farming, looking after the family, collecting water, cooking for the family, making mats, collecting grass, will she have time to come every day to our house?'

'I can, Mama Tristan. I want to work with you,' Rosie proclaims vehemently. 'My girls can do this housework for me. They are old enough now. Then I can learn everything you teach me. Faith you can do my work, can't you?'

The oldest girl smiles proudly and says, 'I can do it.'

I have just met this woman. A Kikuyu woman with no references. I have just committed to her, without even discussing it with Anthony. Am I mad, in view of Mrs. H-P's dire warning?

'What do you think, kids? Would you like Rosie to be your *ayah*?'

'Yes! Yes! Yes!' they shout together, as intuitively attracted to her as I am.

I weigh it up: now that I have been to her home, and met her family, I have more confidence in my own assessment and decide to take the risk.

'Well then, all right. We are going to Mombasa for the school holidays. When I return in one month, I will come and find you, Rosie. We will begin to work together then.'

We finish our drinks and I get ready to leave, shaking hands all round. 'Thank you for the tea and biscuits. I promise we will come and get you next month.'

We linger over that moment, both linked through shared motherhood, in mutual empathy.

'I will wait for you, Mama Tristan, I will come and join your family.'

Our irrepressible children have found a game to play and are cavorting in a circle around Rosie singing

'Rosie, Rosie, a ring, a ring around Rosie, atishoo, atishoo, we all fall down.'

The twins collapse in giggles on the ground. Rosie's children copy them, followed by general hysteria.

'Too much laughing ends in tears,' I warn the children with an old family truism.

Rosie is delaying us as if she is also, like me, trying to prolong the magic of the moment.

'Can you wait, please? One minute.'

She runs off and comes back with a set of her white mats wrapped in newspaper.

'Children, pick some plums quickly.'

The fruits are ripped off the trees by the children and hurriedly stuffed into the car. Now my kids are delaying our departure as they don't want to leave. When they finally get in, laughing and waving to their new friends, we depart like visiting royalty, her kids running along beside us reaching out their hands to grab the hands of our children who are hanging out of the window waving.

'Last touch, last touch,' shouts Wendy to the kids, as their fingers meet.

'Kwa heri! Goodbye!'

'*Asante sana. Tutaonana.* Thank you very much. See you soon,' I yell out of the window as we splash our way back to our grand abode.

❀ ❀ ❀

Rosie: April 1986.

When I am going home carrying a lot of grass for my donkey to eat, I meet a white woman taking her three little children on the way for a walk. I stop where they are to look at them.

The mother of those children asks me, 'How are you?'

I answer her, 'Fine, thank you. How are you?'

She says, 'I am also fine.'

Then I ask her, 'How old are those little childrens?'

She answers me like this: 'The first-born boy is five years old. And the other two are twins of nearly three years.'

I wonder because I am not thinking that English people can have twins.

So I ask, 'Really, can they be twins because the girl is smaller than the boy?'

The mother smiles at me and says, 'Yes. She is small and he is big, but they are twins.'

The children are so pretty with very lovely smiles. I like them very much. I joke with the mother, 'Can you give me one child?'

By that time, I am facing the little girl and she is looking very smart. She has lovely yellow hair like the thread of maize when it is still not ripe. She has those blue eyes that only very white *wazungu* can have.

Their mother laughs a little to hear me ask to take one child and jokes to me also. 'Which one do you want?'

The boy is making a funny face at me. The big boy looks different because he has brown hair like his mother and brown eyes. I point to the girl with such nice blue eyes. 'Can you come with me to my home?' I laugh.

She says in a little voice, 'Okay.'

Then the lady ask me, 'Do you have children?'

I answer her, 'Yes I have six children and that is why I'm asking you to give me one child to play with my children.'

Then the little girl starts walking behind her mother to hide, but the boys just look at me with very lovely eyes, seeing all the big grass pile I was carrying. I am ashamed because I have plastic bags to cover my body because the grass is pouring water on my clothes. So, I think the children are wondering what I am like, covered with dirty plastic and all wet.

We walk together to the big car on the main road. Even their big dog does not bark at me.

I think, is this what they are like, the whites? for I had never met one before. They are so friendly. I have heard from others that white people are very proud and don't talk to black people ever.

The English woman tells me to put my grass rubbish in the back of the car and tells me she can drive me home. I can never get tired waiting to see if she can give me that child.

'What is your name?' She ask me, 'Are you Kikuyu?'

I tell her, 'I am Kikuyu. My name is Ndongu, but my church name is Rosie.'

She tells me, 'Shall I show you where my house is, so that you can come and visit me?' I say, 'Yes, I will come to see you.'

So, she takes the road to her house near the Tigoni village. There is a very big gate, and she opens it and puts the dog at home. It is a very lovely house with nice tiles on the roof and lots of pink flowers everywhere in the garden. I am wondering if I can walk to see her another time, because it is not a place for poor people.

Then she says I can come and work for her and I don't believe what she is saying, as she can maybe hear my mind thinking. I am wondering how she knows that is what I was wanting, I was thinking of asking her for work, when I stopped. But I cannot say such things to her without fear, because I don't even know her. I tell her, I don't even know what it is like inside the English people's house and how to do such things that they do. Then I tell her that I can't work, because I never stay in a real house with electricity.

When the English woman hears that, she laughs so much and she tells me, 'I will stay working with you for one or two weeks to show you everything until you are used to it and also how to stay nicely with the children so you can teach them well.'

When I hear that I will be with her, I accept it, but my heart is still fearing about the electricity. I start wondering: English people is so kind, more than anyone else in the world, except God himself, because he is the Creator of all.

So, I ask myself quietly in my heart: Lord, did you give all your love to the English people? Is it why they are so very rich, and we are poor? They are full of mercy, when our people are so full of jealousy, they can kill you for a shilling. These ones have big hearts. All the time I am thinking about how English people really are. She is still driving. She does not know that I'm thinking about her.

Then we arrive at my road. I ask her, 'Do you want to come and see my home?'

She says, 'Yes. I like to know where you live.'

So, I tell her to keep on driving on the small path to my home. The big car can drive anywhere, even over the fields. Then they met my children and stay with us in my home and so it comes to be a very happy day.

At that time, I am thinking, what can I give them?

I was sewing some white tablecloths that were very lady-like. I give one big one to the English woman, and three little ones to the children. Also, my children find some plums to give to them and it becomes such a wonderful day.

Chapter 3

Big Mama

'*Kipya kinyemi, kingawa kidonda.*'
'Novelty attracts, even if it is not beneficial.'

Virginia: May. 1986.

An intense blue African sky meets the parched scrubland where a moving puff of rust red dust billows up behind our old Land Cruiser. I am scanning the sky above the grey thorn trees, which pass in a blur. The children are hot and squabbling after a long five-hour drive from Nairobi.

'Who is going to be the first to see Mt. Kilimanjaro?' I challenge them to keep them amused.

'You will be very lucky to see it. It's usually covered by clouds,' Anthony tells them.

Determined to see this mystical mountain on the equator, the kids are craning their heads out of the window as we bump along, oblivious of the dust. Then I see 'Kili' just for one fleeting moment, barely perceptible. 'Where? where?' the kids chirp.

High above the heat haze, the towering cloud parts to reveal a blue volcanic cone edged with a thumbnail of pure white. The highest mountain in Africa with snow right on the equator.

'Wow, what a sight. To think we have climbed to the top and walked around the crater, thick with snow,' Anthony reminisces.

'I want to climb Kili when I am big,' announces Tristan.

'Well, you have been up there already,' I tell him. 'When you were a tiny peanut in my tummy, I carried you up!'

'That's quite true,' adds Anthony,' before you were born Mum and I climbed Kili when she was 4 months pregnant with you, so you got a free ride to the top without even knowing how lucky you were.'

Tristan is beaming with an explorer's sense of conquest, 'I have been to the top of Kili, Kili, Kili,' he taunts his little brother and sister, who look sick with envy.

The bushland thickens into a forest of lime-green acacias. Anthony pulls up outside a small bungalow hidden in a forest of indigenous trees. We have come to the home of Mama Gola, the executive director of our organisation. It is the first time we have ever been invited to the home of a professional Kenyan. I have only met Mama Gola once, on arrival, but now I'm to meet her on her home ground. Anthony tells me that it is another test to find out if we are indeed 'real Africans'. I am nervous for this first meeting because we have to pretend to be English, which isn't easy for me. The kids might give us away.

'Children, now listen carefully, you know Mama Gola is Dad's boss, right.'

'Is she really the boss lady, Dad?' asked Tristan, 'You said you were your own boss, Dad.'

'Is she a very bossy lady, Dad?' chips in Charlie, 'like Mum?'

'That's enough Charlie. You are to be quiet and not keep making remarks, okay? Just do what you are told without comments. And remember to say thank you for everything.'

'If you are good, she might invite us again. It's very important that Mama Gola likes our family or Dad will lose his job. And listen to me all of you: If you don't behave this time, it will be the last time we will take you on safari, understood? Next time you will stay at home.'

'We can't stay at home because there is no one to look after us.' Tristan notes triumphantly.

'Well, there soon will be. Rosie is coming to stay with us, and then I will be off round the country having adventures with Dad. So, if you want to come with us, you all have to be very good.'

Mama Gola is outside her home ready to greet us, dressed in a flamboyant orange kaftan with an extravagant twist of glittering orange satin wrapped regally around her head.

'Anthony, Virginia, *karibu sana*. Did you have a good journey?' She pulls us both into a motherly hug, engulfing us in her ample bosom. Then, she makes a show of shaking hands with the children, who respond with great presence. Her husband comes out of the house to meet us and shakes our hands with a gentle touch.

'This is Desmond, my dear husband. My tower of strength.' He is much smaller than her and self-depreciating in his movements, standing back as she bustles us into the front door.

'Come in. Welcome to our humble home.'

She indicates that we should sit down on huge leather armchairs around an ornate coffee table where tea and currant buns await.

In comes a smaller version of Mama Gola, her sister. She is in a sombre kaftan and is much quieter than her extrovert twin.

'Come children let's wash your hands now so you can eat.' She takes the jug from Mercy and pours the water over their hands.

The kids wade into these delights, which are never usually allowed.

'Good, good. Eat up, children. You must grow big and strong like me,' she says stroking Wendy's long blonde hair. 'When you have finished, I will take you to see all my animals: cows, goats and chickens, all for the pot. Then we go to the meeting.'

'Do you live nearby?' I ask, searching for conversation with Mercy.

'I live in our family home in the hills of Taveta, near here. I look after our father there. He is now farming in his retirement but, before, he was a policeman. After school I stayed there.'

'Mercy was the good one that stayed at home. But me, I wanted to change the world.'

'Yes, this one, she is a fighter,' says Mama Mercy, with an admiring look at her sister. 'My sister was very naughty at school, but very smart.'

'We went to a Catholic convent. It was a very good school and I owe the nuns a lot,' adds Mama Gola.

Then I blurt out naïvely, 'I also went to a Catholic convent, in Rhodesia. Anthony was at the Jesuit brother school. His parents sent him up to boarding school in Rhodesia from South Africa.'

'Really?' says Mama Mercy curiously. 'So, he grew up in South Africa? And you grew up in Rhodesia? I thought you were English?'

Anthony looks shocked and tries to cover up my gaffe. 'Well, we are British, *really*. We were both born in the UK, but our parents were working in South Africa, just for a short while, when we were at school,' he dissembles quickly.

Mama Gola exchanges a knowing glance with him.

'People in Kenya think all whites from South Africa are racists. If the authorities find out you are from the south, our organisation would be under suspicion as well.' Mama Gola says sternly. 'Virginia, you must be more careful. I took a risk employing Anthony only because he assured me you would be careful. You do know it will be the end of your contract if anyone here finds out he is South African?'

Heat rises up my neck and across my face.

Mercy brushes it aside. 'Don't worry dear, you are with friends here. But you must be very careful. In Kenya, everybody is trying to trip up the other, especially if they are from another tribe. You will soon get used to it. Come with me and I will show you what we are preparing for the feast tonight.' I nod gratefully and follow her into her big kitchen.

Three women are grating buckets of carrots, onions, and cabbage into a large plastic tub, to feed a multitude, it would appear. They turn out two pots of mayonnaise into the container and stir the mountains of salad with a long wooden spoon.

'Anthony, can I have a word with you?' Mama Gola indicates that he should follow her outside.

A big cauldron stands on the open fire. Mercy whisks off the lid with a flourish and they all peer in. The skinned body is curled up in a foetal position in the huge pot, complete with head and eyeballs. Wendy's face crumples in horror as she bursts into tears.

'It's a dog, Mum,' she howls, rushing to clutch me round the knees and hide her eyes in my skirt.

Mercy hurriedly replaces the lid. 'Don't you worry, Wendy, this is only a goat. This is our African food.'

'Wendy don't be silly, it's not a dog,' says Tristan who is staring at it fascinated, 'I think it is a goat.'

Through the window, I watch Anthony do his charming best to smooth over my indiscretion.

When we come back into the sitting room, he gives me a reassuring pat on the shoulder.

'It's okay, just relax.'

Mama Gola comes in with a parcel. 'Don't worry you will soon learn to be more careful. If in doubt, my dear, it is best just to keep quiet, say nothing. That is the African way. Only tell others what they need to know, not everything.'

She hands me the package with a wide smile.

'Before we go to the meeting, I have a present for you, Virginia, to make you into a real African mama,' she says, with a wink.

I open the package to find a beautiful traditional outfit made from *kanga* material—a wrap-around skirt and matching kaftan top of richly embroidered design. The mood has relaxed.

'Why don't you put the outfit on now for the community meeting? You can use my room there.'

'Ah, you are a beautiful African woman now,' says Mama Gola, giving me a hug. She adjusts the fabric that I have twisted around my head, in a turban.

'If you like, the children can stay here with me while you go to the meeting, as it will be long and boring for them,' says Mercy.

'Will you stay here and explore the farm?' I ask them hopefully. They nod excitedly and I delight at their sense of adventure.

'Come children, let's go and feed all the animals'

They hug us and disappear with Mercy to the farm.

In the generous shade of an immense baobab, a crowd of over a hundred people have gathered. The women are seated on the ground, their legs elegantly criss-crossed like dark stitches against their bright cotton kangas, forming an attractive patchwork. Chubby toddlers sit dozing on their laps, dazed by the heat, while their mothers fan flies from their faces. The crowd of women look up curiously as we arrive with Mama Gola.

The men seated under the awning, lean back comfortably in their white plastic chairs. I feel a hundred pairs of curious eyes turning to see us as we arrive and are shown to our seats in the front row. The master of ceremonies taps the microphone, clears his throat authoritatively and welcomes the crowd. We take our seats as in a church.

From afar comes a high-pitched ululation. All heads turn. From behind the baobab comes a row of dancing girls, snaking towards the front of the gathering, forward and back, forward and back, to the rhythm of their thumping feet. I am mesmerised. They sing a full-throated song of praise punctuated, between verses, by a shrill rallying cry from their leader. They wind up in front of Mama Gola, who lifts her great arms high and gyrates in her seat, laughing and singing to encourage them. The master of ceremonies damps down their excitement and dismisses them. They return to their seats on the ground, giggling and rewinding their *kangas*, which have come loose in their dancing. Some reach for their babies. Squawking infants are plugged by ample breasts, pulled out from Sunday-best blouses.

'Do I need to introduce Mama Gola?' shouts the master of ceremonies in a smart grey suit and bright tie. He points at her like a magician's assistant. 'Who here does not know her?'

There is a long appreciative ululation from the crowd of women. The men bay their deep-throated recognition.

'She is our mother, and we all know her. She is the one helping us so much with getting water. We thank you, Mama Gola, for coming to this ceremony to celebrate the new pipeline, which has brought us water from the hills. Please can you introduce your special guests.'

She gets to her feet and motions us to rise. Anthony and I smile and stand up, unsure of protocol.

'I would like to introduce engineer Anthony Goodall, from Aqua Aid, a UK Charity,' says Mama Gola, carefully fudging our nationality. 'We have been working with this organisation for many years and they are the ones who provide expertise for our water projects. He is our new technical advisor. His wife Virginia is the mother of three children, including twins. You know, in our culture, women who have twins are considered very blessed.'

The master of ceremonies adds, 'So, you are most welcome to Kenya. We thank you for leaving your homeland to join us here to develop our nation.' Anthony and I beam respectfully in response and put our hands together and bow self-consciously in an Indian greeting.

'We have here the chief of Voi, and the whole leadership of our project. Also, the government officials for the Ministry of Water are here. Please, all stand up and show yourselves.'

Each leader takes a turn to address the crowd in *Kiswahili*. We understand nothing of the proceedings, but it is a delight to be here. As the sun sets, the event winds up with a prayer and we are led to a long table under the trees. The children have come with Mercy for the meal and are jumping around with excitement. The women are elegant in matching *kangas* and demure head coverings.

We are escorted to the table where large plates of food are being passed around and I notice I am positioned safely between Mercy and Desmond. Anthony is next to Mama Gola as her chief VIP. He mouths, 'All, okay?' I grin back and then bite my lips as a sign my mouth is sealed. He gives a thumbs-up and smiles.

A huge mound of *ugali*, the thick maize dough, which is the staple food of most of Kenya, is plonked on each plate like at a school canteen. A few fatty lumps of goat meat and rich gravy are doled out and a plate is placed in front of each of us. One of the women rises to give a lengthy blessing of the food. The children put their hands together and pray properly which reminds me of our first meal with Rosie. Everything here seems to be done with the Lord's blessing.

The kids are given a special place with other children their age and readily eat African style with one hand. Tristan makes a ball of *ugali* with a deep thumb print in each to scoop up the gravy, slurping up the food as effectively as any local. 'Hey, hey, your children know how to eat in our way,' says the woman who is serving the food.

If we were really from England, the children would not have known this trick. I realise how hard it is to live a lie.

Chapter 4

The House of Wazungu

'Fuata nyuki ule asali.'
'Follow the bees to get the honey.'

Rosie: May 1986.

When the English family are at Mombasa for the Easter holidays, I am
not thinking about them very much because I am not really believing
that they can come back to my house again. I start thinking not to
go and work for them because I can't manage to do that job with the
children. Maybe I can keep on with picking the green beans instead,
but it is hard work and boring. But now I am thinking, can I really work
in a mzungu home if I don't know anything. I fear ironing because it
can cut off your blood, slowly, slowly, and kill you. I fear to touch the
electricity very much. I could be burnt by that if I work with the
English people.

So, I ask my husband, 'What shall I do?'

He tells me, 'You know it is always good to follow the bees, who knows
what they can give you? The white people can give us money. You must
go and try.'

Then I say in my heart, 'I will go and try and see if I will manage it. If
I can't manage it, I can just run away. But I can try at least.'

Again, I argue with myself, 'If I run away, the lady will come and find me at my home because she knows where I am living. She will ask me why I did run away.' So, I stay thinking that I will just go and try.

Now the school holidays are finished. It is the first week of September. I am sewing my tablecloths outside my house without thinking of them. I hear my children calling me. 'Mama, Mama, here is coming the English woman, with those three children. Come quickly, Mama, and see.'

I don't believe them but, anyway, I walk along to look whether it is true. Before walking one step, I see the little girl running to find me, calling my name, 'Rosie, Rosie'.

I pick the little girl up and my children run to the two boys. We all say, 'Hello' to each other and we are so happy to see them again in our place. The lady has come like she promised. So, it is the time to go to the new job and join the English woman.

The next afternoon, I walk to their house, which is about one hour over the hills from my home. When I reach there, the heavy gate is closed, and their big dog start to bark at me when I knock on the gate. I am fearing and nearly to run away. Then the English woman come to open the gate. I stop fearing the dog very much but, still, I am fearing a bit.

'Welcome, Rosie,' she says, and I am happy because I know she likes me.

When I go to the house, I am forgetting that there is a husband there. Suddenly, she introduces me to her husband, and he says, 'Hello' to me. But I fear him and start to worry a little bit because I don't know how to talk to an Englishman. He has kind eyes and a brown beard. I wait to hear whether he will talk to me again. But for that day, he does not talk any more to me. I am wondering if he likes me or maybe he doesn't want me to come. I start worrying hard about their dad.

On the first day, Mum shows me the children's room. They all sleep in a big place by themselves up the stairs, far from the parents' room downstairs. I am wondering if it is safe for them so far from the mother. I think that they must be very brave children to be so small and to sleep in a bed each one by itself. Our children must sleep together in one place even on a mat on the floor, because they are afraid to be on their own at night in the dark.

When I come to the room, I find the children playing with lots of toys. The room is full of many, many nice picture books. When they see me, they are so happy. I stay with them to look at the books, because I can read a little bit of English from school. I am glad now I was good at learning it. They are talking to each other and talking to me too, but their English is so hard for me to understand. They have their own language for themselves because they are twins and make up their own funny words. It is hard for me to answer them, but they show me things by pointing what they want me to do in action.

I think maybe the father will say my work is no good, because I am not understanding his children. Because he is so quiet, and doesn't talk to me, I am wondering what he is really like. But I give up my heart and say to myself, maybe he will be good when I will stay for some days. And, in the next days, I stop worrying about him.

Then, one day, Charlie messes upstairs. Dad goes and find him messing the room. When I go upstairs, I meet their dad clearing the mess. I open my heart and say to him, 'Can I help you to clear the mess, please?'

Then Charlie's Dad tell me very happily, 'Yes, thank you Rosie.'

My heart comes up very happy and he leaves me there, clearing upstairs. Now I like him very much because he has come to accept me to help him in a good way. I come to know that he is better than every other kind of man. It is only because he didn't talk to me very much. He is not used to being with me like the mother. With her I can talk like she is my sister. I call her Mum because she is not like a Memsahib.

Today, if I see him, I can hug him as my father. He likes me too, as his child. I call him 'Dad'. My tongue is used to that. He can't be called Bwana like the white men are always called in our country by us people. He is not like the boss for me. I can't call them any other name because the children taught me to call them these special names. I am used to making it that way.

The second day, Mum shows me the kitchen and it is a wonderful place, like a factory. There is a lot of space for everything and even a place to put each kind of thing. Like a special drawer for the spoons and forks and knives, and then another place for the cooking pans, and many different plates with sizes for different things. I am wondering if I can remember all this or if the husband will think I am very stupid.

There is also something I did not know. Inside the fridge, it is always very cold and there is also a light. I am wondering if the light can stay on in the fridge all the time. For the light in the room, we have to switch them on and off ourselves. She shows me which switch is for the different rooms. It is very wonderful to have so many rooms. Also, this electricity is not so dangerous. Mum shows me how to do the electricity. I have seen it before, but I didn't have the chance to even touch the switches, so I am learning which is on and off.

There is also a lot of food in the house so that they never go to the shops for each little thing. Many of the things in the tins I do not know because we only eat baked beans in tins. Anyway, I can learn all these things. The English ways will be like my own way soon.

Mum shows me how it is possible to have the clothes washed in a machine, which can be no trouble at all. I wonder, can a machine really wash clothes properly? How can a machine scrub out the dirt? We go to the river and wash our clothes and must scrub many hours on the stones to get out the dirt. Then I see the iron, that dangerous thing I fear most. But she shows me how it can be turned on and off. Even I am now learning how to iron clothes, which can be so dangerous. For all these things, she shows me until there is not a problem in my mind.

Even the first time, I didn't know how to make the bed in a proper way because, in my home, we don't use sheets, only a blanket. So, I have to learn to make it all flat and tidy. She tells me to push the sheet under the mattress, so it is very tight flat. It must be like a hotel, she says, but I have never been in a hotel.

I keep on working harder and harder. I come to be used to do all the work without asking Mum what to do and not fearing electricity anymore. Even I am used to the dog.

Mum likes to do her own cooking and so I just watch so much to see the cooking of English people because it is very difficult with so many things in a recipe. Little by little, I am learning how to do it. Especially I can make the porridge for their breakfast before school. Then Mum shows me how to make scrambled eggs. For their lunch, I can make *ugali* and *sikumi wiki* for the children because they like my food very much. It is so easy to cook on the electric cooker. I am almost forgetting how to cook on a fire when I go home every evening. Electricity is a good thing, I think. I wish we could have it at my home, then we would not have to get firewood every day. My children are complaining now because they have to gather the firewood when they leave school so they can't play on the way home. Also, they must fetch water before they go to school. It is hard for them, but I told them I will bring them sweets when I have more money. I will teach them about scrambled eggs this weekend as we can use our own eggs.

Virginia: July 1986.

Rosie calls us 'Mum' and 'Dad' even though she is the same age as me. I love the way Kenyans often call a women 'Mama', if they look mature, whether they have children or not, but if they know the name of the eldest child, it is polite to say mother of the eldest child, so I am called Mama Tristan. I like to be called just 'Mum' as I don't want to be a *'Memsahib'* to her. For her part she was clear that she doesn't want to be called *Ayah*. I suggested 'Nana', like some children call their Granny, but she said 'That sounds like a nanny. They can call me Rosie.'

It is such fun having her in the house. She adds such energy to our lives with an original angle on the most ordinary things that we take for granted. At times, I feel like Professor Higgins probably felt with the freshness of Eliza in that wonderful musical called 'My Fair Lady.' Rosie enables me to see everything through the eyes of an African Mama.

For example, today when I arrive back from work, I find her looking flustered. She finally corners me and says, 'Mum, I am very worried by something. Can I tell you? Even it is quite embarrassing for me to say this.'

I wonder what it could be. Perhaps some issue with the children's behaviour. Perhaps something has happened at home to her own family. I prepare myself for bad news.

'Of course, Rosie, you know you can tell me anything.'

'Somebody very rude phoned today, Mum. It was an Englishman. I picked up the phone and he said, "I am phoning from England. I want to…" I don't know, Mum, if I can tell you. It is quite rude, you know.'

She lowers her voice, so the kids can't hear, and whispers, 'Mum, he said he wants to fax me.'

Such a rude word she would never use, but she still knows it. She giggles behind her hand, like a teenager, reminding me of her own daughters the first time I visited her.

I laugh uncontrollably. She looks at me, rather offended.

'No, Rosie, don't worry, you've got it wrong, it is a new word for the machine that can send you a document over the telephone. It's called faxing. He's not being rude.'

'*Cooee!* Are you there, dear?' I hear her imperious call. 'Virginia, dear, are you at home?'

Mrs. H-P opens the door and peeps round. 'I thought I would come and see how you are. I have brought you some double cream from our dairy.'

'Oh, how kind of you, thank you,' I gush. 'We are settling in very well, thank you, Mrs. Hunter-Price,' I say, almost curtseying, 'We are still organising the furniture, but do sit down.'

She looks around, surveying our efforts at decoration, which are still very basic, and perches on the only available chair. I offer her some tea. We have survived the first few weeks as her tenant.

'Well, I have some good news for you. I think I have found you an *ayah*. She is an elderly woman who brought up our own grandchildren and she is very reliable. Thank goodness she's still alive. I can personally vouch for her.'

Rosie comes in with a tin tray, with no tray cloth, bearing two large mugs of steaming hot tea, ready mixed with milk.

'Good morning,' she says politely to Mrs. H-P, and places a mug in front of her on the coffee table.

I watch with amusement as Mrs. H-P wonders how to deal with the tea bag that is still dangling in the mug, with the label hanging over the side.

'So sorry. It's what we call 'builder's tea' I am afraid; not very daintily served,' I joke, enjoying shocking her with my lack of decorum. I pass her a teaspoon and plate to fish out the tea bag.

'Rosie is new, and she's still learning. She has only been here a few weeks. She is doing very well,' I say as I know Rosie is listening, 'but you're the first visitor we've had.'

'Shall I bring some biscuits, Mum?' Rosie shouts from the kitchen, with no embarrassment.

I go into the kitchen, and we find some kids' rusks. I arrange them as elegantly as possible, but the dried bread lumps don't measure up to Mrs. H-P's social standards. I remember now how my grandmother used to insist on having a dedicated spoon in the sugar bowl, a butter knife to prevent toast crumbs in the dish.

'No thanks dear, my teeth are not up to munching rusks, and I don't think I have ever dunked one before.' She smooths her silver hair and settles back to find out more. She fastens her beady eyes on the door to the kitchen and whispers quietly, 'I can see she has not had much experience. Where did she work before?'

'Ah, well, this is her first domestic job, I admit. But Rosie is a very fast learner and good with the kids.'

She raises her finely plucked eyebrows and gives me a penetrating stare.

'Did I hear right? Did she just call you, "Mum" dear? Surely the servants called you 'Madam' in Rhodesia, didn't they? She is not your child or a friend, but an employee.'

I get up and close the door into the kitchen so Rosie can't hear, as I know I am in for a lecture on how to treat the 'servants.'

'How can you ever discipline her if you get all chummy? It doesn't work like that. You are young so it is difficult for you to have the required authority, but you must be firm. Start as you intend to continue, dear. Where on earth did you pick her up? Sounds like she is Kikuyu.'

'Um, through a friend of mine,' I improvise. 'She was highly recommended because she's very honest. I don't really mind if she hasn't any experience before. I prefer to teach her my ways.'

She purses her lips and frowns, 'I am sorry to interfere, but I do think you are taking a risk having her here.'

'She is really doing well so far...'

'Well, be that as it may, just remember they are all fine to begin with. Just give it time and they will find out how best to take you for a ride.'

'Yes, I'll see how she goes. She's still on probation,' I continue, wondering how I can embellish the story further, to sound less naïve.

Mrs. H-P is not to be deflected. 'Where does she come from? It is important to know her people.'

'Well, I have in fact met her husband and he looks a very good sort, in fact I think he said he was a carpenter at your tea factory. I've been to her house in the village, and I was very impressed by her family.'

'Oh dear, oh dear, don't tell me you went into the Kikuyu village? It's really not a good idea to do that, you know, it's very dangerous. Let me know her husband's name and I will check up on him with our manager. Meanwhile for goodness' sake at least get her a uniform and maintain a bit of distance.'

'Absolutely, I do really appreciate your advice,' I tell her lying as best as I can.

Now, what are you doing for the Easter holidays? I was wondering if you would like to stay in our beach cottage in Msambweni, just half an hour south of Mombasa. It is a marvellous spot to unwind and get some rest. The children will love it.'

She really is kind-hearted and can't help her snobby ways. I shouldn't be so critical of her. Perhaps she does know a thing or two.

Chapter 5

Seeing the Sea

'Elimu haina mwisho.'
'It is never too late to learn.'

Rosie: August 1986.

I am going to Msambweni near Mombasa. They tell me it is a very long journey – six hours. It is my first time ever to go for such a long time in a car. Before this journey, I was thinking you can't get tired if you are carried by car. It is just an easy time to sit and enjoy it because there is no walking on your own feet, so how can you get tired being in a car? But we drive and drive some more, and my eyes can't stay open. I want to sleep.

I ask the children, 'Are we still going to Mombasa?'

They ask their father for me, 'Dad, are we nearly there?'

'No, still another three hours.'

When we reach a little town that is called Voi, we stop at a petrol station and Dad buys us sodas. Then I see many big baboons. Some mothers are carrying their babies. It makes me feel very much happy to see animals are like us people.

Mum says, 'Rosie, don't go to sleep now or you will miss seeing the start of the sea.' So, I don't sleep.

Then, suddenly, I see something. It is like a lake far away. It is a wonderful miracle that God has made – a big, big sea. I can't even believe my own eyes. We stop a few times to look and go down to see the big boats.

Mum tells me, 'Look Rosie, there is the fairy.'

I am expecting to see a little magic girl, but it is only a huge ship.

I am wondering, how big is it?

Dad tells me, 'This is only a little boat.'

'Why is it called a fairy?'

Then everyone laughs and Mum says, 'Rosie it is a ferry, not a fairy.'

Then, I can't believe what Dad is doing. He drives the car right onto this ferry, to be taken to the other side. I am thinking we are still on a road, but we are moving on a boat. I am scared but I can't say anything.

Then Mum tells me to get out of the car. So, I do what she asks and follow the children to the top part of the boat. Then I see the sea is even bigger than what I was seeing before. Then we start to move and then I think, what about if someone can forget they are on a ferry and just drive off into the sea with the car deep in the water.

Then I start thinking, what about if God could tell the water to cover us, like Moses opening the Red Sea. I see the other side of the river-sea and there is another ferry coming back this way with more people and cars and lorries. No one is worried about being on the water like this, except me.

I am so pleased to know about how the ferry can carry people and cars. It is a very wonderful thing to me. Then we get into the car again. Dad doesn't worry about driving onto the water and the children are laughing. But I am praying because I know we have to come back again to cross the sea, to go back home.

We come to a nice house, where we are going to stay. When we reach there, my eyes can't believe that there is another sea which is even bigger than the first one.

I ask Mum, 'Is this another sea?'

She tells me, 'Rosie, it is the same sea.'

So, I wonder how great God is. Can there be so much water in this world You made, I ask Him in my mind. All that time I stay at the seaside, I am praying to that great God. I am singing loudly to him in praise before I am sleeping. I also see good people here at Msambweni, welcoming me. This is a good place.

Virginia: August 1986.

Tristan plunges fearlessly in and out of the shallow water, surfing onto the shore on a little body board, copying Anthony as he catches the waves.

The twins are in the process of learning to swim and my dear husband's technique to teach them to relax in water is to play roughly with them, so they have no fear of submerging themselves. He grabs Charlie and throws him high in the air, pretending not to catch him. Charlie hits the water with shrieks of laughter as he is a daredevil by nature. Wendy is not so sure if she likes this game, but nothing will stop her trying to match her twin brother. I know all Anthony really wants is to escape his paternal duty to try out his new windsurfer, and once he has exhausted the twins, I take over and in no time, he is off riding the rolling waves offshore, way out of sight for hours.

I potter around the rock pools with Wendy picking up shells and showing Rosie all the wonders of the ocean. Tristan comes back to us and starts to nag Rosie to come into the sea.

'Rosie, Rosie, come on,' he says, dragging her towards the waves.

She laughs and says, 'I can't swim. I will drown.'

'Why can't you swim Rosie?' he asks, 'Everyone who is big can swim.'

Rosie is uncharacteristically quiet and refuses to go anywhere near where the waves are lapping the shore. Instead, she sits down resolutely on a dry rock far above the high-water mark, staring ahead at the sea, watching carefully how the water behaves. It is low tide, and the sea is way down the beach. Charlie is completely absorbed in making a road for his large plastic digger which is his favourite toy. Wendy is pottering around near Rosie fishing things out of the rock pools, bringing back special shells she has found. She makes a pattern with them, decorating the sand. It seems the children are absorbed enough for me to make my escape as well.

'Rosie, can you keep an eye on the kids while I steal a few minutes on my own?'

'It's fine Mum, as long as the sea doesn't come.'

'What do you mean?'

'I am scared that the sea is going to come fast and grab me.'

Then I realise she has never seen the tide come in before and quite logically expects it to be like a tsunami, a great wave rushing up the beach. When I explain how it takes six hours to inch its way up the sand, her response, as ever, is one of wonder, 'How great is God's creation!'

I find a remote spot along the pristine white beach and stretch out my *kanga* in the sand. What bliss to have time off. I cover myself in coconut oil and stretch back luxuriantly, soaking up the heat. I have not forgotten the drudgery of the soggy isle. I think it is possible that I had the SAD disease as now I am here in the sun, my olive skin feels alive.

'If you want children, stay in Africa.' I think, remembering Mrs. H-P's words of wisdom. How wonderful it is to have an *ayah*. What a life of ease, but to allay my guilt at this lifestyle I must pay back in some way by helping other mothers. It's circular reciprocity.

My thoughts return to Rosie's fear of the sea. If I could teach her to swim, she would not be so intimidated by water. The main problem would be to get her to wear a swimming costume.

With these hazy thoughts I fall asleep in the sun, basking like a seal, loving the warmth. Anthony comes back dragging his windsurfer up the beach, full of his exploits. He looks so tanned and attractive, as he hoists Charlie onto his shoulders. How Anthony has blossomed as a father since we got to Kenya, so different from the pale stressed student studying under the eaves of our attic. Rosie hauls Wendy onto her back and ties a *kanga* around her like an African Mama. I relish the fact that Tristan is still not too old to take my hand. We collect our beach paraphernalia and head back to Mrs. H-P's beach cottage, and I wonder if this might be the highpoint of our family life.

The children are soon asleep under their mosquito nets, naked like cherubs. No television, no argument as they drop into a deep tropical stupor after a day on the beach. This is how life should be.

Adult time begins at seven. True to our colonial heritage, Anthony and I are having our customary sundowner. We have taken to the locally made white spirit known as *Konyagi*, the poor man's gin. We are lounging beside the pool, watching the stars come out and enjoying the sound of the sea below us. 'Life doesn't get better,' we tell each other, revelling in all the luxury this wonderful country provides, whilst at the same time feeling almost guilty at our good fortune.

Rosie meanwhile is also counting her blessings and giving thanks for a memorable day so different from her normal life. She is in her room singing her psalms at full volume unabashed at our presence outside her window. I smile to myself, loving her lack of deference to us.

When the nanny of my youth had finished her long day, she was expected to take herself off to the 'servants' quarters' at the far end of the garden, to some dreary room, where she lived alone without her family. As a small child, I would often run off to the unpainted hovel which I knew was socially out of bounds. Even then I felt embarrassed at the difference between 'their' spartan habitat and our comfortable home. The promises we make as a child are those we try to keep when we grow up. I remember well the times I vowed to myself that I would do better for my own children's nanny, and I am determined to keep my word.

When she finally stops praising the Lord, I go to see if I can tempt Rosie into the pool.

'Why don't you come, and I will teach you to swim. The water's lovely and warm.'

She looked stunned at the idea.

'But Mum it is night-time now,' looking for an excuse perhaps.

'That doesn't matter, the water is still warm, and the pool is all lit up.'

'But I haven't got anything to swim in, Mum. Can I swim in my clothes like a Muslim lady?'

'I can lend you a costume.' I suggest, doubting that she would be so bold. Modesty is her hallmark. It might be asking too much of her.

'Okay mum, I can try it and see if it fits.' Once again, I am surprised at her daring.

I find my black costume and give it to her. She holds it up against her body and giggles like a naughty schoolgirl.

'What will Dad say if I come out in this?'

'I will tell him not to look at you. Anyway, don't be embarrassed, he won't even notice.'

In a short while she joins me by the pool, her *kanga* tied around her waist over her costume. I am struck by her elegance. She sits next to me on the edge of the pool, coyly kicking the water with her slender legs. What would Mrs. H-P say if she saw the 'servants' using her own swimming pool?

'*Memsahibs* do not swim with their maids,' I imagine her saying.

'Why not?' I would ask her. 'What happens if one of the kids falls into the pool? They won't be able to rescue them. Surely every *ayah* should be taught how to swim as part of her job, given most families have a swimming pool. Swimming is not only for white people.'

'Put this on, so you don't sink,' I joke, giving Rosie a plastic swimming ring, which she pulls over her bosom. I ease myself into the pool and wade around in the shallow end, waiting for her to summon up courage and take to the water. In a short while, she goes to the steps and climbs gingerly into the pool.

'It's so good here, Mum. I like it. Here the water is warm like the air.'

I show her how to doggie-paddle. She splashes along in the shallow end with her head held high and her lips firmly pursed, to avoid getting a mouthful of water. She is trying so hard and is fearless. Soon she is brave enough to take her feet off the bottom and she enjoys trying to float. Next, I give her the ring to hold in front of her and she kicks along energetically determined to learn.

'Tomorrow I will show Tristan how I can swim,' she jokes.

I get out and sit dripping wet, my legs dangling over the side of the pool, watching her every move, ready to jump in if she goes under. I swill the water around with my legs enjoying her child like excitement of the new experience.

Finally, she has had enough and climbs out by the steps. She looks sideways at Anthony who is lying back on the chaise longue pretending to be studying the stars. She grabs her *kanga* quickly and wraps it around her body, looking at him to see if she has been seen.

I look up and smile at her, 'You did so well for the first time. You must practice every day.'

I motion for her to join me, and she sits down by the side of the pool to dry off, shaking the drops from her braided hair. I realise I seldom see her without a head scarf.

After a few moments of silence she says, 'I wish my mum could see me now, in a swimming costume, learning to swim. She would be very proud.'

I realise I know virtually nothing of her family background. I seize the cue and ask, 'Where is she now, your mother?'

'She passed away two years ago. She was all alone when she died. You know, I was never with her when I was a child. She went away from us, and I stayed with my father. I don't know what really happened, but my father took another wife and she left him. My father didn't allow us to see her. Only when I was grown up, I went to find her, but she was very sick and then she died.'

'That is so sad. I am sorry. And where is your father?'

'He is still alive and living in Limuru with my stepmother. I don't like her too much. All my brothers and sisters are there still, but we never see each other now. We were ten children, but only one brother is good to me now. They say I am like our mother, so they don't want me to be around. Us Kikuyu, we always want to fight with each other.'

I am surprised by her characterisation of her own tribe as it confirms what Mrs. H-P said about Kikuyu. I don't like such prejudice but maybe the old bird does know what she is talking about after all.

'You know Rosie, not only Kikuyu people are jealous. My family is just the same, full of envy, all my siblings have plenty of it. Even white people have the meanness of green-eyed monster.'

'But I think English men are not so violent like our men. Dad can't hit you, Mum. Our men, they beat us, for nothing. It is good Mum that you like us Kikuyu, but you don't know our men. They just do what they like to a wife. You can't even find one good man. You know, I do not see any of my family now.'

'It's the same the world over. Our family is also a real mess. When I was six my parents split up and my mum remarried, not once, but twice, so I had two stepfathers before I left home at 18. My father also remarried, so I had a stepmother. I didn't get along with her either even though she tried with me. Having a broken family is not a Kikuyu custom.'

'But your men are such gentlemen.'

'Huh! Don't you believe it.'

'No, the Kikuyu are no good. I am telling you Mum. Your people, the English, are the best people. I really like the Queen and Princess Diana. She is so good.'

'Well, maybe people just are attracted to the opposite of what they know. You see, I admire *your* people, the Kikuyu, who fought so hard for independence. I am ashamed of my people because our white tribe has caused so much suffering in Africa.'

'Well, maybe you are right Mum. It doesn't matter what country you come from, all tribes have good and bad people. I don't know anything about those problems. I like white people so much. It is good for the children to learn to be friends with all people. I want my children to know your children. Here in Kenya, there are not many white people anymore. You are the first English person I have ever met. I want to learn about your people.'

You know I am not really English, Rosie. I was born in England, but my parents left when I was six, so I have grown up in Zimbabwe, which was then Rhodesia. You won't tell anyone this, will you? We must pretend to be English so we can work here. Mama Gola said we could get kicked out of Kenya if they find out Dad is from South Africa. They might think we're spies or something.'

It feels like we are teenagers, swapping secrets in the playground

'Don't worry Mum, I promise I won't tell anyone.'

Another big risk. Now I am in her power. With any other Kenyan I might be nervous, but I somehow know I can trust her. It is a delight to have this closeness.

Chapter 6

A Muslim village

'Mti hawendi ila kwa nyenzo.'
'You can only move a heavy log with the right tool.'

Virginia: May 1987.

As much as I enjoy basking on a beach in paradise, I have this fascination with the people of this country, and I am desperate to get into the villages. Mama Gola has given me my first real assignment, and with it an opportunity to dip into real Swahili life. I am to illustrate a booklet for one of the water projects, to draw pictures that show semi-literate village women how to repair a hand pump. Enabling women to undertake such a technical task is a ground-breaking departure from normal water projects which assume that only men can do such a task. Today I am going to see how women can take a hand pump apart and reassemble it. I have to illustrate the process and produce a manual so that more women can be trained.

So as not to offend Muslim sensibilities, I dress carefully in a calf-length skirt, long sleeves, and a high neckline despite the heat. By contrast Sara, the Women for Water project officer who is to take me into the village, gets out of her vehicle in an unapologetically tight mini skirt. She teeters across to meet me on stiletto heels like a secretary, puncturing the sand with neat holes. Her hair is intricately braided like an urbanite, her nails long and crimson. Like me she has dressed carefully, but with a very different message. Whilst I desperately want to fit into the local scene, she does not want to be mistaken for a village girl.

This Muslim village is one of many little settlements that lie inland behind the vast tourist resorts, which have colonised the best property along the beach front. Tall palm trees stretch off in all directions, making a dancing lattice of shadows on the bare soil. The drunken lines of their trunks recede rhythmically into the distance, pale stripes against the deep Prussian blue ocean. High above our heads the green fans of the palms sway against the cerulean sky. With these fronds moving the humid air, the temperature is almost bearable in the shade below. The crofts snuggle cosily beneath this green cover. Red mud is smeared on the walls and *makuti* thatch made from palm fronds is used for the roofs.

We are looking for the village health worker. At a distance from one of the huts, Sara suddenly stops and yells at the top of her voice, '*Hodi, hodi.*'

'*Karibu*, Welcome,' answers a strong, deep voice. A large woman squeezes her bulk sideways through the narrow door, hurriedly pulling on her black *bui bui*.

'This is Hadija. She is the village health worker,' says Sara, 'and this is Mama Tristan, who has come to see how you can repair the handpump.'

'*Habari garni?* How are you?' She smiles broadly at me, flashing a lovely strong set of white teeth.

'*Mzuri sana.* Good, thank you,' I reply, pleased to use the right response to the greeting.

Hadija motions us to take a seat on the mat outside the door in the shade, and I explain my mission.

'If you could demonstrate to me how you can repair the hand pump, I could take some photos … if that is okay with you?' I add, aware of the Muslim aversion to being photographed.

'No problem, we can show you. Let's go.' She shouts some instructions to another woman and grabs her tools.

We wander off through the village. As we pass each hut belonging to one of her team, she calls out, 'Mama, come to the water pump. We have a demonstration to do.'

Women grab their *bui bui,* slip on their plastic flip flops, and follow her. By the time we arrive at the hand pump, there are six women. Hadija hands them the large multi-purpose spanner.

'Twenty minutes is their record,' Sara tells me.

'Okay, let's go, ladies,' Hadija exhorts her team. 'Let's show the *mzungu* lady how we Kwale women can fix a pump.' I get out my camera, ready to document the procedure.

Laughing and joking, they throw off their heavy black *bui bui*, revealing brightly coloured *kanga*, like gaudy butterflies emerging from chrysalises. Some re-tie their *kangas* more tightly around their bosoms, draping the other half of the cloth over their plaited hair. They move gracefully, as in a coordinated dance, as they dismantle the pump. I snap photos of them, less interested in technical aspects and more fascinated by their beauty as they flit around the handpump. They twirl the spanner with great panache. First the handle comes off. Next, they haul up the rods that draw the water. Out comes the plunger and Hadija expertly slides off a little rubber seal and holds it up for me to photograph.

'This small thing, it is called an O-ring,' she explains in English with great authority. 'When it gets old, we must change it.'

The women sing as they put the hand pump back together again.

'That was impressive,' I congratulate them, seeing their pride in their technical know-how. It reminds me of the first time I learnt to change the wheel of a car.

'Men make it look so difficult – they pretend this repair can only be done by them. But now we women know what to do, it is so easy. We will keep the water flowing, no problem. We don't have to ask our husbands now.'

The whole process takes less than an hour. Once done, they again pull their *bui bui* over their clothes, disguising their beauty. It has been a revelation to discover that, under their nondescript black attire, these seemingly compliant Muslim women are strong and liberated. The group of women set off for home like a flock of black crows. I wonder why they conform to a dress code that undermines their individuality.

As we walk back, I can't resist asking them, 'Do you have to always wear a *bui bui* when you are in public?'

'That's what we are used to,' says one. 'It isn't a problem.'

'Isn't it hot in this heat,' I ask curiously, 'to have to wear an extra layer?'

'We don't mind it. It gives us freedom to go anywhere without being noticed,' says another woman, adding another dimension I had not realised.

'You know, wearing a *bui bui* shows we are upright, well brought-up women. We wear *bui bui* because it shows we are respectable people. It is our culture,' explains Hadija with more insight.

'But you have no individuality when you all look the same.'

'Well, it is not important for us to show off our clothes to everyone. We think it is very low-class, to expose your arms and legs.'

'We keep our bodies for our own men,' another woman teases me, her eyes glinting with naughtiness.

'Well, sounds exciting, but our men aren't turned on by our arms and legs,' I joke back.

'*Bui bui* are just for going out. At home, we wear what we want to wear. We have so many *kangas*, each one has a different saying.'

'For example, like this one,' Sara adds, showing me the hemline of Hadija's *kanga*. She wears this one today because it says: "*Mti hawendi ila kwa nyenzo.*" This means: "You can only move a heavy log if you have the right tools to move it.'"

'Like what we did today,' says Hadija. 'Give us women the tools, and we can do anything just as well as men. That is our slogan.'

We get back to Hadija's home. Strangers are rarely asked inside a Muslim house but Sara senses I am curious to see Kadija's home and asks, 'Can you show Mama Tristan your place, so she knows what to draw for her pictures?'

'*Karibu. Karibu sana,*' she says, waving me across the threshold into a small sitting room with a couple of wooden chairs and a grass mat.

The walls inside are plastered mud, between a lattice of poles, roughly smoothed over. I am intrigued by a framed photo of the proud patriarch of the house in a gleaming white *kanzu* and *kofia*. He poses assertively, head held high with a serious expression. Seated demurely in front of him is his wife, her face hardly visible under black *bui bui*, with a baby on her lap. Three little girls, all in identical frilly party dresses are lined up beside their mother, whilst two dark-eyed boys standing on the other side of their father. A copper plaque bears a quotation from the *Qur'an*.

I am shown along a short dark corridor through the centre of the house, leading to the back door. On each side is a bedroom with a king size four-poster bed supporting a mosquito net like a vast exotic Arabian tent. The headboards of each bed are grand, with tiles set in the elaborately carved and high gloss varnished wood.

Then we are through the tiny house to the yard, where a pot bubbles on an open fire, balanced on three blackened rocks. The women sit on the ground nattering companionably, weaving palm leaves into mats, grating coconuts. The smell of spice fills the air. I am given strong milky, ginger *chai*. When I have finished the tea, I ask if I can sit quietly somewhere to sketch. They give me a chair in the shade outside the little hut. I immerse myself in the scene lulled by the quiet rhythm of a young girl sweeping the leaves from under the trees. She shakes out a large mat of woven palms. Chickens cluck around, pecking up the rice grains that fall from the remains of the meal. A group of young children chase each other, inventing games without any toys. A piece of string becomes a skipping rope. With a few bottle tops and some stones, they play 'jacks,' the same game I played as a child.

As I watch the children play, I realise that this culture appeals to me deeply, not only visually but emotionally: the security that these women seem to project is something I have never experienced as a modern woman. I yearn for this sense of strong identity. They know who they are and how to navigate their life. These women are not the mindless drudges I imagined Muslim women to be. In fact, from what I have seen they are very powerful in their own households, admired by their men for their home-making skills. Perhaps traditional gender roles do not necessarily disempower women.

I imagine my mother's response to such romantic notions. 'Good God, Virginia, with all the advantages of your background and education, your ideal life would be to be an ignorant Muslim wife!' My father would have made a good Muslim patriarch. He was of the post-war generation that still had no expectation of a career for a daughter. When I left school, he told me that the only two options for women to earn a living were to become a secretary or a model. When he said that I was not quite attractive enough to be a model, my future was decided.

I was sent to England to learn shorthand and typing although I had no interest or aptitude for clerical work. I agreed to do the dreary secretarial course in Cambridge only because it allowed me to get to Europe. My mother's hidden agenda was that I would meet a well-educated, classy Englishman from the prestigious University and hopefully make a good marriage. Having no intention of complying with her Victorian schemes, instead I imported my rather unclassy French boyfriend of the time. When I left the technical college after failing even after a year of mindless practice to get up to the required typing speed of 70 words per minute, I vowed to myself never to be a secretary. Instead, I opted to go to art school in Cape Town. My father refused to support me, imagining I would become a drop out hippy, so I got a scholarship and supplemented my meagre income by working in a framing shop.

Now at last, I can put my artistic training to good use, as I sketch the scene before me. I watch how women go about their daily tasks and see there is so much they could do for themselves to improve their family's health, simply by improving their home hygiene. I start thinking about how I would like to illustrate books for mothers about issues that would improve their lives. Many have not a single book at home, and I sense there is a kind of intellectual starvation in their lives. Even if they are semi-illiterate, they can look at the pictures and learn. Perhaps it will be the children who read to their mothers, now that most children go to school in Kenya.

When I get back from Kwale, I am filled with enthusiasm for my idea which I term 'ethnographic illustration', a style of drawing that depicts the culture of the readers so that they can identify themselves in the picture. To achieve that I have to observe every detail of their kitchens, what their pots look like, where and how they wash, how they care for their children, how they collect water, and where they relieve themselves, how they tie their kangas. To convince Mama Gola I decide to offer to do a mural on the dreary corrugated iron fence around the car park at the office. I copy all I have seen in Kwale showing women in the bright kangas doing their household chores.

Each day when Mama Gola arrives at work, she stops and watches me and offers suggestions on how to make it more authentic. Now she has given me a part time job as an 'Ethnographic Illustrator' to document hygiene behaviour and produce training materials for two different projects. This gives me a chance to travel throughout the country and an excuse to get into the villages. With Rosie handling the children at home at last it is possible to travel.

The Afridev Handpump: designed for Community Management (Booklet Cover) 1988.

Chapter 7

Harambee

'Pesa zitumiwazo kuposa sizo zitumiwazo kuoa.'
**'The money that is used for an engagement is not
the same as that used for a wedding.'**

Virginia: June 1987.

Mama Gola's daughter is getting married at the Anglican cathedral, with the Archbishop of Nairobi himself officiating. Wendy is to be one of the bridesmaids, and Charlie and Tristan are to be pageboys. I am excited that we have been asked to be part of a local Kenyan wedding. Now we have been invited to join the family in a Harambee, but I have no idea what this entails.

'It is an absolute racket,' explains our old African hand, Mrs. Hunter-Price. 'If I were you, I would make an excuse and duck the whole thing. After independence, *'Harambee'* was the government's rallying cry to encourage all the tribes to forget cultural differences and join hands to build a new Kenya, based on a shared national identity.'

She laughs rather sarcastically. 'It might be a good idea in theory, but the reality is, it's just a fund-raising event to squeeze money out of your friends, so everyone possible is invited. You are the token whites so they assume you will have pots of money.' As usual her derision of Kenyans annoys me, and I decide to go and find out for myself how *Harambee* works.

When we arrive, the hall is already packed. Mama Gola is seated like a solid baobab, overshadowing her husband, Desmond on her right, and to her left is her daughter and the groom with his parents next to him. No one would know that this is a picture of intertribal harmony, the Kikuyu sitting down with the Taita. The women all look exactly the same with modern cocktail dresses, most with the new fashion of padded shoulder pads like Princess Diana. Once again, I am looking more African than they are in my ethnic attire, an extravagant West African fashion with an oversized linen turban wound round my head. I have to hold onto this mountain of cloth as I walk, as it is not well tied with the result that I look as if I have a splitting headache.

We are shown to Mama Gola's table. She gives me a warm smile and hugs us both, as my turban finally unravels. 'What a lovely outfit,' she compliments me as she helps me rewind the headdress more tightly. 'You are a real African Mama now, Virginia.'

She introduces us to her daughter, the groom and the in-laws and then we are shown to our table nearby. Mama Gola sits back and folds her chubby hands over her stomach and gives me a wink. The loudspeaker crackles and pops and the introductions begin. We are indeed the only whites in the hall and soon are asked to stand up and greet the crowd with others at the top table, after the Minister of Health, prominent CEOs and directors of non-governmental organisations. Where a few months ago I had been flattered at such attention, it now irritates me to be constantly singled out so publicly.

The elders are each given time to lecture the young couple on how to make a perfect marriage while the soon-to-be-weds nod humbly and look genuinely compliant. Finally, the speeches are over, and the music starts up with a lively beat. The master of ceremonies invites everyone to line up for the donation, like a procession to receive communion at the altar. As each person hands over their wad of shillings, he publicly flaps the notes above his head and shouts out how much is being given. It is distinctly un-British. I realise listening to the vast amounts being generously donated, that although we were warned by Mrs. H-P, we have not brought nearly enough money.

Acutely embarrassed, Anthony counts his notes under the table, gritting his teeth.

'What's the matter?' I whisper.

'Have you got any money on you?' he hisses into his beard, 'I have only 20,000 shillings.'

'No, of course not. I didn't bring my bag, as it wouldn't have gone with the outfit. I thought you had the money. Can't you write a cheque?'

'I left the cheque book behind. Maybe I could write an IOU,' he jokes.

'Ask Mama' I whisper in his ear.

'Of course I can't.'

I look up and see Mama Gola has seen our dilemma. I give her a big smile and open my palms to the roof and roll my eyes.

She winks with an exaggerated grimace and rubs her eye. Then she opens her large black auntie bag and scrabbles inside for some time, counting notes. She flaps her hand telling me to come over to her and passes me a fat wodge of notes. I am reminded of my parents dishing out for the collection in church on the few occasions we went at Christmas.

'Virginia, can you take it up,' Anthony begs me. As usual, he doesn't want to make a spectacle of himself, whereas I have no such qualms. I coil my turban more tightly, and squeeze between the chairs to the MC to hand over the cash. He counts the bundle of notes flamboyantly, flicking out one at a time, and shouts triumphantly, 'A hundred thousand shillings from Mr. and Mrs. Goodall.' The audience ululates in thanksgiving. This is extortion by social embarrassment.

Mama Gola leans across to Anthony and teases him, 'We will be deducting that from your salary.'

Rosie: June 1987.

The daughter of Mama Gola is very brave because she is marrying a Kikuyu. She has been to university so her bride price must be very high. I don't think she will be happy with a Kikuyu. Her parents are from the coast. I think they are Taita or Taveta group. The family of the groom won't be very pleased unless they are very educated and don't care about things like totem. I don't think Mama Gola is happy either because I heard she was joking with Dad saying, 'My child is marrying the enemy'. We are everyone's enemy, because Kikuyu are very powerful because Kenyatta was Kikuyu, and he is the father of the nation. We Kikuyu take everything and don't care about the other tribes at all.

I think it is better for people to marry in their own tribe. I hope my daughters will marry Kikuyu even if they are not so good. Even my sons have to marry from our tribe. Now the first born is circumcised he can get married soon. He has his own hut next to ours already.

When I married Kimendi, he paid a high bride price for me because I was smart although I didn't have senior school. I think it is something quite good, this bride price because men cannot marry the girl they love without a big effort. They have to work hard to save up to get married. At least enough to give a cow or a goat to the parents of the bride. That is the way we do it. Also, a new wife has to try hard to stay with her in-laws because if she runs home then the bride price has to return to the man so her family makes her stay if she can. Also, bride price means families are happy to have daughters because they will get money for them, so it gives them more value.

When I see our children looking so smart to go to the wedding of Mama Gola, I am very proud of them. They are very beautiful childrens. Mum and Dad are so happy to go to such a big wedding as well because I see they are very much honoured to be invited. It means they can stay in Kenya now, maybe. I hope they forget about Zimbabwe so I can always be with them here. They are so near to me now, more than my own family.

🌀 🌀 🌀

Virginia: June 1987.

On the day of the wedding, we drive to the heart of Nairobi, and wait outside the entrance of the Cathedral. A gaggle of dark beauties awaits the bride. The maids-of-honour are tense with expectation, flattening wisps of their intricately braided hair. They adjust their outfits, smoothing tight dresses over voluptuous hips. When we arrive, they swoop on our children with genuine delight. Wendy, in a purple, multi-layered, taffeta creation, her blonde hair hanging almost to her waist looks like Alice in Wonderland. She is paired up with another little flower girl with hair tied in two little pom poms with huge purple bows. Tristan and Charlie, dressed like Lord Fauntleroy in miniature purple velvet suits, accompany the little girls down the aisle. Anthony and I are ushered to the front of the church next to the family pew, feeling so honoured to be here.

The organ starts up, playing the mandatory 'Here comes the bride' in full throttle. All heads turn. Mama Gola's daughter gets out of a smart hired car and arranges her expansive dress of billowing chintz. The bridesmaids cluster around her. With a roll of drums, the ceremony begins. The gospel choir raises their voices to the drumbeat as the procession begins.

'Father, according to our tribal traditions, the mother also gives the bride away,' Mama Gola had told the slightly confused priest the day before. Mercy had laughed and had told me, 'Typical Mama, that is not our custom at all!'

So now the nervous little bride takes both her mother's and her father's arm to walk her to the altar. Mama Gola, in purple headdress, sails down the aisle, as confident as a schooner under full sail, while her daughter trails slightly behind her, resembling a little puff of steam, while her humble father tags along on her other elbow.

The bridal trio are followed by two little purple Iris flower fairies. Wendy's face is flushed pink with anxiety as she tries to keep hold of Charlie's hand. He is enjoying the spotlight, marching along with an impish smile on his face. Tristan follows, acutely embarrassed to be holding hands with a pretty girl whose deep purple dress is the same tone as her glowing skin. As they pass each pew, the women in the congregation melt at the symbol of idyllic inter-racial harmony.

Behind the children comes a crocodile of six elegant young couples. The women are in Lenten purple silk gowns with 'fascinators' floating like butterflies above their bee-hive hairdo. The men in velvet waistcoats are suavely old-fashioned, like Fred Astaire guiding their girl on their right arm, with the other folded arm neatly behind their backs as they proceed to the front of the church and splay out to each side of the altar, girls on one side and men on the other.

When the drum begins the hymn is transformed, each beat uniting the congregation in one sound as they sing with gusto. Sun streams in through the stained-glass rose window, shedding rainbow colours over black and white skins alike. When the bride joins hands with her husband and receives her kiss there is a riot of delight.

Mama Gola is standing to the side of the great gothic doorway as we come out into the sunshine. She embraces me and whispers, 'Our nuns, both yours and mine, would have been so proud of this wedding.' I know what she means exactly: the new Africa of the 'born free generation', where all the tribes and races intermarry without prejudice. Both of us have this ideal.

Chapter 8

Nairobi

'Macho yaliona milima hayashtukii mabonde'
'The eyes which have seen mountains are not terrified by valleys.'

Rosie: June 1988.

I have been with the family for two years. Now the children are big, they have to go to a proper school. So, Mum and Dad decide it is better to move from Limuru to the big city of Nairobi. I didn't think they would want to take me with them. I was worried because I had left the job picking beans and could not return there. Then Mum ask me if I can go with them. It is only one hour away from my own home. I can stay with them in the town all week and go to my home at the weekend. So, it is good.

It is not a problem for me because my girls are now teenagers, and they can look after the smaller boys at home. The school for them is nearby. For me to see them on the weekend is enough. Also, staying without my husband is no problem for me. He is also fine that I should go.

He said to me, 'Go. We must have the money that you earn. The white woman gives you many things. Already we have a new roof for the house. Already we have a new bed and so many clothes from them each year. Those whites are like gold. You must stick to them. If you stay there in Nairobi, we can get money to build a new house with cement. Even our first born needs his own house now he is circumcised.'

When I hear the plan of my husband I rejoice in my heart because I am tired of managing for so long in our small hut. So, I take my clothes and tell the children to be good, so I can earn money for them. Then I come to Nairobi with the family. I am not leaving my family, only I am working to get money for them.

It is quite funny being by myself without my family now, but I say to myself, I have a new family. Maybe they will help us with school fees to help my own children, or even give us some money for building a good house. Then I say to myself, 'Rosie. It is not good to think about those presents, you have come to help Mum and the children.' I don't work with Mum for what she give me like my husband thinks.

Mum is like my sister. We look after the children together. That is my happiness, not the money. But anyway, we can see what will happen. I just pray to the Lord to stop me thinking of how we are so different. She is a rich woman and has everything and I am a poor woman. I only have my blessings to give to the rich. Also, maybe I want to know what makes them to be so clever. I don't know why we people are so poor in Africa. I think maybe it is just that God loves the white people and bestows his love on them but for us, he sees we are jealous and have no good behaviour, so we are punished.

When I tell Mum my ideas, she tells me, 'Rosie, it is not like that, it is because everyone needs help to get started in life.' So, this is the work Dad does. He gives people water so they can get started but still black people don't get rich. Mum tells me to make sure the children work hard at school and get some certificates so they can get a good job. That is the best way for us to change. Each time a child goes to university they can save their family and look after the parents when they are old. But I have six children and I wonder if even one can make it to a good job. The youngest one, Kariuki, maybe. He has the best brains, but for the others, I don't think so. These are my worries, so I will stay with the family, and they will show me how to live so my children can prosper and get a good job.

Rosie: October 1988.

The house in Nairobi is not far from the new school. Sometimes Mum asks me to get the children. That is my happiest time. I run quickly across the road and find them. There are lots of smart cars with the parents taking their children home.

Sometimes our children are asked by their rich friends, 'Do you need a lift?'

They say, 'No thanks, we want to walk with Rosie.'

I came to know that these children are a bit different from the other English children. It is the way they were taught by their parents. To me, it is wonderful that our children never mind going on foot even though their father has two cars. They are like my Kikuyu children who must walk a long way from our home to school.

The Kikuyu people along the road who see me walking with these white children call to me, 'How clever is that Mzungu mother? One day a time can come when they cannot be in a car because there are some problems, and they have no money, then those children will know they can always walk. They cannot be stranded.'

I say to them, 'She is like a Kikuyu. She never minds anything. They are people who know how to help our people properly.'

Tristan asks me what the Kikuyu were saying. I tell him, 'They say your Mum is teaching her children in a clever way. That is to make you walk home, and not use a car.'

The children were happy that my people are liking the way they do things. So those children are growing bravely. I have seen there is no big difference from our people and the English people even if they have money and we have little. It is only what you make yourself to be.

Sometimes on Saturday, I take the children to ride their bicycles at the school to enjoy themselves. I have to be very careful about them crossing the main road because it was having a lot of matatus driving like crazy. Charlie is a very careless riding boy. He is going so fast and not caring for himself if he can fall down. I think what can happen when he is riding. I am scared for him. What can Dad say to me if I let him get hurt.

I tell him, 'Charlie don't ride so fast.'

He is a very joking boy. He don't like to listen to anyone.

He just laughs and says, 'Okay, sorry Rosie.'

Then he rides slowly, slowly for the first round, when I am watching. Then he goes around again. When I am not looking, he starts to go as fast as a car.

When I look at him, I pretend to be cross, he say, 'Oh! sorry Rosie. I just forgot!'

Then he goes slowly and comes to ask me, 'Am I being good now Rosie?'

I say, 'Yes, you are a good boy now.'

The children are getting so big now. The first born, Tristan, is almost seven years old now and enjoying very much to climb trees. He goes on the roof and is not fearing anything. One day I am in the kitchen. They are all outside. It was only one minute I left them alone. The little girl is so helpful. She runs to me and says, 'Rosie can you come quickly because Tristan is climbing to the top of a tree.'

So, I come and I see Tristan at the top of a very high forest tree. He is hanging on one of the branches and swinging on it like a monkey. When I look at him, my body starts sweating and my heart pumps so hard when I see where he is. Very, very, high up.

I say, 'My God, please help me get this boy down safely.'

When Tristan sees how I am, he starts laughing and says,

'Rosie don't worry. I can't fall down. I am a monkey. My cousin is a baboon.'

He starts doing lots of funny things like monkeys do. He takes one hand off the branch and scratches under his arm, going 'Hoof, Hoof.' and laughing too much. I feel so scared for him when he is so high in the tree.

I think, 'What can I do, so he doesn't know I am worrying too much? So, he can come down.'

So, I just joke with him so that he can come down slowly without falling.

I call to him, 'Tristan, love, please come down slowly. I have seen that my child is growing big. I can see he can climb far up into this tree like the monkeys in the forest.'

I play that game, even though I am shaking all over my body with fear for my nice boy.

Then Tristan is happy to hear that I think he is so grown up. But me, my eyes are big with worry. I am watching and thinking he can fall down. But he starts coming down, slowly by slowly. My heart stops pumping when I see he can do it easily. When he comes down, I hug him and tell him, 'You must not climb so high in the trees. The branches can come off and you can fall and kill yourself or break your legs.'

Dad's parents have come, and I am so happy to meet his family because now I understand why he is so quiet because he is like his father who just smile to me but doesn't talk. His Mum is a very smart person with good clothes and something like the Queen because she has very good manners. She told me she like to go to Church very much and she honours the Pope who is important for Catholic people. She said she can come with her to church on Sunday, but I say I will be going home then. Every night she says prayers with the children, so it is making them to be more holy, because Mum never does that even though Dad try his best. I wish Mum could become a Catholic, but she said she can't do that because any religion that believes only their people go to heaven can't be a true religion. So I keep praying for Mum to find Jesus and be saved.

Virginia, November 1988.

Anthony's parents, Angela and Michael have come to stay and have bravely offered to look after the children for a few days, with Rosie's help of course. It is their first time in black Africa and there is a certain anxiety as to whether they will cope with the chaotic traffic in Nairobi and are nervous to venture out without us. Angela has had six children herself and is not fazed by the task of handling our three, but she is worried in case she has to pretend that she is not from South Africa as she is incapable of the sort of deception that now is second nature to us.

Mama Gola insisted that they come to the office and welcomed them like part of the family, showering them with presents and compliments about their son. 'Anthony is a great asset to us, and a wonderful technical advisor; we only hope that he will stay on with us for a few more years.'

They were well primed not to mention that they lived in Johannesburg, and Mama Gola studiously avoids asking them too much. They are charmed by their reception at the Women for Water office, which is so unlike anything in South Africa, where the idea of a black person being an Executive Director is unthinkable let alone that director being a woman. It is an eye opener to them to see such a powerful lady in charge and they are trying to make sense of it all.

Angela is so impressed by Mama Gola.

'I can see why you enjoy working with her, she is quite unique, such a character, isn't she? You can tell she is a mission product. We had a good talk about the dear old nuns, and I told her all about our Centre of Concern at our church.'

'They are much less complexed than our locals who have such an axe to grind that it is difficult to get through to them,' Michael observes quietly.

Chapter 9

Homo Habilis

'*Heri shuka isiyo kitushi, kama shali njema ya mauwa.*'
'Better an honest loincloth than a fancy cloak'

Virginia: November 1988.

In the far north-east of the country, on the border with Sudan, lies the Turkana desert, one of the most inhospitable areas of East Africa, and a chance to see 'real tribals' and to meet people who still roam the wilderness virtually naked, much to the embarrassment of the government. I have always been intrigued by people who resist modernity. What is it that is preventing them? Is it due to lack of exposure or are they just fond of their own ways? A great opportunity has arisen giving Anthony and I the opportunity to explore the most deserted region of Kenya.

We set off at first light for the twelve-hour drive. From our home, we drop down the dramatic escarpment past Kijabe hospital, past the rabbit sellers on the high misty passes, past the patchwork of shambas along the fertile crescent of the highlands. We dodge dangerous potholes as the road snakes around the active crater of Mount Longonot, down to the bottom of the Rift Valley. It is like something out of National Geographic: Mount Kenya rises above us to the right. Migratory birds flock to Lake Naivasha to the left. Pelicans circle overhead, catching the thermals as they rise like heavy flying boats into the air. We drive on, resisting the temptation to stop and admire the shoreline of Lake Nakuru, flushed pink with the flamingos that congregate in their millions in this soda lake.

Three hours later as we head north, the tarmac has deteriorated into a moth-eaten coat over the dry dust. The countryside becomes ever more barren, pastel shades of pale blue, hazy heat, on an empty road to Lake Baringo. We see not a single car on the road the whole day. And no petrol stations. This is just hard, dry Africa, which few can endure. 'MMBA', the explorers called it - 'Miles and Miles of Bloody Africa'.

Young shepherd boys lazily goad their goats as their charges nibble their way along the paths, picking off the last leaves off the thorn bushes in this overgrazed land. We overtake a couple of Turkana girls carrying water on their heads, their strong necks encased in beaded necklaces. They wear large circular metal earrings. I am riveted by their natural beauty and long to engage with them somehow.

'Stop the car,' I urge Anthony, 'maybe they'll trade.'

'Oh God, not your bangle business again. Can't we just keep going?'

'No, just stop,' I beg him, 'it's a pretext to meet them. I've got bangles from only six tribes so far.'

'We're already going to be driving in the dark.'

'Come on, it's fun. All women love jewellery. Just indulge me.'

He stops in front of them, and as the dust settles, I get out of the car and greet the girls.

They laugh behind their hands looking shy, like wild deer about to run. Their athletic bodies are barely covered by skirts of hide and loose tops.

'*Jambo. Jambo,*' I smile. Connection. Possibilities.

They smile and stare back at me. The teenagers are as curious as I am. Their hair is shaved except for a ridge along the crown like a mohawk, and they wear large brass earrings.

I put my arm out and jingle the bangles towards them: one from a Giriama woman on the coast, a copper one from a Maasai, three rubber bangles hewn from a bicycle tire from Tanzania, a woven palm bracelet made by Swahili kids on Lamu island, and a carved wooden Kikuyu bangle.

Taking off two manufactured bangles, intricately woven with copper and brass, I hold them out towards them.

'We swop?' I mime, pointing rapidly from my bangles to their earrings and back to me. Their eyes light up. Intrigued, one lowers the water containers from her head and giggles to the other, who whispers to her.

She unhooks a huge plain bronze earring from her lobe and wipes it on her *kanga*. Then she holds it out to me. I take it and smile. It is homemade, beaten into a thick ring by hand. She puts my bracelet on her long slender dark arm and holds it out to show her friend, like an engagement ring. They clink their wrists together and laugh, white teeth glinting in the sun.

'Okay?'

'Okay. *Asante sana.* Thank you.' The trade is done. I am delighted.

'You see,' I prod Anthony playfully, 'that is what it's all about, making personal connections.'

We drive for hours in splendid monotony, on and on. No mountain provides scale. Forty degrees in the shade. Nothing moves in this heat. Just us. This is camel country, where even goats won't thrive. If we break down here, we will not survive. There are no trees, just termite hills. These are towering, wobbly creations, like crazy Dr. Seuss constructions. Tall chimneys, some over three metres high, are built by hard working termites to create a draft below ground, to cool their queen and her millions of larvae: the hotter the year, the higher the chimneys. Below these towers the termites feverishly carve out passageways deep underground to where the soil is still damp.

'Hey, there's the turn-off to Koobi Fora, Richard Leakey's dig. Shall we go and see where he found his homo habilis skull?'

'It feels like the dawn of the world here.' So remote and timeless.'

'I wouldn't be surprised to see an early man wandering along with a bow and arrow.'

And then we do. In the middle of this lunar landscape, a dark silhouette of a man is standing beside the edge of the road. He has a shaved head and virtually no clothes on, just a hide hanging over his right shoulder, scarcely covering his bare backside. In one hand he carries a spear, a panga and a long stick and in the other a headrest. He slowly shoos his camels off the track, raising his stick in greeting. With long, elegant hands, he pats down the air, motioning to us to stop.

'Come on, let's stop.'

'Oh no, not again. We're never going to get there.'

'Well, you would be glad to see him if we had a puncture, wouldn't you?'

Anthony pulls up the car beside the man, unwilling to get involved. I roll down the window.

The dark stranger bends his head down to my window, looking around the inside of the car quickly, inches from my face. His breath is overpowering. I back off. He makes the classic 'food' sign, bunching his fingers together in front of his buck teeth.

'I should think vegetables and fruit are luxuries in this part of the world,' Anthony says.

I reach for a plastic bag of mangoes. His eyes light up.

'Do you like mangoes?' The man grins, nods and reaches for the plastic bag.

His wrist knife gleams on his wrist, and I touch it and point to Anthony. He points to the mangoes, grinning. I am surprised he would want to trade his only knife for a mango.

Then the man takes the knife off his wrist, stretching past me, he hands it to Anthony. With his other hand, gives a thumbs-up sign, '*Mzuri?* Good?'

Anthony smiles sheepishly, holds up both hands and motions away from the man.

I take the rusty knife and examine it: a disc of rusty steel, with the lethally sharp outer edge protected by a sheath of worn leather. I give him the bag of mangoes.

'*Hakuna matata.* No problem.'

Then he holds up his neck rest, a curved seat just wide enough to lay his head on at night when he dosses down. He pushes it through the window and points to a new T-shirt lying on the back seat, with the WfW logo which is given to people in our water projects. He grins and bangs his chest.

'Can I give him one?'

'Go on then, in for a penny, in for a pound. You're fleecing the poor guy.'

The nomad's eyes glisten as I hand him the T-shirt. He makes a thumbs-up sign. He pulls it over his bare chest and is transformed. I instantly regret it. He was so manly in his leather wrap. Now he looks like a foolish vagabond without trousers. I am embarrassed to see his genitals hanging unceremoniously below. He has no such shame: he is on a shopping spree, special delivery. He points to my plastic bottle of water.

'You want *maji?*'

'He probably wants the plastic bottle as much as the water.'

'Eh, eh!'

I give him the bottle of water and he takes a sip, smacking his lips together, savouring it like fine wine.

'*Maji safi. Mzuri sana.* Clean water. Very good.'

He steps back and waves. As we drive off, he turns tail, his hide swinging around his backside and wanders off into the desert. The WfW logo he now wears will link us to this stranger for years to come.

'I can't understand this compulsion to leave bits of yourself around Africa,' Anthony teases me.

'It's fun. I want them to remember me.'

'Incredible how these pastoralists can exist in this desert. He just walks off into no man's land with nothing.'

'All they want from the modern world is a handful of tea, some sugar and a bag of maize meal each month.'

Anthony shakes his head. 'It won't be long before the Turkana will have to wear clothes by law and go to school. In a few decades they will all be educated and move to the towns.'

'Then Turkana will be deserted. It's such a pity as it is such a unique culture. No one else could live here if the nomadic way of life dies out.'

'We must be near the lake now.'

The sun plops down behind the white heat haze on the horizon like a molten blob, silhouetting thorn trees and anthills like a kitsch rendition of an African sunset on a cheap poster. Night drops like a fire curtain and, instantly, the land is pitch black.

We have absolutely no idea where we are, and Anthony is loving it.

'This is a real adventure.'

'What do you call an 'adventure'? I tease him, 'being stuck in the middle of nowhere at night without any food or water?'

'An adventure is when you set out with no idea where you will land up.'

'Well, this is certainly one. Where are we? Have you any idea?'

'Absolutely none but if we follow the car tracks, we are bound to end up somewhere.'

Skidding down the sandy road for a kilometre, we are finally led to a man flashing a torch, guiding us between lines of painted white stones, carefully laid out in the thick sand. He seems to be expecting us as if this is all quite normal. There are two other cars parked but no sign of habitation anywhere.

'Jambo, Memsahib! Jambo, Bwana.'

'Jambo. Is there a safari lodge near here?

'The boat will come now to take you to the camp.'

He flicks his light across the water. I catch the sound of a motorboat chugging closer. When it reaches us, we load our bags into the little boat and speed across the lake into the deep night.

A promontory appears on the other side of the bay, where a generator is thumping out light. A restaurant is perched over the water, lit up like a stage. A waiter, dressed in white 'number ones', is serving dinner to a young white couple, who look like they are on their honeymoon. An original choice for a memorable escape.

'Hmm, just when we thought we had escaped civilization. Spoils the sense of adventure a bit, when you land up back in civilization after driving through a desert all day.' They are probably as disappointed to see us, as we are to see them. We smile and nod at the other guests from across the large empty dining room. We are shown to a tent overlooking the still water of Lake Turkana gleaming green from our lights. The king size bed is hung exotically with a mosquito net and fluffy white towels beg to be used. After a day's dusty drive, the lukewarm shower is the ultimate luxury. Anthony opens the cool box to find a beer and sits looking at the stars rising in the dark sky. This is the honeymoon that we never had away from the children for the first time since arriving in Kenya.

We awake to the blinding white light of dawn. White sand, white water, white light. Even at sunrise, the temperature is unbearable. We go down to the crusty salt line of the lake and take the speed boat across the shimmering mirror of water. When we get to the car, the askari directs us to the only school for miles. We set off on a track across the sand to the school buildings that we can just make out on the horizon, shimmering in the heat haze.

The headmaster meets us. He is a tall dark man who looks Nilotic. His expression is of patient endurance of one used to very little, almost too shy to communicate. We shake hands warmly. The school has five classrooms under a tin roof. There is no flooring, just sandy ground, no glass in the windows, no desks, no chairs, no toilets, no water.

In one room, dusty six-year-old kids wear little clothing, all chalky white from rolling around on the sand floor of the classroom. A teacher is holding hands with them in a ring as they circle round just like our own children sang when they first went to Rosie's home.

'Ring a ring of roses. A pocketful of posies, atishoo, atishoo we all fall down.'

They roll onto the dusty ground and add another layer to lighten their skins. So far from little England, these naked babes of Africa are singing songs composed in England centuries ago to describe the great plague that killed so many without understanding its meaning. When I join in the singing, they shriek with excitement, amazed that I know 'their' song. How cultures can be shared through music, I think to myself.

In the next classroom the young teacher is lining up her class of 7-year-olds, in front of her desk to perform for us. She utters a crystal-clear note to start them off, her voice like a lark in dry savanna.

'Row, row, row, the boat gently down the stream, welly, welly, welly, welly, life is but a dream,'

While they sing, the children mime punting a dug-out canoe in Lake Turkana, and I imagine the great turquoise sea in the middle of a desert. They clap their hands in delight at the end.

The children seem to get progressively more alert with each older age set. When we reach the top class, a male teacher, a tall dark skinned Nilotic with fine features, motions the students to rise with the same majestic sweep our nomad used to stop our car. I notice that most of the students are now boys. I spot one bright girl who catches my eye and smiles shyly, dropping her gaze as she has been taught by her parents when addressing an elder. The children push back their chairs in unison and politely rise to their feet.

'Good-morn-ing-teach-er-how-are-you?' they intone together in English. Some are as tall as I am.

I see careful handwriting in the book on the nearest desk in front of me with an essay entitled, 'What I want to be when I grow up.'

I pick it up and ask the little boy to read it aloud, he gives a wide smile, with perfect pronunciation says:

'When I leave school and grow up, I want to be a *matatu* driver in Nairobi. I want to have a big car and drive people to work. I will be very smart and have good clothes. Then I will get a Turkana wife who will be a teacher and she will give me many children. I want to live in a big city like Nairobi.'

! wonder what girls want to be when they leave school. When I ask the bright girl to show me her book, she opens it for me at her best page. She shows me the illustration of a nurse, and a dying child. I ask her to read her ambition aloud.

She smiles coyly and in perfect English she reads, 'I want to be a nurse when I grow up to help my people survive. My brother died of malaria. I want to learn how to stop malaria. I want to help children grow up strong and healthy. I want to stop disease in some way. I want to teach people to be clean and have a good home. This is what I can do when I am big.'

'That is also my dream.' I tell her and there is a spark of connection between us.

I have a strong urge to help her, to adopt her. How are her parents ever going to pay for her education to that level? But I argue with myself immediately, I can't take on every hard luck story. If anything, I should sponsor Rosie's children to become qualified.

'Can we go and see where you could sink the borehole?' asks Anthony sensing I am getting in too deep. The tall teacher sweeps his arm in a majestic orbit and points to a slight dip in the sand. Twenty paces into the baking midday sun and we are looking for shade. We look at the selected site and hurriedly return to the shadow of the classroom.

'How will the children benefit if you have a hand pump here?' Anthony asks the headmaster, wanting him to frame his request in his own words, so he can assess the need, and justify the project to Aqua Aid.

'If we get water, then we can provide accommodation for pupils so that, when their parents roam with their herds, the children can stay behind at school and complete their education properly.'

'How can their parents manage with their camels if the kids stay at boarding school?'

'Yes, it is a problem for the parents, but they want at least one of their children to get a job. It is their traditional insurance policy. At least one child must succeed to reach the city. Those who are not bright will stay at home to guard the herds. The children also prefer to live in the city where modern life is more interesting.'

'Does this type of western education have any relevance to their immediate needs as pastoralists? Surely these kids will just join the endless drift of labourers flooding from villages into the town?'

The headmaster looks at me blankly, unable to agree, 'Okay, perhaps, but you see, we all must change. The key to progress is literacy. We cannot end poverty until we end illiteracy.'

'Turkana herdsmen too want their children to be part of the modern world even if it means forgetting their language and their culture,' adds the young woman teacher quietly. I listen to her and think how I want to talk to Rosie about the value of education and to hear her own experience.

'It is possible for them to be well-educated, as well as locally connected with their own unique culture,' argues the elegant Nilotic teacher, 'that is how I am. My father and his father were nomadic. I could also herd camels if I wanted to. But it is a boring life. I prefer to teach and help others escape such hardship. 'You *wazungu*, come to the desert to escape the city, but we are trapped here.'

Anthony promises to follow up and submit a proposal to Aqua Aid. We shake hands all round and make our way thoughtfully back to the car. The air inside is hot enough to roast a chicken. I sit down and yelp in pain. The seats are red-hot, and my thighs are seared.

After a few minutes of silence, we drive past a little encampment of stick shelters in the sandy wasteland. Thin sticks are bent over close together, tied in an arc like a crude nest, not even as high as a man. There is no grass in the area to use for a thatched roof, so the frame is covered with a few hides. The entrance is so low that a person must crawl in on hands and knees. So basic are the little shelters that a tin shack in the urban slums of Nairobi would be like heaven.

'I hated boarding school,' Anthony recalls, 'it was the worst thing that ever happened to me in my childhood, having to leave the comfort and warmth of my family at eleven years old, while my siblings stayed at home. I have resented it all my life, but if I had been a Turkana kid, I wouldn't mind going to boarding school - it would be a luxury compared to their little hovel. The best thing we can do is provide water here.'

※ ※ ※

Rosie and I are walking back home from school with the children beetling ahead on their bikes and I seize the opportunity to hear her story.

'What was your schooling like Rosie? Did you do well at school?

'I loved school, Mum. I was very bright, but I only did primary school.'

'Is that what *you* wanted, to leave school?

'No Mum, I wanted to be a teacher.'

'Why did you leave early then?'

'Because my parents could not pay for so many children at school.'

'That is so sad. You would have been such a good teacher.'

'There was nothing I could do. Kimendi's mother came and asked my parents for me to marry him. That was the old way. I had to do what they told me. So, we got married when I was only sixteen.'

'Ten years earlier than I did. I had Tristan at 29 and you had Ezekiel when, at 17? So, you had all your children before I even started having mine. In fact, Kariuki, your youngest child is the same age as Tristan, my oldest.'

You know women always marry soon because we can't stay alone without protection, or we can get pregnant. Then it is hard to find a husband. That is normal in our culture.'

'And your girls, Faith and Mabel?'

'Well, they are not so clever, but they just try.

'How are your boys doing at school, Rosie?

'They are doing fine, Mum. They are in senior school. Ezekiel is to leave school this year now he is 16. He wants to be a mechanic.'

'And Joseph, Ebrahim and Kariuki? How are they doing at school?'

'I think Kariuki can do well.'

'Rosie, I really want to make sure that at least one of your children gets a good job. I will help you to get Kariuki properly qualified.'

'Can you do that Mum, really? God bless you for that.'

'What is his best subject at school?'

'The teacher says he is good at everything. I will show his report to you. He is such a hard-working boy. I am very happy with him.'

'Do you think he would look after you when you are old?'

'I hope so Mum, that is what we expect.'

Chapter 10

Polygamy

'Kidole kimoja hakivunji chawa''
One finger cannot squash a flea.'

Virginia: February 1989.

There is to be a water project near Kisumu, the very heart of the continent, on the edge of Lake Victoria, the area where HIV/AIDS was first identified. After the success of my illustration of hand pump maintenance in the coastal villages, Mama Gola has asked me to set up women's groups and a hygiene programme on a remote island in Lake Victoria. I am excited to see inside the homes of another tribe.

This is the land of the Luo, the lanky, dark-skinned people who originally migrated south from South Sudan, and who according to our reliable informant Mrs. H-P are great talkers. From the shores of Lake Victoria, we are to take a boat to the islands, where a small offshoot of the Luo, called the Luya, lives in neglected fishing villages. This area has the highest levels of infant mortality in Kenya.

Just as my own mother believed, most rural mothers believe they should stop breastfeeding and give nothing to eat to babies with diarrhoea, so as to give their stomach a rest. As a result, the infants literally dehydrate to death. Their families visit the *n'anga* who gives them magic amulets to save them. There is so much simple stuff they can do to save them.

I feel bad about leaving the children, but Rosie says, 'You go, Mum, I can look after them. They are so good with me. You know that children are always naughtier with their own mother, but I am their second mother, so they are very good with me. I can manage fine. I will walk them to school, make their food and it's no problem.'

'If you are absolutely sure that you can manage, that would be wonderful.' I realise how lucky I am to have someone like Rosie. Once again, I justify my absence: by caring for my children, she enables me to help other mothers look after their children. Then I think with a pang of guilt, that the only children who suffer are Rosie's children. Who is looking after them in her absence? She never allows me to worry about her family, and I push the guilt to the back of my mind.

To the west of the great central plateau of East Africa, the road climbs up to the Kisii highlands, an area of equatorial rainfall, one of the most densely populated parts of Kenya. Here lies a quilt of tiny *shambas*, where every inch of red mud is intensively farmed, much like Rosie's home area, with neat hedges between the green plots of every hue. The energy of the farmers is palpable and invigorating. The rectangular mud huts are made by pressing orange clay between a lattice of sticks and plastering the floors with the soil from ant hills. The women are tough, hard-working peasants who grow everything needed to feed their families. Living standards could be good here as the land is fertile; the torrential rains are reliable, and fish abound in the lake.

Men near Lake Victoria are mainly fishermen, while the women farm the land. Dugout canoes bob on the placid lake water, little more than logs. Alongside them, the water *matatus*, the long thin skiffs with their sharp prow and pointed stern, wait patiently to ferry customers across the largest lake in Africa. Painted thickly in sky blue, they are as bright as the iridescent kingfishers that dart across the waters. On each beach are wonky lines of racks, where Nile perch are hung to dry in the sun. The men pedal their old bikes to market each morning with their fresh catch of tilapia dangling from their handlebars. All along the rutted roads where the buses circumnavigate the lake, young boys hold up bunches of silver fingerlings for sale. The lake provides bountifully.

Father Tielen meets us as we pull up at the mission. A great bear of a Dutchman, strong and vigorous, he looks more like a boxer than a priest. He has developed an oasis of activity around him. In the villages beside the lake the main health threat is cholera which claims people's lives daily. It is an irony that the population, unlike most of Africa, have ample water living as they do beside such a large body of fresh water but because this water is polluted by their own lack of sanitation it is killing them. So, he has requested help to provide clean drinking water from boreholes and Anthony has come to assess the groundwater to see what should be done.

The tough old missionary takes us down to the lakeshore, where a large motorboat is being made ready. We roar off like wealthy deep-sea game fishermen across the lake, which stretches through a pale haze to the far horizon, where the low-lying island of Mfangano, can just be seen. He tells us it used to be a leper colony in colonial days, and there is still leprosy to be found as well as polio.

It is exhilarating to race across the lake in this speed boat. We are both savouring the opportunity our job provides to get beyond the usual tourist route into the dark heart of Africa that few foreigners ever see.

There is a smudge of brownish cloud drifting fast to meet us, changing its shape like a ghostly flapping blanket.

'Is that smoke?' I ask.

'Quick, go inside the cabin and close the hatch. Those are lake flies coming our way.'

We duck inside the cabin just as the boat is engulfed in a dense cloud of tiny lake flies, like the swarm of midges I remember once encountering in the Scottish Highlands. They cluster wing to wing in group flight. Within a moment or two they are gone. On opening the hatch, we find a carpet of tiny corpses clinging to every surface of the boat.

'Ugh, they're a real nuisance,' says Father Tielen. Being the only female on board he hands me a brush to clear the debris. I am tempted to pass it on to Anthony, but instead comply meekly.

'You will see on Mfangano Island how the dead lake flies cover every leaf on every bush. In fact, it is a lot of protein waiting to be used,' he jokes. 'No one knows why they swarm like this. Perhaps to protect themselves from being eaten as they search for mates.'

We are nearing the island now and can see the flat rise visible just above the water level.

'Whoa! Hey, we have some friends,' Father Tielen says with a laugh, pointing out a pair of hairy pink nostrils snorting out sprays of water. He dampens down the engine, and we drift at a safe distance, watching a pod of hippos wallowing lazily offshore.

With a giant bow wave, a large hippo lunges up out of the water towards another pair of nostrils, then they both sink luxuriantly into the green depths together. When they resurface, they pop up in different places and fix us with their knowing little eyes, watching at a safe distance. The male stretches his huge jaws open in an impressive display of seniority, flaunting his vast incisors and puffy pink throat before submerging beneath the surface with a disgusted 'harrumph'.

The priest revs up the engine and swings away from the pod.

'Enough sightseeing. We must get going or we'll be late for Mass. Can you take the helm, Anthony? I must change.'

The bulky Dutchman disappears below for a few minutes then emerges like a giant moth in flowing white robes. Yanking his dog collar into position around his thick red neck, he winces.

'I don't like having to wear these things, but you know, I have to meet expectations sometime.'

He winks, then clambers clumsily onto the deck. He goes to the front of the boat, and carefully loops the rope into a lasso and hands it to Anthony.

'Chuck this rope to the guys on shore when we come up to the jetty.'

Father Tielen takes the wheel and swings round to avoid a large stretch of water hyacinth that is blocking the way into the bay. A small landing jetty protrudes from the green water, where a few local dugout canoes are moored.

A huge crowd has gathered along the shore to welcome us. Father Tielen strides through the gathering like a visiting potentate, shaking hands warmly with the men, patting children on the head, while the women dance before us, leading us to the 'altar' under a tree.

A small table has been set up beside a bench. We are introduced and sit self-consciously with the altar boys to the side, very conspicuous.

Father Tielen lays out the white cloth and arranges the chalice with the paten sealing the top, to prevent the lake flies contaminating the holy contents. Then he drapes a square of embroidered *kanga* cloth elegantly over the top. Another use for the ubiquitous kanga. He sets out the precious book on a stand next to a plastic container full of chunks of bread which are to be distributed in place of the usual communion hosts.

The women spread out their *kangas* on the ground and sit in the shade, while the men seat themselves on a few benches which have been pressed into service from a nearby school. Father Tielen straightens out his cassock over his rounded paunch, looking up with the might of Moses about to part the dead sea. He holds up his right hand and blesses the masses before him in Luo, then spreads out his arms, Christ-like, to embrace the congregation. A man comes forward with a large drum and squats in front of the crowd, like a conductor, to keep the beat. A woman shrills out the first note and the rest join in with a surge of joy, like the swelling cloud of the lake flies as it rises and falls in the muggy air.

After mass, Father tells me I am to be taken to the village so I can do my survey of households, while he goes off with Anthony to look at the water options.

My guide will translate for me, and I can teach him how to do the survey. This is the moment I have been waiting for.

'Can I take photos?' I ask.

'Of course, just always ask the people first. They usually love to have their photos taken but nothing sensitive, you understand, no photographing topless maidens washing in the lake,' he jokes. For a priest he seems so worldly.

From the direction of the lake come four women, each with a bucket of water balanced carefully on her head. Their necks remain rigid while their bodies sway with each step. A couple of young girls overtake us, each carrying a huge stack of firewood on their head. A young woman is pounding maize in a pestle and mortar outside her hut, kids scrabbling around in the dirt beside her. We continue past several huts to the largest dwelling, where an elderly woman sits over a large pot on an open fire, stirring the *ugali* for the midday meal. Nearby, an old man is fixing a wooden plough, chatting to a younger man, mending his fishing net. We are welcomed with traditional grace and shown a place to sit under the tree. My guide explains that I have come to meet the man's family. He nods and greets us, '*Karibu sana.*'

I start the survey by asking him how many people he has in his household.

'Many people. I can't count them.'

He calls over to his wife who is standing at a distance to help him make the tally. She smiles and greets us shyly.

'This is number one, the oldest wife. She has eight children herself but there are other wives.' They can't agree how many people in total live in their compound but around thirty. Three sons, their wives and children are here permanently.

A young woman comes into the compound with a baby strapped to her back. She lifts the bucket carefully off her head. Drawing a small packet of salt from the front of her blouse, she hands it over to the older wife.

'This one number two wife,' says the old man, grinning with toothless gums.

'Very good girl,' says the old wife in English, patting wife number two, and smiling at me.

'You have two wives?' I ask the old man. He creases up with laughter and holds up three fingers, beaming proudly.

'Wow, impressive. How many wives can you have?' I ask through the interpreter.

'Many, many wives. Only I need too much money.' He hunches his shoulders, his mouth disappearing between his nose and his chin, and rubs his finger and thumb together looking like a crafty old miser.

Wife number two smiles and takes her baby off her back. She gives the child to the wrinkly old woman, who croons over it lovingly, a second mother.

'How many grandchildren?' I ask the old man. He doesn't know and immediately asks his wife. They start to tally them up: at least twenty-five grandchildren, it would seem.

'Have you been to school?'

'Primary school - two years, and I can read, but not so much.'

'And wife number one? Can she read?'

'Ah no, she did not go to school. The old wife can't read. But *she* can...' He grabs his young wife playfully by the wrist. Her eyes sparkle at his attention.

'I can read,' wife number two pipes up in English, smiling brightly.

The interpreter explains, 'Education has improved very much now. Most mothers under 30 can read.'

'So, in this house, everyone has a different way they can help the family.' I suggest.

The interpreter draws a diagram on the floor with his walking stick, 'Exactly. It is the strength of many parts. You see, this grandfather is the head of the household. It is a big job. He must rule like a cockerel rules his hens. Then, you see this grandmother, she likes to look after the children for the younger wives.'

The young girl mimes sweeping the ground, 'We young wives must clean the house and cook.'

'You fetch the water and firewood also,' I add, 'What do the young men do?'

'Ah, their job is to plough, fish and herd the cattle.'

'... and drink beer,' I joke, which makes them laugh heartily.

'We make beer to keep them happy,' says the young wife, shooting a daring glance at the old man.

'Do you mind your old man having a younger wife?' I ask the old lady, who by this time is warming to the theme.

'Ah no, I don't mind. Then he can leave me in peace,' she jokes looking cheekily at him. 'We women like to be together.'

'Okay, but what is it like for young wives?'

'We help each other. It helps us to survive, like when we are pregnant, for example.'

I am impressed: this arrangement seems too good to be true. I can see the value of sharing the chores, but I'm not entirely convinced it is that easy to share a husband, even if he is old and boring.

✿ ✿ ✿

We walk along an overgrown path to a clearing where there is a single hut with a badly thatched and dilapidated roof. No cows, no goats, no chickens. Nothing in the compound moves except the flies around a mangy dog, lazily scratching fly-bitten ears. There seems to be no one about.

'*Hodi, hodi!*' shouts my guide, attempting to raise the house owner. No one comes.

'This man, I know him, he is a Jehovah's witness, and he is away now. But his wife should be here.'

Finally, the face of a woman pokes around the door, just roused from sleep. She emerges, stomach first, very obviously pregnant, a hand on her arched back to support the load.

'*Karibu,*' she says nervously and offers us stools on which to sit on outside the hut. A couple of small toddlers appear at the door, snivelling at their mother's legs. They look up at me with the abnormally big eyes of malnourished children, their little pot bellies sticking out. The scrawny dog licks up the remnants of rice on the ground. Cooking pots lie unwashed in the dust.

She tells me that she is about 28 years old and has only two years of schooling. In response to the questionnaire, she explains she has only two surviving children.

'One boy died of malaria when he was one year old. Another small girl, she got measles and didn't live. Another one she died in childbirth because the cord was around her neck.'

She puts her hands around her neck and sticks out her tongue grotesquely.

'*Pole sana, Mama,*' I sympathise wishing I could comfort her better.

'Last pregnancy, I tried to fix the roof. I fell and there was no one here to help me so I lost the baby.' She looks thin and anaemic, probably as a result of bilharzia.

'And the child you are carrying? Will you go to the health centre to have this baby?'

'I can't go there. My husband cannot let me go to a clinic. It is not in our religion. What can I do?'

I look up at the hole in the thatch, through which the rain would pour in.

'What about if your husband got a second wife?'

'Ah no, he can't do that. We are Christians. Only one wife.'

I am at a loss for an answer. I realise how hard it must be for a woman to be the only wife, carrying the whole burden of the household. I think of my time in England looking after the children alone. Mothers need the help of other women to raise their large broods, especially if they live in a village. It strikes me that monogamy is fine for the rich. On balance I think I would opt for polygamy if I was a rural woman. I must talk to Anthony about it, see if he wants a second wife.

Rosie: February 1889.

I love to be left in charge when Mum goes away. The best time is the evening. I am always carrying the twins on my back. I love to fold the little girl, Wendy, inside my kanga on my back like we do with our children. She comes to bed so happily when I carry her like we Kikuyu carry our children. I am playing games with her, like I am a horse. She enjoys this very much.

Sometimes I watch TV with them. There is a funny story about a little boy in the forest who grows up with animals. They love this story the best. Charlie scratches under his arm like a baboon, and says, 'I am Mowgli, hoof, hoof', like a wild boy. I have to put them to bed at the right time. I am watching for when it is the time to sleep and I start telling them, 'The time is nearly to go to bed.'

I tell them each time how many minutes is remaining before they must go. Sometimes the little boy Charlie pretends that he has fallen asleep on the chair. I know he wants to be carried on my back to be taken to bed. It is making me happy to see how he enjoys being helped by me. I go where he is on the seat. I say, 'Charlie, love, are you asleep?'

Then he pretends he is sleeping when I start to carry him. He thinks I don't know he is pretending. So, I carry him to his bed. When I put him down, he starts laughing in a happy, jokey way. He is such a funny boy even now. I am like a child with them and enjoying their good games.

Then I come to get Tristan he says to me, 'Please Rosie, my turn, my turn!'

I take them to their bedroom, and they are so good. I sing songs to make them sleep

When they come back from safari Mum asks me, 'Were the children good?'

I say, 'Yes, they were very happy.' I am thinking about what a nice game we had.

Virginia, February 1989.

I can't wait to ask Rosie about what she thinks of polygamy, given she is a committed Christian. I drop the children at school, and I put the kettle on to make us a cup of tea, determined to have a conversation and learn how she sees things. I put two mugs of sweet hot tea on the kitchen table and then settle down. She is washing the dishes with her back to me.

'Rosie, come and have some tea. I want to ask you something. Would you ever let Kimendi have a second wife?'

She drops the saucepan she is washing and turns round to me with her eyes wide with surprise. She wipes her hands on her apron and sits down at the kitchen table with me, shaking her head in disbelief.

'How do you know *that*, Mum?'

'What do you mean?

'Kimendi *have* got a new girlfriend. She was even in my house when I came home last time I was there! He wants to marry her.'

'Oh, Rosie! No, that is not right, you can't allow that.' I respond without thinking.

'Mum, you know something? I don't even care about this woman. She can stay there. It is good for me too. It is long time that I don't care much about Kimendi. He can go with her. It's fine, Mum.'

Rosie smiles at me bravely, as if it were the most natural thing to accept another woman in her husband's bed. I gape at her, surprised that she is so broadminded. Rosie is a devout Christian, yet she accepts polygamy so lightly. Very pragmatic. 'So, you just left them there together, your husband and his new woman, with your children?'

'What can I do Mum? At least I know who that lady is now. Before I was always wondering, where does all his money go? He gets some money from his job as a carpenter, but he never uses it for our family. He spends his money drinking beer. Without the money you give us for my job, we would have nothing at all. It's only my money that we take for the food. Now, I think it is because he buys things for this lady.'

'Has this affair been going on long?' I take a gulp of tea and stare into the mug trying to imagine myself in her position.

'Maybe. Perhaps that is why Kimendi is telling me to work here, I don't know. I can't trust him so much now. Anyway, it doesn't matter. I don't want to go back there now. That lady can even help with the children. She can be the young wife. She is not so bad, Mum. She is very polite to me, not shouting at all!'

Although I am surprised by Rosie's resignation in the face of this rebuff, I don't want to comment. Her life is so very different from mine, and although I am starting to see the world through her lens, I know I will never really understand her properly. If Kimendi takes a second wife, without divorcing Rosie this is polygamy. My positive assessment of polygamy for the rural poor seems to dissolve when I hear Rosie's story. I feel incensed that she should be usurped.

'Rosie, what about the children, what do they think about this woman?

'They just say nothing. Nobody can tell Kimendi what to do. He just shouts at them and tells them to go away. He wants to be the one who decides. He doesn't care about the children.' She drinks her tea. There is a long silence.

I never considered for a moment that her marriage would collapse, or that she might leave her family if she worked with us. They seemed like such a perfect family. Maybe she has been longing to escape for years and my job offer gave her a way out. Am I getting too close to her, getting involved in a private aspect of her life which is none of my concern? My mother never made any attempt to get to know or understand her employees, they were two dimensional shadows in our lives, like *Mpishi* is to Mrs. Hunter Price. As a child I remember my embarrassment at her disregard for underlings. To compensate I have become the very opposite. I can't help getting involved and seeing things from their perspective.

'I think you should go back home and look after your own family. Don't feel you are letting us down. The kids are much bigger now and we can manage fine. I think it's too far for you to travel each day on that dangerous road. For goodness' sake, Rosie, go back home now. I honestly won't mind. It's better if you stay with your own family. Kimendi is taking advantage of you being away from him now.'

'Mum, you remember I told you six children were enough. He didn't want me to use contraception. So, because I refused to have more children, he wants a younger wife and another family.'

I feel slightly responsible for the breakup. If she is leaving her own family to join ours, what will happen when we leave Kenya? At some point soon we will have to return to our home country. We are not allowed to work in Kenya indefinitely and our contract is almost complete.

Healthy Living beside Lake Victoria (Cover of Booklet) 1986.

Chapter 11

Maasai Mara

'Uchungu wa mwana aujuae mzazi'
'A mother's pain in pregnancy bonds her to her child.'

Virginia: August 1989.

It is six hours down a long, corrugated dirt road to the Maasai Mara, the most well-known game reserve in East Africa. This vast plain of savannah grassland, straddling the border between Kenya and Tanzania, hosts one of the greatest migrations of animals in the world. Over two million wildebeest travel north from the Serengeti plains in Tanzania and cross into Kenya in July each year in search of fresh pasture found in the Mara, before migrating back again in October. Wildebeest cows give birth to their calves in January and, two months later, the calves set off with the adults from the far south on the long gallop north, which will take them eight months to reach the grasslands of the Maasai Mara. We have come in August in the hope of catching up with the herd as they cross the Mara River into Kenya.

The unimaginable number on the hoof is difficult to absorb. In all directions, dense herds of grey wildebeest graze the infinite grassland. Other animals move with them: the stately kudu with their corkscrew antlers, nimble rust-red-and-white Thompson's gazelle, the black-and-white zebra, all cross the plains together in the same direction. A range of predators lurks patiently in the fringes of the long grass, picking off any stray calf. Slope-backed hyena crouch around the periphery, waiting for the lordly lions to have their fill.

Packs of silver-backed jackals and painted wild dogs lick their paws, watching, their dark muzzles twitching with every scent. The herds graze calmly. Like the lake flies in their swarms over Lake Victoria, this abundance of prey on the plains of the Mara reduces the odds of each individual being killed.

Like a vast green sea, the plains stretch interminably, as far as the eye can see. The shadows of clouds passing overhead make it seem as though the pasture itself is heaving, like the swell of an ocean. No fences mark the man-made boundaries between the two countries; the animals have no nationality.

I am taking a turn at the wheel of our Land Cruiser with Anthony and the children sitting on the roof on a rough bench welded to the luggage rack. This makes it easier to spot game in the long grass from a high vantage point. The boys are desperate to see some lions, excited by the danger it implies. Vultures fly in from all sides, whirling high above us in the sky. We bump over the savannah to where the scavengers are homing in on the remains of a kill. They skip around, scruffy feathers drooping, necks bent low as they try to snatch a morsel of the remains. Lying in the shade of a thorn tree are four languid lionesses flopped on their side, stomachs bulging from a recent meal. A couple of young cubs are still chewing on bones scattered around. One cub is playing with its mother's tail, which twitches with irritation at the disturbance of the playful young. The lionesses look up lazily as I pull up beside them. I inch closer for the perfect photograph, fiddling around with my camera, intent on capturing the playful cubs.

'Mooooove! Drive!' Anthony yells from above.

I drop my camera. A lioness is crouching, the black tassel of her tail flicking like a bad-tempered cat, her ears flat. Her mean eyes are focused on the children above. I hit the accelerator just before she leaps and the car skids away.

The kids yell in excitement, 'She almost came for us.' Anthony is visibly shaken and insists on taking back the wheel.

The further south we get, the denser the herds become. As far as the eye can see are wildebeest, a million black tails flicking flies, the continuous cow-like mooing of multitudes of mouths. We head for a trail of dust across the plains.

The herds are gently cantering along, each behind the other in lines stretching from one horizon to another. Nose to tail, they pound along, their calves keeping up beside them. The smell of fresh rain and new grass drives them on.

We shadow the herd to where the worst challenge of the whole migration occurs: the infamous crossing place of the mighty Mara River, where wildebeest launch themselves frantically into the gushing torrent. The drive of the herd forces them to leap towards the predators below. If they hesitate, they are crushed by the ever-increasing pressure of the herd which builds up behind them. On the edges of the muddy torrent, crocodiles wait, ready to snap up those that fall. Too soft to watch such carnage, we leave before any tragedy occurs.

The open prairies of the Mara have belonged since time immemorial to the Maasai. When the land became a game reserve, the Maasai were allowed to remain on their land because of their traditional ability to co-exist with the wild animals. The young men still live out in the wilds, guarding their valuable cows from lions and other predators. To provide employment and lessen the temptation to poach wild animals, the Maasai morans are trained as camp guards, using their traditional skills to protect visitors from lions at night as well as teach survival skills to foreigners who are fascinated by their culture. As children, young Maasai boys are given regular beatings, which they are expected to endure without complaint. Teenagers are banished to the bush for years and must survive on their own wits. The young men usually live off the fresh blood of the cattle they herd, puncturing a vein of a cow to syphon the off blood, which they mix with milk to drink. Every few years, a group of boys between twelve and twenty-five are initiated together and circumcised without painkillers. Boys do not dare cry out in pain. Circumcised Maasai are the warriors of the village and can only return when they are considered strong enough to marry and protect the family.

We have been allocated two such hardened morans as guards for our camp. They come sauntering in at nightfall, like elegant Roman gladiators in their red togas. They are the peacocks of the Kenyan tribes, whiling away the long hours in the bush creating their elegant hairstyles, using red mud smeared into their matted dreadlocks, braiding them into elaborate loops around their ears.

The morans enjoy the chance to show off to our kids how they can leap vertically into the air, bouncing increasingly higher until they look like puppets on springs. They teach the boys how to start a fire without matches to cook the meat. Like other pastoralists, they preserve their livestock and only eat them on rare special occasions, so the slabs of meat we share with them are consumed with relish. The boys sit with them round the fire, listening to their stories of encounters with wild animals. Tristan asks to hold a spear, and practises lunging forward, pretending he is killing a lion single-handedly. How much better than playing spiderman on the slide in the village playground, I think to myself. I love to see the children in the wilds of Africa.

When it gets dark, the children crawl into the little pup tent and snuggle into their sleeping bags with much excitement. We zip up the fly screen to protect them from mosquitoes while we stay up watching the stars, listening to the sounds of hyenas whooping in the distance, falling asleep to the haunting sound of a distant lion groaning his way through the night. The men sit around the fire and chat far into the night, their gentle voices warning lions to stay away.

Only a few hours later we awaken to the hysterical screaming of the children. They claw their way out of their tent, scratching themselves in panic. Horror-stuck, I imagine a snake, or a scorpion. We find that an army of ants has invaded the tent through the tiny hole where the three zips meet. We pull off the children's clothes to see them covered in monster black ants.

The Maasai come sauntering across, unperturbed.

'*Siafu*, ants,' our morans explain calmly, pinching their fingers and thumb together. Picking off the *siafu* from the children is a nightmare as the thousands on the ground keep up the attack on us with their big pincers. They are renowned for setting out in long lines 'on safari' and eating anything in their path.

The Maasai think the whole incident is hilarious. They jump around, pretending they are being bitten, imitating the children to make them laugh. Since we cannot get all the ants out of the bedding inside the tent, the kids must sleep in the car, with the window open, but now they can't get back to sleep because of the mosquitoes that dive-bomb them all night.

The next morning, a band of Maasai girls come into the camp, exquisite with their petite noses and oval faces. They are adorned in beads like overladen Christmas trees: each has different decorations to show us. Their hair is cropped close to their heads, with bright, beaded headbands round their foreheads. One has strings of beads looped from her forehead around each eye to her ears, where they are attached to the headband of glinting beads. Another has fashioned little tin arrows, which dangle down like a crown around her head. They all have at least one large neckband, stretching like a plate to their shoulders. They are hoping to sell their bead decorations and soon, we are festooned. Once a necklace is around our necks, they won't allow us to take off. I exchange their beaded jewellery for my manufactured bangles. Each new bangle marks the extraordinary diversity of cultures in Kenya.

Rosie: September 1989.

I told Mum, 'Tristan is burning up with fever: he has malaria.' It is a problem for the *wazungu* who come to Kenya. We people are used to malaria, and we don't get it so easily from mosquitoes. Some get malaria every year when it rains, and we know when we have it. It gives such a bad headache and bad fever. You feel so tired in every place and want to lay down and sleep. Even it can kill you. So many children here die from malaria.

I tell Mum and she says 'It is ten days since we came back from the Mara. So, it must be malaria. He must take malaria pills. He will be fine by tomorrow. He doesn't have to go to the doctor.'

Then Tristan sleeps and sleeps but the next day he is still sick. He is too too hot.

So, Mum says, 'We must put him in the bath to make him cold.' So, we do that, but he cries and cries. My poor boy is so sick. I tell Mum, 'We must take him to the hospital because he can die.'

Dad is away, so we go together, me and Mum. Tristan is too weak to walk. I give him a piggyback to the car. He has such a sore head. His mouth is so dry. He shakes all the time in the car. We go to the children's hospital, which I know because one time I was there before with my own daughter. The nurse comes and she is very kind. They put him in bed and put the tubes on him.

Then Mum leaves me by the bed with Tristan as she must get the other children from school, so I stay there and I pray all the time. I cry and I beseech the Lord,

'Why Lord, do you make this happen to this family? Is it because there are some people jealous of Mum maybe. Please lift off this sickness from my good boy.'

I know it is now serious because it is three days of fever, and he is still so hot. Mum comes back and the doctor tells her, 'This Malaria is the worst kind because the *dawa* cannot work for him. Our mosquitoes are used to this *dawa*. They have something like 'resistance' she tells me. So, now he must have the strongest *dawa* to cure him.'

Mum goes home to be with Wendy and Charlie. So, I stay with Tristan all night giving him water and I try to keep him cool, but he sleeps so deeply he could be dead. I am worrying too much. The next day Mum is calling Dad, but he is far away in one of the water projects. So, she starts to fear as well. Then I pray some more. I tell her, 'You must pray Mum,' so even she starts to pray, and I tell her, 'Only the Lord can save him now.'

When the doctor comes, he says we must keep him cool, or he can have a fit if his temperature is too high. That is called cerebral malaria, he says. I know that one too, as my uncle did die from that. Mum is very scared now, and I do hug her and say 'Its fine Mum. He is a strong boy, not like our African children who are so thin and weak and can die. He will be fine.'

She starts to cry very very much. I have never seen her like that. Even, I don't know if the English ladies do cry, but now I see they are the same as us. All mothers fear for the life of their children.

'Don't worry Mum. Malaria is like this. You know it can be so bad one day, then the next day they are fine. Tristan is very strong. I will pray for him.'

I sing my prayers aloud; I will make a miracle to save him.

Mum is stroking his head and singing to him, 'In the jungle, the mighty jungle the lion sleeps tonight...' but I tell her, 'Why don't you pray to Jesus, not to the lion, who knows how to kill people. The Lord is our Saviour.' Then she hugs me and says, 'Rosie, God only hears the prayers of those who believe in him. I know your prayers will work, but I don't think mine will.

Suddenly Tristan sits up, his eyes open without seeing. He stares ahead shouting like a crazy boy.

'Go! Go! Lion! I will kill you!'

He tries to get out of bed in his sleep. He is breathing hard with fear. We soothe him and I rock him to sleep like a little baby. Tristan lies in hospital for two days. He is white, white, white, like he is dead. Then, his temperature goes down slowly, slowly. Next day he sits up and looks around like he is coming from another place, and he don't know where he is.

I tell him, 'Tristan, you are fine now. You are in the hospital. Mum is coming soon. Never fear.'

Then he asks for some orange juice. Soon he is eating one biscuit. He is weak on his feet when we get him home. Mum comes and we are happy together with Tristan, and we hug him with joy.

I tell Mum something funny.

'Do you know that prostitutes are called mosquitoes! *mbu*! Because they come out at night and spread disease.'

Tristan asks me 'Rosie, what are prostitutes?'

'They are a type of mosquito that make men very sick. Now my big boy is well again, there are many things you have to learn. Like how to avoid mosquitoes in life if you want to survive.'

He tells me, 'When I grow up, I am going to be strong and maybe even kill a lion.'

'Tristan when you are a man, you don't have to kill a lion to be strong, you just have to avoid mosquitoes, 'she says laughing at her own joke.

Chapter 12

Tana River

'Dalili ya mvua ni mawingu.'
'If there are clouds, expect rain.'

Virginia: September 1989.

The missionaries who came to Wema Mission did not expect to survive long. What drove them to leave their safe countries in the northern hemisphere for this godforsaken part of Africa, beyond the rule of law, beyond redemption? Father Spiro is Maltese, a tough little man who left his perfect Mediterranean island to join the White Fathers, one of the earliest religious orders to come to Africa. Pursuing a childhood dream to serve the people of Africa, he was sent to Wema Mission in the Lower Tana River delta to deliver the word of God to the heathen. The two priests who preceded him had both died of cerebral malaria.

The two white nuns, Sister Romana and Sister Agnes, are both from North America, from families who themselves left Ireland to escape the potato famine in the nineteenth century to start afresh in the brave new world. As the Catholic descendants of tough Irish peasants, they are prepared to forfeit their comfortable lives in America to run the hospital for the Orma in one of the outposts of the lost British empire. The sisters throw themselves into this difficult task with little outside support.

Mama Gola was delighted with my training manual for Mfangano Island and now has asked me to do a similar story book for a hygiene programme in

Wema Mission. The project aims to sink 50 boreholes and to ensure they store their drinking water properly, but the Orma people need to learn the same hygiene messages as the Luya in Mfangano. The people here have a totally different culture being an offshoot of the Somali tribe who live north across the border. This is the most remote place I have been to since arriving in Kenya and there is an element of risk which I am trying to ignore, especially as I have come alone without Anthony.

I think what my father would say if he could see me now, a woman alone hundreds of miles away from 'civilization' without another white person in sight. To put this in the context of my upbringing, I need to explain the extreme paranoia over the apparent appetite of black men for white women at the time I grew up in the colony of Rhodesia in the 50's. As girls we had never been allowed to socialise with locals, and women were never allowed out alone or as a group without a white male escort to protect them. When I left my strict Catholic convent, and went to Europe, I was amazed to see that girls went out by themselves at night without any concern for their own safety.

Despite my wild bohemian years as an art student, I still have this residual wariness of being alone with males. Here I am, the only white woman in the middle of nowhere in the hands of a bunch of unknown men with an AK47 gun. I don't even know where we are going. My deeply hidden fears start to surface as we bump down one of the most remote roads in Kenya. An armed guard is hanging off the back of the truck in case of an ambush by Somali bandits, known as '*shifta*'. Every time we hit a pothole, his rifle dips casually towards me. I am hoping it is not loaded. What if the ruthless *Shifta* stop the car like highwaymen on this lonely road?

As the hours pass and I am largely ignored by my travelling companions I begin to relax. I feel like intrepid female journalists must feel when they are reporting from a dangerous war zone. It is a liberating few hours as I realise that these men have absolutely no thought of taking advantage of my situation.

We trek across the scrubby coastal plain, through the wetlands of the lower Tana River as it fans out to the sea. On either side of the road, the bush is thick with game. The dusty road itself shows the trails of fresh antelope spoor, mingled with the heavy prints of Zebu cattle. There is also evidence of predatory hunters – jackals and hyenas. Occasionally, the impressive seal of a large lion's paw can be seen, stamped in the sand. Massive elephant footprints, the size of dinner plates, imprint the road, punctuated by their grassy turds the size of bowling balls but we see no wild animals.

After four hours, we draw up in front of a cluster of nondescript buildings with whitewashed walls and red-tile roofs. The fly-screened door is opened by Sister Romana, smiling a gracious welcome. She leads us into their convent house. Like every other mission in Africa, it is a modest bungalow. We follow her into a tidy sitting room with red, polished cement floors and crocheted antimacassars on the few plastic-covered sofas that line the walls of the room. We sit down and are plied with strong tea and Marie biscuits.

Sister Romana has bright blue eyes and a strong face. Her hair is hidden modestly under her veil. She sits forward on the edge of her chair, a long crucifix dangling around her neck. She explains that there are no wells in the villages, so the women must fetch water from the Tana River. No one ever boils or treats their drinking water, so many people die of dysentery. They face other dangers when collecting water: not only children, but adults are being taken by crocodiles almost weekly. Sanitation in the area is non-existent. They still just use the bush.

I munch slowly on the biscuits, feeling completely out of my depth, wondering where to start in such a challenging environment. Daily life is extremely dangerous here. Women are abducted by the shifta, who take them for their wives. If the shifta attack, the men fight back. They don't come into the hospital unless the wounds are serious and, by that time, they have septicaemia, and it is often too late.

'We are all at the mercy of the *shifta*. We are hoping that, because we provide them with medicine, we are safe. They come here to the mission when they are sick. In fact, we "religious" seem to be safer than the police. They attacked a police car yesterday and killed two of the policemen. They are angry because

Kenya has been helping the Somali government against radical Muslim warlords.'

'It really is beyond the rule of law here, isn't it? It must be terrifying for you.'

Sister Agnes arrives, looking tired. 'I am so sorry. I was called out to treat a child who was taken by a python this morning. He is so brave.'

She offers to take me on a tour of the hospital to give me an idea of the local health issues. The little hero of the python attack is lying on a bed, rigid with bandages, stony quiet. His petite mother is sitting like a Madonna by his bed, rhythmically flapping flies off his beautiful face.

'She was on her way to fetch water, with her sister, and the little boy was following behind them. She heard the boy scream with terror to find a python had already coiled round his legs, pinning him down. It must have been at least five metres long. The two women between them managed to kill the python with their pangas but, in the process, the boy was cut badly.'

Hugging the young woman, Sister Agnes says, 'She is a very brave woman. This boy is so courageous.' She pats him lovingly on his head.

The boy is exquisite. He looks up with large dark eyes blank with fright.

Patients lie in rows, with relatives squatting beside them, giving them food. We pass through a ward full of expectant mothers, holding their aching stomachs, waiting to deliver. Everyone is thin to the point of emaciation. Most women look malnourished with thin faces and sunken cheeks like anorexic supermodels.

'There is a big risk of mothers haemorrhaging in childbirth due to anaemia,' Sister is explaining. 'This is the only hospital for many miles where they can get proper care during childbirth. They often try to walk here while in labour. If the baby is born on the way, there is a high risk of complications in the birth. We are trying to get the mamas to come well before their babies are due.'

I have been attached to the drilling team to enable me to observe the culture of the Orma, so that I can develop some pictures for hygiene training which reflect their own village. We set off in the pale dawn light to drill a new well. Women are already awake, winding down the dusty roads to fetch water and firewood ahead of the scorching sun, which will make such trips even more exhausting. The coastal humidity builds up during the day. As we approach the first village, a colourful group of women, each balancing a bucket of water on her head, returns from the new well. They weave along the dusty paths back to their homes like models on a catwalk – some of the most beautiful women in Africa, tall and slender with elegant bones, small ankles, and wrists. Their long aquiline faces are set with lively dark eyes. They have delicate mouths with wide smiles, showing strong white teeth.

We come to the first Orma compound in a nondescript stretch of thorny bush. The tall grass domes, which are their homes, pop up above the stunted thorn trees like inverted weavers' nests. Chickens scatter and goats jump out of the way as we drive into the centre of the village. We pull up next to a dead cow, hanging from a branch, being drained of blood. As the vehicle is coated with a fine layer of white dust, I step down to the ground, careful to avoid getting it on my clothes. Skinny yellow curs bark in a frenzy while a few men, as emaciated as their dogs, curse and chase them away. Dusty children peep curiously out of the huts at me, stomachs unnaturally swollen from the worms that live perennially in their guts.

Women tread past quietly, raising their hands in greeting, coyly sheltering half their faces. They wear two *kangas*, one wound tightly round their bony chests, to cover their bodies, the other draped demurely over their heads. The bright colours give them the look of psychedelic Madonna's. Only their husbands can ever see their long fuzzy hair, pulled back into high buns at the back, giving even more elegance to the shape of their heads. The women hardly bother to wave away the flies feeding on the *ghee* used to oil their skin.

So many of the mothers are still teenagers. They have babies slung from one shoulder in a *kanga* which matches their sarong. I note their way of carrying a baby is different from normal, a detail I must capture in my drawings. Most mothers I have seen in many parts of Africa, strap their babies firmly on their backs. The babies have noses caked in dried snot and their weeping eyes are thick with flies and I wonder if there is much trachoma as a result.

We stop in the middle of a village where the water diviner has already done his work, walking across the field with a forked stick held out above the ground. A likely spot for drilling the borehole has already been located. The rig has been brought to the village on a donkey cart and is being assembled. Six women climb up onto the crossbar to provide the weight to sink the augur blade, whilst the men push them round and round like a merry go round in a playground, enabling the villagers themselves to provide the weight and the power for the drilling. There is much suggestive joking with the men teasing the women as they push them round. The women sitting on the crossbar shriek and slap the men away when they try to sneak a touch of their bottoms. With each turn, the corkscrew sinks further into the ground. Then the men shake out the mud from the augur and reassemble it for another round of drilling. It is a long and tedious process, but the water table is shallow in the area. After a few hours, the earth gets damper, until finally the mud gives way to water.

There are whoops of joy from the team. The oldest woman has the honour of the first taste. Like a priestess she holds up the glass to the sky to check the clarity of the water. Wiping her wrinkly old lips, she takes the first sip making a noisy slurp like an expert wine taster.

'*Mzuri sana*. Very good! '*Maji safi*, clean water,' she pronounces at the top of her voice. The women ululate.

There are shouts of triumph from the men, who now all take their turn to taste the water passing it from one to another, each one shouting with appreciation.

Now the drilling is over, the men cluster around us, curious to know what a white woman could be doing in this desolate place. Orma men are tall and stringy, often bare-chested, with emaciated long legs. Most wear scruffy T-shirts hanging over their *kikoy* of fine striped cotton, which is the male version of a *kanga*. They tie this cloth untidily round their thin hips. They all carry large knobkerries over their shoulders with a *panga* tucked conspicuously into their belts. Many of the men regard me with haughty disdain. It is likely that this is the first time they have been close to a Western woman.

The Orma men are as tough, although not as elegant as the Maasai. Their initiation ritual also trains them to be fearless and they too are expected to fight lions to protect their herds of Zebu cattle, moving through some of the wildest territory in Kenya. In the lower Tana, lions and elephants live alongside the Orma settlements. Unlike the lions of the Mara, who fear nothing from the camera-carrying tourists, the wildlife here is hunted and therefore extremely shy and seldom seen.

We are ushered to the shade of a tree, and I am invited to sit down to formally explain my business.

'I want to draw your village, so that we can make pictures about how to protect your drinking water properly,' I tell them, through an interpreter.

'Are you married?' They quiz me suspiciously. They require my credentials before they give away any information.

'Yes, my husband is the one assisting you to get *maji safi*, clean water, in your village.'

'Do you have *totos*?'

'Yes, I have three children.'

'Who is looking after the *totos* if you are here?' another elder quizzes me curiously.

'My husband is looking after them.'

That raises eyebrows. 'What man would look after children, while his wife travels alone into a place which is full of strange men?'

'A good man. Because my husband cannot talk to your women, he has sent me to learn from your wives. I make pictures so that people can learn.'

I show them some drawings and they cluster around curiously.

'We would like to make a book for the Orma people. Every family in the village will be given a book of pictures to teach the children. This can help your women understand how to make your children strong.' The old men point at the black-and-white sketches and shake their heads, unimpressed.

'These are not our people. We don't cook like this. This is the home of *Giriama* people. We make homes just of sticks and grass, so we can move to change pastures when it is dry here.'

'Exactly. I will change these pictures so you can see your own village. Are these your women, here in this picture?'

The wizened old man screws his eyes up and brings the picture nearer to see more clearly.

'These are not our women. Our women are tall and beautiful with long *kanga* to cover their legs. They do not wear these clothes. They cover their heads.'

The next picture shows cattle standing in a river and defecating, with a woman nearby collecting water.

'You have not done a good job drawing these cows. These are not our *Zebu* cattle,' he notes, more interested in the cattle than the implications of poor hygiene. 'Our cattle have very big horns.'

'This is the kind of information I am looking for. Thank you so much for all your help. Can you now allow me to meet your women and see inside your houses, so I can draw everything as it really is in your village?'

'*Sawa*. It is permitted. Please come with me,' says the village leader.

He takes me to his own house. As a village leader, it seems to be his prerogative to monopolise strangers. As I stroll beside him, the children cluster around me like bees round a honey pot, eyes wide with interest, nudging up to me. A teenage girl shyly tries to touch my brown curly mop of hair. The village consists of about twenty tall grass, egg-shaped shelters looking much like elongated birds' nests.

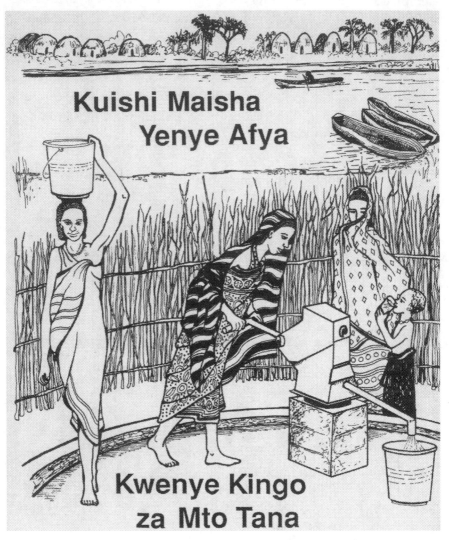

Healthy Living beside the Tana River (Cover of booklet) 1987.

The chief's thin wife slips in through the narrow slit between the thatched walls and bids me to follow. I take off my sandals and just manage to squeeze through the door. Inside, it is dark and cool, scented by the sweet smell of fresh straw. The flies and children remain outside. Being in the hut is like being in a womb, a calm retreat from the heat and the glare outside. My eyes rove around the walls of the hut, adjusting to the dim interior. I suck up the scene. Flexible ribs of vine are bent around the inside of the hut like a Chinese lantern, to provide the framework for the thatch.

I smile and point at things. Beside the door, a few *pangas* are wedged into the straw wall, ready in case of intruders. Other than a couple of plastic buckets and some cheap plastic sandals, there are few manufactured goods. Big black cooking pots and a wooden spoon are piled on one side. There is no water stored, no shop food to be seen. A small sack of millet-like grain is stashed in a corner of the hut. Most food here is grown by the family and consumed immediately. There are a few cuts of meat hanging from the roof to dry.

Imagine living without any means to preserve food, I think to myself, no electricity for a fridge, no tin cans. They have virtually no goods of material value, their total wealth consisting of their cattle. On each side of the hut is a high platform of straight canes, covered with cow hides over a bedding of grass. One platform is for the parents and the other for the children, who sleep together like sweaty little puppies sharing body warmth, bed wets and skin parasites. There are chickens roosting comfortably on both platforms. The two women giggle at my interest but are too shy to speak to me directly. I mime my thanks wishing I could communicate properly with them.

As I leave the Orma village, the sun is setting, and the women are sweeping the dried cow dung into heaps of fuel before lighting little bonfires to fend off the mosquitoes that plague them all night. The village will soon be covered in a haze of blue smoke, which will curl into the slots of the huts to protect the children from mosquitoes. If the infants survive malaria in summer, in winter they may succumb to pneumonia, aggravated by the smoky air they must breathe all night. Even if the Orma families are provided with mosquito nets, they will seldom be used to protect children from malaria. The men commandeer the nets for fishing.

Children cannot thrive in this foetid climate and many toddlers do not make their fifth birthday, dying unnecessarily from one disease or another. Mothers try to protect their new-born babies from disease by tying grubby leather amulets around their fat little tummies, under their grossly protruding belly buttons, in the hope that they will be safe. If that fails and their children sicken, they must carry them on the long and dangerous path to Wema Mission. I put myself into their position and realised how Tristan would have died of malaria if I lived here. What would happen to these remote communities without the sister's help?

PART 2

LAMU ISLAND

Dhow race off Lamu Island. Watercolour. 1993.

LAMU ISLAND

Chapter 13

Hakuna Matata

'Bendera hufuata upepo'
'A flag flutters the way the wind blows'

Virginia, October 1989.

Lamu Island, lying off the mainland of Kenya, became the East African equivalent of Marrakesh during the 1960s, attracting alternative truth seekers from across the globe. Its ancient Arabian culture appealed to the international hippy community, resulting in an eclectic mix of off-beat wanderers, who have taken root, living a simple lifestyle beyond the reach of western materialism.

For centuries Lamu Town on this Island was the main port for the Omani traders who plied the length of the East Africa coast on the trade winds. Although there is now a dirt road up the north coast of Kenya to the border with Somalia, only the most adventurous of travellers still risk the decrepit local bus service that transports goods and provides the only means for the poor to travel cheaply. The Northeast Province of Kenya is remote and beyond the law, as the police cannot contain the cross-border *shifta* insurgency fuelled from across the border in Somalia. Following a string of attacks in the area, no tourists are allowed to travel by road and local buses from Mombasa to Lamu have to be chaperoned safely by heavily armed convoys. As even these buses have been ambushed, I realise now that the risk of travelling in Tana River was not my imagination. To get to Lamu Island with our family the only way is to fly in a light aircraft, which departs weekly from Nairobi.

'Can Rosie come too?' Wendy begs, 'So she can go in a plane?'

'Won't you be afraid to fly, Rosie?' I ask her, thinking how delightful it would be to give her such an experience.

'I can come with you Mum. I can't be scared of going in an aeroplane. If you and Dad are there. I can show the children that I am very brave and fear nothing.'

The little domestic airport outside Nairobi is a glamorous place, frequented by attractive young safari guides and hunters flying opulent American clients to the Mara in private planes. After four years in the country, we are starting to feel more like Kenyan residents than 'two-year-wonders'. We walk straight onto the little runway where a small nine-seater Cessna waits for us. The children are jumping up and down with expectation. Rosie is holding the twins' hands and laughing with excitement. One at a time, we bounce up the quaint fold-down stairs and squeeze into our seats. Tristan and Charlie grab the front row behind the pilot, enjoying the satisfying click of opening and closing their seat belts, fiddling with the air nozzles to spray each other with cold air. There is no air hostess; we are the only passengers. The pilot gables off the mandatory briefing, how to buckle up and bail out.

Rosie is sitting next to Wendy, who is showing her how to put on her seat belt. The pilot wheels the little plane into position for take-off. We bounce down the tarmac to squeals of excitement. Rosie's eyes grow large with expectation as we whizz along the runway. She is hugging Wendy with her eyes tightly closed. The two boys are peering out of the window to catch the moment when the wheels leave the ground and our plane separates from its earth-bound shadow.

We climb into the skies; the pilot amuses the kids by swerving between the towering cumulonimbus clouds like a slalom skier. Rosie is beside herself, gasping between her expressions of wonder. We fly over the long brown plains of the Tsavo National Park. Within an hour the tropical coastal plain is below us, with the lush Tana River delta fanning out across the wild bush. I recognise the buildings of Wema Mission and think how remote it is from the modern world. Minutes later we are above the river as it reaches the sea:

the low-lying islands of the Lamu archipelago, floating over the mangrove swamp. Then we are over the ancient port, circling round to the neighbouring island of Manda where there is enough flat land for a runway. The little plane is manoeuvring closer and closer to the ground, wings tipping to each side as the pilot steadies for the approach. With squeals of terror, we hit the dirt below and bounce to a standstill.

The pilot turns around and beams at us all. 'Welcome to Lamu Island, where the temperature is 35 degrees in the shade.'

He clambers out of his seat and lets down the steps. As the door opens, a wall of muggy air hits us like a blast from an oven. Towards us comes a man pushing a wooden scotch cart. The bags are handed down to him. We wander across the narrow tarmac like movie stars in a remote film location, to the little *makuti* shelter at the end of the runway. There are no customs to clear, just a couple of officials guiding us through a gate to pick up the baggage that is being dumped under a vast mango tree. Muslim men in dirty *kanzu* have been lounging in the shade chewing *miraa*, waiting for this flight. They close in on us as we approach, all talking at once, jostling each other to get our attention, all pushing their offerings inches away from our face.

'You want room? Very nice room in Lamu Town. We have very good toilet.'

'You want henna drawing on your feet? My sister very good for Swahili design.'

'You want boat? I have very big boat. Please come with me.'

'I take your luggage, please, you come this way,' says one, yanking our bags from us.

It is invasive and unnerving.

Just as our patience wears thin, a good-looking young man with very dark skin, dressed neatly in dazzling white shorts and shirt, comes forward. Above the confusion of the mob, he holds up a handwritten sign with our name on it.

'Good afternoon, Sir. I am here to meet you from Palm Tree House. I am Solomon. Mama Clarissa sent me. Please come this way, I have a boat waiting for you.'

The crowd of touts disperse, and relieved, we follow Solomon down the dazzling white sandy path to the edge of the sea.

ֆ ֆ ֆ

Rosie: August 1989.

I close my eyes as that plane starts to move and I call on the Lord.

'Please God, can you give me strength to go up into the air as I am afraid now Lord. Protect me and this family so that we can go safely.'

Wendy says to me 'Hey Rosie, open your eyes and see what is happening.'

'Look Rosie, we are taking off!' Charlie also tells me.

I think that it is like being in a car. The plane goes along the road easily. The pilot gives us very nice sweets. Then very quickly we get into the air, and I can't believe how it can do this without problems. Then my ears start to go funny, and I can't hear properly.

Wendy tells me, 'It's okay, Rosie, don't worry, just suck the sweet hard so your ears go pop, pop, pop.' So, I suck the sweet and I can hear much better. Even if she is only five years old, she has been so many times in a plane that she can help me very much.

Then I see Nairobi under the plane. All those houses. I feel like shouting to my friends down there. 'Hey, look at me here above you.'

Even, we are above the Ngong hills. It is a very wonderful thing to be so high.

Then Mum says, 'Look kids! Can anyone see any animals?' I try to look out of the window, but I am very much afraid to go so close to the glass because it makes me to be a bit dizzy. Tristan tells me, 'I can see giraffe.' I ask him, 'Is it possible to see animals from up here? Won't they run away from the aeroplane?' Then I look down and see many very tall giraffes just walking along, like they don't care.

Then Charlie say, 'Look Rosie, I can see a rhino.' I am thinking he is just trying to beat his brother, but then I see that it is true. There are even big rhinos walking along the roads in that park. It is the first time I see such animals.

I say to Mum, 'Is it possible? Am I really here, me, Rosie, in this aeroplane? It is so good. Thank you, Mum, for taking me in this plane. How great is God to let me do this? Me, a normal person. My children never thought I would ever do such things.'

Then, I get a big surprise. I see this big, big, mountain right up in the sky. It is even above the clouds; it is so high.

Wendy tell me, 'Rosie can you see the snow on Mount Kilimanjaro?' I can't believe my eyes. I didn't know that snow could be seen from far away like it is there. So white. And the mountain so high. It is a beautiful world, I can say. So, all the time I am now looking out of the window to see what I can see.

Wendy is asking me, 'Do you like being in this aeroplane, Rosie?' and I say that I like it very much. Only it is a bit scary when we land which is to make me pray again and close my eyes. But with God's grace I survived this trip.

I come down from the plane and I feel like I am very dizzy, because it is very hot. Even if I take off my pullover, I am still very hot. There is no sun like that hotness. I am sweating and my fingers are sticking to my body. When I am thinking about the sun, Mum says we have to go in a boat. I wonder if I can do that even though she has taught me to swim. I ask myself what happens if the boat is turning over. I can only swim in the pool, not the big sea. I will surely drown. She tells me, 'Rosie, go down into the boat.' I am fearing because the boat is moving all the time.

The people who are working in these boats are very kind and welcome us. People with good tongues. But the problem is that they are talking in a different kind of Swahili which is too hard for me to understand. But at least they are understanding my Swahili. So, I make them to know that I am Kikuyu and have come from somewhere near Nairobi. It is difficult to understand these coast people. So, I am sitting quietly in the boat next to Mum.

I am fearing for the children because they are being quite naughty, climbing all around this boat. But Dad is there with them, and he doesn't worry. So, I am thinking, if they fall off Dad can swim and get them. Then, when we start into the middle of the big sea, it is worse because the boat sort of tips over to one side. I think we are going to fall out, but no one care much. They just put a big plank sticking out over the sea on the side which is high up. Then many young men sit upon it to make the boat go more straight. It is not so nice really. I have to say some more prayers so we can survive this trip.

Mum ask me, 'Are you okay Rosie, are you feeling sick?'

Then I answer, 'No, I am not sick. It's fine Mum.'

She tells me, 'You are doing so well. Sometimes people can vomit because the moving boat makes them to feel sick. So, you are a good sailor.' That makes me feel quite proud to be doing this thing. I say to myself: 'Is it really you, Rosie, going on a big sea like this when, a few years ago you didn't even know there was so much water in the world.'

So, I come to know there is so much in this world to see that I don't know. Staying with Mum I am learning so much.

Chapter 14

Shela

'*Hauwezi kuvuka ziwa hadi uwe na ujasiri wa kutouona urefu wa pwani.*'
'You have to step off the land if you want to go in a boat.'

Virginia: August 1989.

The jetty has collapsed and is covered in jagged barnacles. We clamber over broken plinths and rocks to get to the little dhow which is bobbing on a rope tied to a reinforcing rod sticking out of the sea. The baggage is manhandled chaotically down from the quayside into the wooden boat. The skipper of the dhow, looking like a pirate, welcomes us roughly to his ship.

'*Jambo. Jambo. Karibu sana.* I am Captain Tufani.' He leans towards us, handing us all down into the dhow with charming gallantry. Our baggage is stashed under the deck in front of the mast to keep it dry. He directs us to sit at the back, to avoid the vast lateen sail that can swing across at any time. There are no floorboards in the belly of the boat, now sloshing with oily seawater. Since time immemorial, dhows have been the donkeys of these seas, shipping mangrove poles cut along the mainland, or coral blocks hewn from the ground at Manda to Lamu island. But now these small dhows are used mainly to ferry people from one island to another. Captain Tufani sits on the deck controlling the tiller casually with a dexterous foot, pushing it back and forth in a steady rhythm, constantly adjusting the wind in the sails above him. I look at Rosie to see how she is managing this adventure, her first time on a boat, and she laughs happily.

The channel between Manda Island and Lamu Island is dotted with elegant white sails of the dhows skipping back and forth between the airport and the town. The captain steers the boat across the channel, into the calm water under the lee of the island. We veer away from Lamu Town and hug the coast, just offshore, heading for the little fishing village of Shela.

There is a constant stream of people along the path that links Lamu Town to Shela village: a boy on a donkey is jogging along, whacking the poor beast to maintain its busy trit-trot to town; a group of black-shrouded women plod along with their wares, goading their children and shrieking to each other as they pass their friends going in the opposite direction. Bare-chested labourers, like biblical slaves, push huge carts along the road, laden with gallons of cooking oil, gas bottles, and boxes of tinned food. There are a few bicycles but not a single car on the whole fifteen-kilometre island.

Old men sit along the seawall, ruminating as they stare absentmindedly at the ocean, flicking flies lazily, watching the women who in turn boss the children.

The town's generator sounds like an erratic pulse. Thud. Pause. Thud, thud. Pause. Thud, thud, thud.

'We are lucky there is electricity today,' says Solomon. 'Many days no power in Shela.'

We sail on past a lavish new building, looking like a palace.

'Hospital for Lamu Island,' says Captain Tufani, 'Very big building but not working. Nothing. No *dawa,* no medicine. The Saudi they give us hospital but no doctors, only big building!' he adds, rubbing his thumb and forefinger together, raising his eyes to heaven miming bribery in high places.

A large, long building labelled the Lamu Cotton Ginnery is the next ferry stop, but it is deserted.

'No cotton growing here now,' says the captain. 'They built a factory for making *kangas.* But now it is cheaper to get the cotton from India. So, this factory is dead now. No work in Lamu. Only tourist trade.'

Next an elegant white patrician abode, crenelations edging the flat roof like a sandcastle appears. Green lawns reach down to the high wall above the sea.

'This, French house. Plenty, plenty, money. Also, empty.' Once again, he rubs his fingers together looking like a crafty Arab merchant.

'You like alcohol?' asks the roguish pirate.

We assure him we do.

'No alcohol found in Lamu. Only at Rafiki hotel. Muslim people no like to have alcohol here. No good for men. Me, I allow you to take wine in your bags on my boat, but other strict captains, no!' Perhaps he is a smuggler.

Shela village comes into sight. A quaint collection of *makuti* roofs beneath an oasis of palm trees. A fleet of small dhows, bobbing on their moorings, slanted masts, beside the jetty. Captain Tufani swerves towards the land whilst the crew expertly drops the sails to glide in alongside the jetty without an engine. It is a smooth operation, done countless times before.

'*Hakuna Matata*. No Problem. Me very good captain.'

He chucks a rope deftly in a single well-timed movement to a helpful lad on the jetty, who catches the line and secures it to a large ancient bollard. We clamber off the boat, entranced by the whole experience. The elegant balcony of the Rafiki Hotel lends a colonial grandeur to an otherwise simple fishing village. A sleek sloop lies luxuriantly in front of the hotel, surrounded by a collection of little speed boats waiting to take visitors on expensive outings. Glamorous women waft around on the balcony in wispy clothing, sipping cocktails.

Solomon leaps ashore and picks out a bunch of young boys to carry the bags. Our belongings are being whisked off on their heads, out of sight. Just relax, I remind myself.

'*Hakuna Matata*' says Solomon, noticing our European angst. 'This is not Nairobi. Here you can trust people.'

We are led along a sandy path through Shela village, past the old mosque on the seafront, hugging the narrow lanes of shade beneath high white walls of grand houses. We are led to an old carved wooden door marked 'Palm Tree House.' I am reminded of those idyllic cottages under the palm trees of Kwale, and my dream to live like a Swahili mama. Solomon shows us our simple little rooms, hung with mosquito nets, and cooled by roof fans. Cats scatter in all directions as the kids try to catch them. Anthony and I sit entranced under the coconut trees with a glass of cold water and gaze out to sea, watching the dhows flit past.

When I reach the place where we are to sleep, I am so thirsty. I go to the tap to take some water. When I try to drink this water, it is a bit salty. Then, I spit it out from my mouth. That water will be making me vomit.

'What am I going to drink until I go back to Nairobi, with this water tasting so bad?'

By good luck it started to rain in the afternoon. I start to think, 'How can I catch that rainwater?'

Then I take a biscuit tin and leave it there in the garden. It continues raining. When I go to the garden to get the tin, I found it full of nice fresh rainwater, all clean and tasteful. I did not even take the time to boil that water, so much I was missing fresh water. I just put it in the glass and drank it. Then I put the rest of the water in a bottle, and I hide it for only me to drink. I had it for two days and with that water I feel like I am at home in the hills of my place in Limuru. Now I don't mind to be here at the coast.

Virginia: August 1989.

Rosie and I are cooking together in the kitchen at Palm Tree house. The electricity has been off all day. 'Mum this is just like my home, no electricity!' Rosie laughs.

'Remember when you first came to work for us how you were so terrified of electricity. Now look at you, you don't know what to do without it.'

'Mum, I was so scared to come to your house. Now I am used to everything. I go in cars. I go in boats, and now I even have been in a plane. I think I am so lucky. How is it that we met like that, and you found me? You know Mum, it is God's doing that we met. He answered my prayers.'

'If you say so Rosie, but I think it is just because we know how to take advantage of good opportunities. People make their own luck from things that are right in front of them, staring them in the face.'

'That is because God had arranged for you and me to be on the same path.'

'Well, if that's what you think, I won't argue, but I think it is our choice. We could have just walked past each other. I didn't have to give you a lift home that time. You didn't have to agree to come. Look at your friend who didn't stop to greet us. Where is she now? Has her life changed like yours? She ignored the opportunity to meet us, but you took a chance and stopped, and look what happened as a result. The reason you are lucky is because you are curious to try everything.'

'And so are you, Mum. That's why we are sisters.'

'You also like to take a chance, Rosie, look at the big risk you took coming to work for me when you had not even been in a modern house before. You aren't scared to try anything.'

'I am scared of one thing.' She chops the onion with a sudden vigour.

'What am I going to do when you leave Kenya?'

She wipes her eyes with the back of her hand,

'I am not crying Mum; it is just the onion making me cry.'

The next morning Wendy wakes up with a sharp ache in her ear. There is nothing we can do to ease her agony. Her little body is tense with pain, and her bright blue eyes red with crying. We go to the village health centre. One tiny room with a scruffy veranda where a queue of women and children wait for the attention of the only male nurse who looks exasperated. He is surprised to see *wazungu* coming to him for treatment. The Swahili patients smile and wave us to the front of the long queue of women patiently waiting. No one objects as the nurse takes us into the consulting room before them. He looks down Wendy's ear but has nothing to suggest.

'I am sorry, I can't help you. I have no *dawa* here. Maybe you can go to the hospital in Lamu Town.'

George Feegan is an eminent doctor, known for his pioneering work on varicose veins and was one of the first foreigners to buy up property in Shela Village. We have been curious to meet both him and Dr. Anne Spoerry the famous Flying Doctor of Kenya, the two most well-known white residents of Lamu Island. Every morning when Anthony goes for his morning run at dawn, he sees George walking far down the beach, accompanied by his bodyguard, an elegant Maasai youth. Yesterday Anthony managed to start a conversation. When George establishes that Anthony is not a tourist but is working in Kenya as a water engineer, he invites us for a sundowner.

We climb the twisting flight of stairs to the top of the eyrie and shout '*Hodi. Hodi,*' at his door, as we catch our breath.

'Come in come in,' he calls out in his broad Irish lilt. He is sitting with his feet up on the extended armrest of a carved Swahili chair, watching the sun go down over the dunes behind Shela. 'Hello. Hello,' he says, pulling himself to his feet and coming over to greet me.

'Ah, your young lady,' he shakes my hand warmly and pats the children on their heads. 'What will you have to drink?'

Despite his gruff appearance, he is tolerant of our children who are exploring his place with open curiosity. The couple of rooms are spartan, little more than a glorified bachelor bedsit. The décor consists of a huge Swahili carved bed, a hammock, and a large, cluttered desk with a commanding view over the whole island.

'Can I give you a whisky, or gin and tonic?' he indicates the crystal decanters on the sideboard. A handsome young boy is in attendance, more companion than servant. He brings the tray forward and serves up the drinks like a well-trained bartender, producing cokes for the children. We nibble on Indian *chevda*, a snack of aromatic nuts and grain.

'So, you work for Aqua Aid, is that right?' George asks.

'That's right, we have been hand drilling tube wells in the Tana River area.'

'Excellent, that is what we need here. Absolutely no concept of water protection in Shela or any other village as far as I can see. We all get the trots from the well water. You better meet the chief.'

We tell him about our concern over Wendy's earache, and he immediately suggests we see the "Flying Doctor."

'Anne Spoerry can give you something to ease the pain,' George suggests. 'Don't be put off by her manner. She is a tough old spinster having been in the French resistance and captured by the Gestapo. She is my competitor,' he jokes, 'between us we are buying up Shela. So far, I think I have the upper hand. Actually, we are going to the grave together. Anne and I have secured a spot halfway down the beach for our graves. If you want her help, just tell her I sent you, or she might not open the door.'

We walk along the cool lanes between the high walls of the stone houses, to a grand patrician abode on the seafront.

'*Hodi. Hodi,*' we call, as we bang on the exquisite carved door in the coral wall.

The Flying Doctor herself opens the door. A squat little matron with short, cropped hair and intense beady eyes. She appraises us for a long moment, rather unsympathetically.

'*Oui?*' she says without warmth, clearly not encouraging visitors.

'So sorry to bother you, but George Feegan suggested you might be able to help us,' I gush, dropping his name unashamedly, the only way to gain entry.

Rather grudgingly she opens the door wider.

'*Karibu, Karibu,*' she motions us inside impatiently, indicating we should sit on the bench in the *barazza*.

We explain our worry about Wendy's ear wondering if it might be too banal to warrant the famous doctor's attention. Her regular clients are the Maasai warriors with severed limbs, Turkana raiders with gaping head wounds. She sweeps Wendy's long blond hair roughly to one side and looks down her ear with a torch. 'It is not serious. Just a bit of coral ear from swimming. You should put a bit of pure alcohol in each ear after you have been in the sea.'

She squirts some brown antiseptic down the ear and gives Wendy an almost affectionate pat on the head. 'That should fix it.' Then she wants to know about our business in Kenya. When Anthony explains that he works for Aqua Aid, she softens noticeably. Like George, she is devoted to improving the village and can see how he can be of assistance.

'*Bon!* You can help the clinic. They have no water because their pump has collapsed and needs repair,' she raps out briskly. I will send the Chief over to Palm Tree House, and you can see what you can do for him.' It is a command not a request. Anthony promises to investigate it. We back out, apologising for taking her time - almost bowing out in deference.

The Jetty at Shela. Watercolour. 1989

Chapter 15

Paté Island

'*Waarabu wa Paté huelewana kwa vilemba*'
'The Arabs from Paté communicate by the way they tie their turbans.'

Virginia: August 1989.

The next evening, as we are sitting under the palms gazing out to sea, forbidden gin and tonic in hand, there is a firm tap on the outside door.

'*Bwana, Memsahib,* the Chief of Shela is here to see you with his councillor,' reports Solomon.

In come two local men dressed in freshly laundered white *kanzu* and *kofia*.

We shake hands and motion them to take a seat. They decline to drink alcohol but accept glasses of water. After the usual exchange of pleasantries, they get down to business.

The Chief seems to understand only a little English, so Councillor Nilah speaks on his behalf.

'*Daktari* has asked us to come to talk to you about the needs of the clinic. We are having problems with the water pump because it is old, and we cannot repair it here.'

Anthony offers to take the pump back to Nairobi and get it fixed, and they readily agree.

'There is also much difficulty in the school which has no water either. Can you come and see some other places with us?'

An irresistible opportunity to get beneath the surface again.

The next day we go with the Chief on a *dhow* from Shela village to Lamu Town. From the street, the stone houses rise three stories high, forming a continuous strong wall along the narrow alleys which are cool most of the day. The shady central square is built around an ancient tamarind tree which reaches as high as the monumental fortress behind it. Men sit around idly on the steps, eyeing the henna patterns on the soles of the black shrouded women who flip flap along in their plastic sandals, dragging scruffy little children in their wake. Cone-shaped turrets tower high like a mediaeval castle, with an imposing flight of steps up to the giant carved wooden portal. In the shadow of the fort, narrow streets lead off in all directions. The west wall of the fortress supports the market stalls, lines of little *makuti bandas* selling bright arrays of vegetables and cheap plastic goods.

The Chief takes us through the narrow alleyways to the Friday Mosque. He explains it was built centuries ago, when the first Omani traders arrived. This makes it the oldest building in Africa we have ever seen. The off-white coral plaster walls are like dirty sponges, grey with mildew and damp.

'This is our famous Madrassa, the best school in East Africa for Muslim learning,' we are told. 'Most famous Imams are teaching here. Most pure knowledge of *Qur'an*. If a boy comes here, he is a very lucky boy, he gets the best education.'

Next to the imposing white mosque is a large playground backing on to classroom blocks.

'This is the main government school for boys and girls in Lamu, maybe 1,000 children here. Here is the well. Very special water, from the sand dunes.'

Anthony looks down the hole and sees plastic floating in the depths. Water is hauled up by rope with a bucket which is now lying on the ground amongst the donkey droppings.

'Do you drink this water?' asks Anthony, thinking of the notorious "Lamu trots".

'Ah, yes.'

'Do you chlorinate the wells?'

'No, we don't use any chemicals, because we don't like the taste.'

There is little sanitation in the town. Most of the large houses have indoor 'long drops,' open pit latrines, and washrooms. Soapy grey water from washing is ejected through a hole in the wall, flowing straight onto the street where it mixes with pungent mounds of rotting garbage and is washed down the drainage gullies to the sea.

The next day we are taken to Matondoni, a tiny village on the northern side of Lamu island. The *dhow* drifts silently along the channels between the mangrove with the wind in its large grubby sail. Visually the village looks like paradise, but in reality, it is far from comfortable. When the boat stops moving, the heat is suffocating. People lie around indolently waiting for the evening breeze before attempting any physical work.

We clamber out of the boat into the shallow sludgy warm water and onto the baking soil. The foetid smell of dead animals rotting nearby hits me; lazy little flies settle on every sweaty bit of my exposed skin. This remote village is home to a few hundred families of fishermen and known for the building of *dhows*. We duck under the palms where the temperature is tolerable and take a quick look at the well. It has the usual scum of debris on the water at the bottom. The chief of the village is introduced and summons a couple of miserable looking men to answer our questions. Everyone is affected by torpor. They chew twigs of *miraa*, a local stimulant, which is used to stave off fatigue. As they watch us in undisguised curiosity, they periodically spit out a shot of red saliva, which peppers the soft sand.

Anthony explains that the well has first to be drained, cleaned, chlorinated and then lined before he can provide the headworks. Would this be possible? The men spit and complain, then agree rather half-heartedly to do the job.

'When?'

Sometime soon, unspecified.

I sympathise with the task ahead. It is not surprising that nothing gets repaired in this heat.

❀ ❀ ❀

The *dhow* sails up a creepy narrow alley of green mangroves on the high tide between Manda Island and the mainland, then up the west coast of Paté Island. The water is still deep enough to sail into a hidden coral creek to reach the town of Sivu. Protected by the tides for centuries it is cunningly situated against marauders. There is no access by plane, so few foreign visitors ever come to Paté. The people of the island are quiet and diffident compared to the lively, entrepreneurial people of Lamu. Information is given dryly, in short bursts.

The school buildings are neglected. No latrines, nor a working well at the school.

'Do you want some help to rehabilitate these facilities?'

'Well. Yes, maybe,' is the general feeling but no hurry.

Most of the older children are sent to the senior school in Lamu Town that we have just visited. The island leaders seemed content for Paté to remain lost in time. It is difficult to believe that in the 18th century, Paté Island was a centre of great wealth and refinement. There are ruins of impressive stone houses decorated with elaborate plasterwork. Ancient carved doors still hang off derelict houses, long since abandoned.

'This is the grave of very rich men from Oman. They came here over 1000 years ago to trade using the *Kusii* winds to drive the *dhows*. They wanted mangrove polls from us.' The chief shows us the ancient tombs where long epitaphs describe the glory of a past Arab empire.

Our guide tells us proudly, 'We people from Lamu, we took over the control of the islands from the Paté people. We beat them in a very big fight at sea near Shela. In 1813. Then came the Sultan of Muscat, to govern Lamu. Paté no good after that.'

'We are just quiet here. *Hakuna matata*, no problem,' says the Paté chief, making a virtue of living in a backwater.

The tide has gone out rapidly whilst we have been talking. To avoid getting stranded on the mud floor of the creek, the *dhow* captain has had to sail off on the retreating water without us. If we want to get back to Lamu Town on the same day, we have to walk to the seaward side of the island where the *dhow* can meet us. Nothing daunted, we set off on the baking path for the six-kilometre hike.

Within a few minutes, I am reeling under the sun. My head starts to heat up and I wind my *kanga* thickly around my skull for protection. My brains seem to be bubbling with heat like a pressure cooker waiting to explode. Then my face flushes puce red. I gulp back my water. Anthony is striding ahead, and I get more and more agitated. When two hours later, I spy the glint of the sea between the mangroves, I lumber towards the promise of water exhausted and dehydrated submerging into the sea fully clothed. My brain inside my skull seems to fizz like a sausage in a hot frying pan. The captain is waiting for us, sitting patiently on his *dhow* in the shallows, fishing with a simple line wound around a block of wood. I surface like a hippo from the deep. He greets me and smiles in sympathy, knocking his head, then pointing to the sun.

'*Kali sana!* Very hot!'

'Yes, very *kali*,' I agree, thinking of the Hindu goddess of war. I am reminded of a song from my childhood, 'Mad dogs and Englishman go out in the midday sun.'

The Stop Over in Shela village. 1996.

Chapter 16

Putting down Roots

'Ukitaka kula nguruwe, kula aliyenona.'
'If you are going to eat a pig, at least eat a fat one.'

Virginia: October 1989.

'It's paradise on earth, this place,' says Anthony, taking a deep breath and breathing in the warm frangipani scented air, watching a dhow drift silently past as the sun sets quietly over the Manda Channel. The palm tree canopy above rustles in the breeze and a donkey brays its forlorn objection somewhere deep in the village.

'Don't you wish we could stay here forever? Just put down roots and submerge ourselves in this little village. It is how the world used to be before it was all covered with industry.'

The muezzin singer clears his throat preparing for the evening call to prayer. We listen charmed by the melancholy notes as they glide on the air, incomprehensibly alien and yet so alluring. It is as romantic as the notion of Arabian nights.

'Be realistic. Do you really think we could put down roots in such a deeply Muslim community?' Anthony muses.

'I would love to live here with these people: they have such a quiet dignity about them'

'It is their code of honour I really admire. It is so old fashioned, a sort of gentleman's agreement that once uttered can't be broken.'

'Hm… it's a sort of old-fashioned patrician chivalry about them, so refined: '*Noblesse oblige.*'

'It must be the effect of the Omani culture.'

'Remember when we dreamt about buying a *dhow* and thought of sailing to India on the trade winds. We could buy a little dhow here and just drop out.'

'I would love to have a little fisherman's cottage here in Shela, with a *makuti* roof. Our little hideaway beside the sea.' I lie back against Anthony dreaming out loud. He kisses the top of my head, and we snuggle against each other, sticking together in the damp air. 'What about bringing the kids up here?'

'Well, this is the only place I know in Africa where the colour of our skin does not seem to matter.'

The prayers end at the Mosque, and we listen to the soft patter of feet on sandy lanes as the men return home for the evening meal.

There is a knock on our door. Solomon answers. A muted exchange. It is not a fisherman at the back door.

Then Solomon comes in with the Chief and Councillor Nilah.

'*Karibu sana.*' We welcome them, shaking hands and offering them a seat.

They come in respectfully and sit down. We go through the formality of the long Swahili greeting, inquiring after each other's families. Solomon brings in some soda water for their refreshment. Anthony asks how the new water pump at the clinic is functioning.

The Chief bows gently with his hand on his left chest, 'We are very happy with all you have already done for Lamu. It is for this reason that the leaders of Shela now invite you to come and live here.'

I look at Anthony astonished, eyes glowing with excitement. I try not to look too keen.

Anthony is being deliberately hesitant, but I know he is beaming under his beard.

'What do you mean?'

'We can offer you a piece of land to build your own house in Shela.'

Anthony and I look at each other. Without any discussion, we both nod simultaneously,

'Really? My goodness, that is a very wonderful offer,' my husband says enthusiastically on our behalf.

'There is a plot now available right in the centre of the village. You can buy it cheap,' says Nilah.

'Can we really just buy some land here, even if we are foreigners in Kenya?' Anthony asks.

'Not on the beach front but this piece of land in the village is possible for you to buy as a foreigner.'

I smile in disbelief imagining my little fisherman's cottage. After five years in Kenya, searching for an African haven, we have been offered this extraordinary opportunity. We can put down roots in a part of Africa that seems to want us to stay. There is no need for discussion between us. 'It can't be that easy to build here. What about all the government permits?'

'*Hakuna Matata.* You have already been approved by our council. That is why I come here to formally invite you to settle in our village. Please, you take this land. It will be your home.'

'Come, we will show you the plot.'

I had a vision of a seaside plot like Palm Tree House, with coconut palms above the beach and a little gate to our dhow bobbing on the waves below but instead we are shown to a neglected village common between little mud huts which is clearly the dumping ground of the village.

It is not inspiring. There is a mound to one side of the square, just outside the perimeter of the proposed plot.

'Is that not a grave?' Anthony asks dubiously, looking for potential obstacles.

'Yes, yes, that is a grave. But you know, it is good to have a grave. In our culture, it is forbidden to move a grave. So, no one can build on this plot, it will always be vacant so your view will not be spoiled. says Nilah.

Anthony is pacing out the size of the land, 'Twenty metres by thirty,' he estimates, 'and only one block of houses between this plot and the sea.'

'Yes. You take this plot. It is a good place. From the first floor, you will always be able to see the sea and feel the fresh breeze. That is good, yes? We know, you white people like to have a view"

'Who does the plot belong to?'

'It is my family who owns this land, so I will give you a good price, *hakuna matata*,' says Nilah.

'Well, okay. If it is your family's land that would be good. *Bei gani*? How much?'

He looks up to the sky and says, 'For you it is just five thousand dollars.'

A rubbish dump in the middle of a fishing village where we can live side by side with some of the most welcoming people we have ever met.

Anthony nods sagely, 'It sounds too good to be true, but Nilah, how can I possibly build here when I am working in Nairobi.'

Nilah takes both his shoulders like a long-lost friend. He stares deeply into his eyes, and with touching conviction says, 'Anthony, you are my brother. This is my family land. I sell you very cheap. Please accept it as a friend. It is our present to you for the trouble you have taken to help with our water supply here. You will not regret it.'

'Thank you … well of course we accept your offer.' They shake hands.

Then Nilah makes an even bigger offer. 'Anthony, I myself will supervise the building of your home. It is my pleasure.'

'What?' I gasp dumbfounded. 'How can this be true?'

'I want no money for this supervision.'

'We must give you *something* for your work.'

'That is your choice. You know in our culture you can repay a favour with another gift. Like that we make a long friendship.'

'What can we give you as a present?' asks Anthony, patting him lightly on the shoulder, deeply touched by his generous offer.

'OK. Well, here is an idea. My wife very much wants to have a video machine.'

'All you want is a video. You will manage the building for us for a video?' asks Anthony incredulously.

'Exactly, and the materials you will get at cost price from my own sources. You will not be made to pay as a foreigner. You will see. This is a good deal, brother.' The offer is irresistible.

We pause to take in the enormity of the project. I am happy to be mute, watching my dream come to life. Anthony and Nilah shake hands and the deal is done.

I notice a little girl quietly picking the buds off a scrubby Jasmine bush growing wild between broken bottles. She is threading each bud onto a safety pin. Nilah sees my interest, 'The village girls love to pick these flowers from the Jasmine bush.' He calls her over. She comes up shyly and presents me with the little brooch of Jasmine buds.

'This is for you, Mama,' says Nilah, and attaches it onto my kaftan.

I thank the little girl and she smiles charmingly up at me. 'You can always come and collect flowers, even if we build a house here,' I tell her. 'We will keep this bush and build around it.'

'We could call it Jasmine House,' says Anthony.

'That is a very good name,' says Nilah, 'In Swahili culture, Jasmine is put between the sheets of the marriage bed of newly married couples. The crushing of the flowers spices the love between the couple. I think you will enjoy a lot of love here,' he teases us.'

The chief who has been silent throughout says quietly, 'I will give you a climbing rose bush for your garden,' as he shakes our hands solemnly to leave. We are being taught to dance to the beat of a different drum. Three wise men once came from Oman bringing gold, frankincense and myrrh to the west. This golden opportunity of a scented garden are the treasures we are receiving from the descendants of Omani Arabs.

We have actually been given a foothold in paradise. It may be a cliché, but how else to describe it? We have actually been asked to belong to this village, our own place in Africa.

Jasmine House is to be built in a typical Arab style with high external walls and all rooms facing inwards around a central courtyard which centres around our jasmine bush. Like all the local houses, all the building materials are from the island: foundations and walls of coral blocks from Manda Island; ceilings held up by mangrove poles from the mainland; *makuti* thatch from the village of Matondoni. The only thing from outside the island is cement, and this is to be delivered by lorry from Mombasa and transported by *dhow* by the donkeys to Shela.

It is good to feel that this construction will employ countless people from the area, co-ordinated by Nilah the mastermind. He is always thinking ahead, directing a well-choreographed dance of command and effort as he orders his young assistant Fahari to make our dream a reality.

'Fahari, arrange for coral blocks,' Nilah demands, as a large chunk from a wad of notes is counted, with dextrous merchants' fingers, flicking notes in a fan, his thumb peeled back with practice. There are moments when we wonder, 'Where are his accounts? Are we being taken for a ride? Is he getting his cut?' but when the accounts come in, they are reasonable. We throw all cynicism to the wind and put our faith in Nilah.

'Fahari, more lime for the foundations,' orders Nilah, peeling off more layers from the wodge of shillings. From the edge of the quarry on Manda Island, where kilns slowly burn, the coral rock is burnt into a fine lime, an ancient form of cement. The dhow load of lime is dished out into shallow metal basins hoisted on the heads of porters who wend their way along the lane to our site and dip the coral lime mixed with water into the foundations, an ingenious method. As the walls above become heavier, the foundation sinks ever deeper into the earth expanding sideways like an elephant's foot.

On Manda Island, ebony men, stripped to the waist, wearing only white loincloths, bash away at the ground to extract thick lumps of coral hewn from an ancient quarry. I remember the heat stroke when we walked across Paté Island and wonder how they manage to slave away in this heat. The men pad their strong shoulders with a sack to protect them from the rough coral blocks, and trudge back and forth along the baking white sandy path to the edge of the mangrove swamp, counting the pennies they earn from each trip as school fees for their large brood back home. They flip their loads manfully into the wooden belly of an old dhow. Each evening the wind fills the sails and shifts the heavy cargo across the choppy channel to Shela.

'*Hakuna Matata.* Don't worry about them. They are Luo, from Lake Victoria. They are used to it,' Nilah reassures me with the authority of an ancient slave driver. Like his Omani forefathers, he has no difficulty with the belief that Africans are born to provide labour, whilst Arab traders are born to profit from such work, a feudal mentality which on this remote island is still very much alive. We are too overawed to interfere.

Arriving on Shela beach, each donkey is loaded with two heavy blocks in a pannier of woven palm hanging each side of its back. The train of donkeys waits patiently, heads down, knees tense, until all of them are loaded and then they turn obediently, to trip up the little sandy path through the village in a line, back and forth, until all the blocks for the walls are neatly stacked. Another caravan of donkeys arrives with their paniers bulging on either side with fine sand from far down the beach.

Within three months the coral walls are completed. We fly in for a few days to position the windows, framing the best views in each direction. There is not a single pane of glass in the whole building. The jasmine-scented sea breeze will waft straight into our master bedroom on the rooftop.

Next Nilah arranges for poles to support the ceiling slab to be cut from deep in the mangrove forests where unseen the workforce stack the poles for sale. Well-seasoned by every rising tide over the years, mangrove poles are immensely strong.

The cement floors are paved with terracotta tiles from Mombasa transported through the corridor of shifta-infested bush. Each tile is passed on and off dhows and donkeys until they come to rest on the floors of Jasmine House.

Matondoni, the moribund village we visited with indolent *fundi's*, is now a hive of activity, as the women now sit in the shade, knotting thousands of palm fronds like Hawaiian skirts. The *makuti* panels are tied in lines along the purlins of the roof and before the rainy season the house is thatched.

Late one evening, a truck arrives from Nairobi with plumbing and electrical fittings. The cardboard boxes are off-loaded into the soggy bilge of a dhow at Mpeketoni port, and the contents spew out all over the boat. The fittings are collected in local baskets, not one brass nail filched from the cargo. 'The honesty on this island is phenomenal,' Anthony muses, enchanted by the ease of the whole endeavour. Nilah smiles, 'What do you expect,' he says, 'from good Muslims?'

Chapter 17

Jasmine House

'Ndege asiyeruka hajui mbuga ioteshayo ulezi.'
'The bird that never flies, never finds a field of corn.'

Virginia: December 1990.

The profile of Jasmine House breaks the skyline of this magical village. The captain veers into the dhow harbour. I stand on the prow, hanging onto the forestay as the dhow noses into the turquoise shallows, flying my *kanga* in the wind like a kite. Anthony and the children jump over the edge of the dhow and splash ashore without hesitation.

I see Nilah, Fahari and Shani, his assistant, who have come down to the shore to meet us. They wade into the warm sea up to their knees to manhandle all our luggage ashore on their shoulders.

'Mama, here I can carry you ashore. I am your donkey,' says Nilah but I refuse his chivalry, embarrassed to be carried like a sack of rice.

I hitch up my *kanga* and jump into the warm tropical sea. In a state of delight, I wander through the village in disbelief that our ideas have been transformed into bricks and mortar. We have a home in real Africa, a foothold on this wondrous island, amongst the warmest of communities.

Our new neighbour's wave and call out as we pass, '*Karibu, Mama. Karibu sana, Bwana.*'

An ever-increasing band of barefooted urchins trail us shouting '*Mzungu, Mzungu,*' reminding me of how far I had come since the first time I drove into Rosie's *shamba*.

The entrance to Jasmine House is decorated with long branches of rich red bougainvillaea woven into a tall arch encasing the ancient Swahili carved door that we had brought from Pâté Island. We duck under the flowers, bursting with suspense. The chief is waiting in the *madaka*, the traditional archway to an Arab style house. He greets us as we sit on the built-in concrete benches and take off our sandals. We wash the sand off our feet in the shallow basin of fresh water with floating white frangipani blossoms. He picks up a large rose bush bursting with pink flowers and presents it to me very formally, '*Karibu Mama*. This is your home now. Welcome to Shela village.'

I am charmed, floating on a wave of delight as we are ushered into the dusty courtyard of our Jasmine House, enjoying the rite of entry. We look around and take it all in slowly. On the ground floor the arched kitchen windows open onto the courtyard and dining area. The proportions are perfect, the arches frame every view. The children are dashing around exploring every corner. There in the corner of the courtyard, still covered in the remains of building rubble, is the noble Jasmine plant still in flower, despite its lime-dusted leaves.

From the first floor, we overlook the sea through palm trees, whilst dark alley ways lined with little village huts stretch to the sand dunes to the rear. To the left the shop owner and his family are gathered around their fire outside where a large pot of coconut rice is cooking sending the rich flavour drifting up to us. Behind us is the oldest tavern in the village, a tall rather seedy backpacker lodge. To the other side is the empty village square now crisscrossed with well-worn footpaths.

Nilah and Fahari are chatting urgently, looking over the wall to the empty plot below. Anthony joins them and shakes their hands, effusive in his praise of the building.

'I have some good news for you,' Nilah announces. 'This plot is up for sale.'

Anthony stares at him in disbelief. 'What about the grave? I thought no one could buy it?'

'Ah well the grave will remain there, of course, but the family is now happy to sell the land with the grave, as long as it remains undisturbed.'

'Who is the family? Surely, we should meet them and get their permission in writing?' I suggest.

'Actually, it is my grandfather's grave,' confesses Nilah with a sheepish grin, finally revealing the whole truth about the mysterious ancestor. He is the descendant of one of the pashas who came here over a hundred years ago. I have asked his permission,' he jokes.

'However, you must buy this plot immediately. Otherwise, you will lose your sea view.' Doctor Feegan has already offered to buy this plot.'

He sees our horror and smiles, 'but I would prefer to sell it to you.'

'Nilah, how can we do that? We have used all our savings to build Jasmine House.'

'I am sure you will find a way. *Insha'Allah*.'

She arrives with a flourish, first down the steps of the little aeroplane, waving like a movie star. The kids rush across the runway to meet her. With her dark brown eyes, olive skin, and strong profile with a large, rounded nose, Babushka could be an Arab woman. She has come for our first Christmas in Shela. I am intrigued to see how my class-conscious mother will react being fully immersed amongst the fishing folk of our village. I need not have worried, as she also has a fascination for people and a natural common touch when she approves of someone.

She is immediately captivated by Captain Tufani who sails us across the straits to Shela. He starts chatting her up. In no time she is sparkling away, enjoying his roguish charm.

'Anything you want, you come to me. I take you to see the ruins of Manda village. You call me. You want go to Lamu Town? I take you. *Hakuna Matata.*'

She steps off the rolling dhow, making a theatrical entrance onto the quayside in Shela, steadied by Anthony and Captain Tufani.

'God! It's hot here!' She fans her face, sweating copiously. She talks nonstop at the top of her voice as we wind through the village alleys to the less salubrious quarter. Feral cats are everywhere like vermin, picking the scraps from the garbage embedded in the sand. As we pass a village woman opens the door, greets us, then hurls a bucket of dirty water onto the sandy path just behind us.

Babushka picks her way around the debris remarking, 'It is real village life, isn't it? Are these all the fishermen's houses?'

'These are our neighbours,' I laugh, knowing what she is thinking. 'Not far now.'

Around the next block and across the open wasteland of the grave, and our wall looms high above us, still raw from the recent construction.

'Here we are.' I announce as we push open the great wooden carved door. The boys carry her bags across the courtyard, and up a spiral staircase to the little guest annex.

Rosie opens the door, 'Babushka, *Karibu sana.* I am so happy to see you.'

'Rosie, dear, how good to see you. I hear you have even gone in an aeroplane now.'

They hug like old friends. I think to myself that Mrs. H-P would never have hugged a maid. In the past few years my mother had been working with

'Women for Peace' in the Soweto township and can now be trusted not to behave in the high-handed way I remember as a child, when she had newly arrived from England and treated her servants like chattels.

'Yes, now I am a well-travelled person, like you are,' Rosie jokes without any shyness. She takes Babushka's bag to her room.

'Oh, how quaint! My God, this is heaven!' she says collapsing on the seat on the balcony overlooking the palms to the sea beyond.

'I am afraid it is only a cold shower' I point out, 'but you probably won't need it as it is so hot here. We can boil up a bucket of water if you need it.'

'Right, well let me change and settle down a bit.'

She comes out of her room, bare feet, in a large orange tie-dyed Kaftan, her silver hair wild and curly, the look of a gypsy about her. The sun drops down suddenly behind the sand dunes like a blob of red molten glass, and a fresh evening breeze wafts the smell of coconut fish across from our neighbours. Time for our usual sundowner drink.

Wendy has prepared the specialty of the island, known as '*madafu*' for her granny's arrival. It is a decapitated green coconut with a straw to drink the fresh juice straight from the nut.

'Mmm! What a treat. Isn't this fun.' She hugs Wendy and gives me a huge smile. 'You must be thrilled with this wonderful house. What an achievement.'

Anthony comes up the stairs with a tray of drinks. 'Try a dash of this local gin with it. It is called '*Konyagi*.' He dollops a tot of alcohol into the coconut juice, and she sips it with relish.

'I must have a cigarette.' Her chunky rings click while she lights up, exhaling smoke then taking a deep breath of sea air, she breathes in the humid atmosphere, 'This is the life.'

'I am dying to show you Lamu town. It is so full of history.'

We flit across the narrow strait from Shela to Manda in time to catch the high tide rising so we can get through the shallow mangrove channel that leads to the ancient settlement of Takwa ruins. As the tide is still very low, we could not sail to the jetty and so have to walk the last bit squishing in mush up to our ankles. The children go sloshing on ahead, but Babushka treads carefully, escorted with great panache by Captain Tufani and she leans on his shoulder, feigning terror as crabs skittle sideways from her feet. I am amazed she is so familiar with him as she slips her way along the channel. Then she declines to walk across to the seaward side of the island.

'I am too hot to go further. I will just sit here in the shade for the moment.'

'I will look after your mother, *hakuna matata.* Mama, I will show you the ruins of my village. My family came from here,' says Tufani with great authority.

In South Africa, it would have been dangerous to leave her alone with a local sailor, but here things are different and she herself seems completely unfazed. I am rather amused by her daring and knowing how honourable Captain Tufani is, I feel confident I can safely leave her to be entertained. We walk through the ancient ruins to the wild ocean raking the beach on the seaward side of Manda Island. She is still chatting away with the captain when we get back an hour later, clearly intrigued by his stories.

'Tufani has explained all the history of the Islands to me, what a fascinating place. I have never been anywhere in Africa with so much history. They are not really *proper* Africans here, are they?

'They are Arabs originally from Oman. They consider themselves superior to us whites.'

'Yes, they are quite, quite different. Captain Tufani is most attractive! Like Zorba the Greek!' she confides, enamoured by his wit, 'I can understand how you get on with them. A real cut above our locals down south, who are so servile. A different breed.'

Rosie

Babushka has come. I am so happy to see her. She always comes at Christmas time. She is the same size as me, so she has brought me some of her clothes that she doesn't want any more. Also, some bras because she has big boobs like me.

It is a very happy time with the children. Dad pretends that he is Father Christmas, and he puts some presents by their bed, but Charlie and Tristan mock Wendy. 'Why do you think Father Christmas is going to come to this island? It is too hot for him. Anyway, he doesn't come to Muslim children.' 'Is that true, Rosie?' she asks, and I say to her that I am sure he is coming, let's pray that he can come. So, we pray together, and in the morning, she finds some presents at the bottom of her bed. She runs to find me and says, 'Rosie come and see my presents.' Then she shows me the mark of a deer's foot on the floor and says that Father Christmas landed there from the sky. I think it is very funny, so I just say. 'That is right.'

Charlie laughs at her. But he also got so many presents, some more Lego because that is what he likes. I think of my children who don't get presents like that. I don't even tell them about Father Christmas because we can't pay for presents. There is so many presents when everyone brings theirs for each other, that the floor is covered in paper. I fold it up because it is such pretty paper.

They have also brought me something for Christmas, a very nice kanga and also a new pair of shoes. Wendy brings it for me, and I hug her so much. Then I give them the presents I have got for them. Each one has a T-shirt that I found, and also one for Mum and Dad. For Babushka, I found a necklace because she likes jewellery so much. She is a very funny lady and is always joking with me. I like it when she is here because she likes cooking, and she shows me so many things. Here in Lamu, we can't get pork because Muslims don't like to eat it and also bacon, we can't get so we prepare very big crabs for our feast. Then I go and cook the crabs which we are having for the meal, with coconut rice and special things Babushka has brought, like a huge cake of nuts and raisins and dates.

After the big lunch the children ask if they can go to see Nilah and take him some special Christmas cake. He tells them to come and sit inside because they are having a good film on his new video that Dad has given him. So, the children go to watch but it is a very bad film. I don't know why Nilah lets our children see things like that. Tristan is so good because when he sees how violent the film is, he tells Nilah, 'Sorry we have to go home now'. I am happy to see he is quite grown up now. I say to him 'Good, good boy!' and I say to Mum, 'You see what a good boy Tristan is. He is looking after his brother and sister. He will be a good head of the family when he is big.'

Captain Tufani has his boat already for the sail to Lamu Town. The wind picks up and we drift down the coast, in the lee of the island and tie up alongside the lines of ancient craft as they bob together in the old harbour. We clamber over the boat to get to the narrow stairs onto the promenade along the seaboard. Everywhere people are plying their trade. Scrawny old men are pushing wooden carts back and forth to the dhows, bare-chested with only the classic white loincloth. They look like Egyptian slaves, patiently unloading everything that is needed to sustain this island community: crates of sweet drinks, boxes of tomato paste and milk powder, cement, tools and bathroom fittings, but not a drop of alcohol passes through this port.

We walk along the front and find a seat at the old hotel under a cool *makuti* thatched veranda overlooking the dhow harbour. A fan clunks mechanically above us, stirring the humid air just enough to dry off our sweating faces. Flies are busily sucking up the remains of food on the sticky tabletops. We watch the cooks, through a hatch into a chaotic kitchen, where they are chopping the mangoes. The deafening roar of an ancient liquidiser drowns our conversation. When the two heavy mugs arrive with the thick mango juice, we suck it through straws greedily.

It is easy to sit indolently hour after hour, watching a parade of real-life patter past: a stream of lovely women in vibrant *kangas*, carrying food on their heads, dragging children along the seafront. Merchants in white *kanzu* with long lean fingers counting wads of grubby notes, their darting eyes on the alert for a chance to score. A young tourist drifts past, irritably trying to shake off the hustlers who follow in his wake, offering cheap rooms, dagga, and fishing trips; thin old men worn out by a life of labour drive the donkeys onwards or push their body weights into the loads on their carts.

We finally tear ourselves away from the mesmerising trickle of life and go along the main alley to the carpentry quartier. Each little cubby hole in the wall has a man tapping away at wood, with slithers of shavings piling up below his benches as he carves intricate designs into the hard timber brought from the mainland. I have come to pick up two carved chairs which we have ordered modelled on the one we saw at George's. As the arm rest can be opened out to act as leg rests, enabling a comfortable rest to spread one's legs and put one's feet up, the design is known as a 'rude' chair. The chairs are sent on the heads of yet more porters to our *dhow* waiting in the harbour. I order new doors of solid mahogany which are to be traded for the century old ebony doors from Paté which will give antique charm to our otherwise brand-new house.

We walk to the market for fresh vegetables and soon fill our large basket with cabbage, tomatoes, onions, potatoes and eggplant. Huge pineapples and mango are added. A young boy has appointed himself as our skivvy. He seizes the basket and hoists it onto his shoulder, following us as we continue the shopping spree. At the Indian *duka*, we purchase some provisions. Mr. Patel waves us away when we come to pay,

'No problem, *Memsahib*, I will add it to your account.' Nothing is ever written down, but we know we will pay eventually. His young son joins the caravan of porters as we proceed to the dhow.

Captain Tufani is waiting patiently and jumps onto the quay side to take our goods. The man with the chairs is also waiting for us, and the *dhow* is loaded with our day's shopping.

'Ah. That is good. You have new chairs. How much do you pay? Where did you get them made?'

'You have been robbed' he exclaims, 'Why did you go to that shop? If you want some furniture, my cousin has a good shop. That one is a thief. Next time I will come with you.'

Chapter 18

Scorpion in the Sand

'Huenda malishoni zikiwa ng'ombe hurudi zikiwa nyama.'
'They go to graze as cows, but come back as meat'

Virginia: January 1990

The village has been awake since four o'clock, when the haunting call of the *muezzin* wails out, *'Allahu Akbar ašhadu 'anla ilāha illal-Lāh, wa 'ašhadu 'anna muḥammadan rasūlul-Lāh,'* summoning the men to prayer. I leave Jasmine house an hour later just as the sun rises. Women are up sweeping and singing in their courtyards, preparing food for the men who are returning from the mosque. The neighbour's children cluster in the dark doorway. I pick my way through the littered alleyways to the sea front. Wooden *dhows* are coming in from the night of fishing and the tired men look up and greet me, surprised to see a white woman alone at this early hour.

Negotiating the anchor lines and shards of ancient Chinese ceramics, pebbles and fish bones, I stroll through the narrow passageways, passing beneath the deserted balcony of the hotel, as the staff sweep the beach. Most of their guests are still asleep beneath their mosquito nets. I am ahead of the basking sunbathers.

This is my annual challenge to myself, to circumnavigate the island on my own. It will take me about four hours to walk along the pristine white beach stretching for 14 kilometres to the other end of the island where I hope to find a fishing boat to take me through the mangrove channel to Lamu Town and then back to Shela.

The beach is freshly washed by the receding tide. I am barefoot, with the freedom of the deserted beach before me. No footprint but mine spoils this sandy solitude. Translucent pink ghost crabs skitter sideways on the lapping edge of the ocean, as they sense the rhythm of my footfalls. I unwind my *kanga* and hold it high in the soft tropical breeze, like a flag reaching for the sky. Limbs taut with joy, I run down the beach splashing through the waves as it flutters above me in the cobalt sky. The sun rises white hot on the horizon.

It is at the precise moment of joy that I see the figure of a man cutting directly towards me down the dunes, in uncharacteristic haste. The core of my brain jerks to life. It flashes a warning. Danger. I stop dead in my tracks, dropping my arms helplessly, and watch him. A fisherman walking to the ocean has no urgency in his gait. This man is thrashing through the curvaceous hips of the sand dune with uncharacteristic haste. He is coming to intercept me brandishing a panga. I sense as instinctively as an impala being stalked by a lion, that I am his prey.

I wrap the *kanga* anxiously around my waist and walk on fast, head down. Thank God I am wearing a proper costume and not a bikini, is my first thought. When he disappears behind a dune, I break into a jog. Perhaps I can get ahead of him before he hits the beach. Then suddenly he jumps out in front of me – a small, wiry coffee-skinned man in dark glasses. He has sloped shoulders and the look of a hyena.

He hails me: '*Jambo*'.
Innocuous? I don't think so.
I greet him weakly.
I don't make eye contact.
I stride on, feigning calm.
He moves too close to me.
'*Ngoja, usienda.* Wait, don't go.'
'*Kwa nini?* Why not
'*Simama!* Stop!'

180

'*Kwa nini?* Why should I?
He points with the tip of his blade at my kanga.
'*Ninataka hiyo,* I want that'
'*Ni yangu.* No, it's mine,' I stand high,
Clutching my *kanga*, staring at him defiantly.
'*Nataka sasa!* Give it to me now.'
'*Nitafyeka wewe.* I will slash you.'
I see the blade glinting in the sun
I rip off my *kanga.* I fling it at him,
Like a bad-tempered wife having a tantrum.
'*Sawa.*' I back off,
Clutching my breast in horror.
He lurches at me and grabs me,
Dark hand grips my black costume,
Boobs bunch together in his angry fist,
A tight cleavage beneath his dirty hand.
I am about to be raped.
This is happening to *me.*
I am stunned. It is surreal.
I watch my own attack from above
fascinated floating like a spirit.
I think - God, this is it! I am going to die.
My head boils with rage.
The cheek of it. Little shit. No way!
I am not scared. I am incensed. I fight back.
'Hey, leave me,' I shout in his face, blazing angry.

Like a drunk husband, he grabs my arms with both hands.
'*Kufyeka wewe!* I will slash you'
Nose in my face as if he knows me.
His teeth are stained and rotten,
His breath is rank. Stale coconut.
Repulsive man! I am incensed.
I am cold – like ice.
Blade glints again, not far above my head.
He will slash my face. I don't flinch.

181

He tries to twist my arm.
I will beat this man.
He tries to push me onto my back.
I wedge my feet in the deep sand,
leaning hard towards him.
He hooks his foot around my ankle,
hoping to topple me.
I resist. My muscles tense.
I shove back with all my weight.
He shunts me slowly backwards.
Off the open beach, behind a dune.
If he gets me onto the ground,
I am finished.
I throw my full bulk against the stranger.
We wrestle back and forth.
A despicable little runt of a man.
I push him backward.
Two scorpions fighting in the sand.
He pulls me forwards.

A Buddhist saying calms my brain.
Wash off the mud to find a diamond.
Disarm him. Seek his humanity.
Uncover his soft core.
I change my voice to a weak simper
'Jino lako nani? What is your name?'
His slime yellow eyes blink in surprise.
'Ali.'
'Sawa, Ali, Okay'.
'Hezi hapana mzuri. This is not good.'
He cackles like a sick hyena.
'Mimi, Mama mzuri. I am a good mother.'
'Toto tatu. I have three children.'
'Wewe baba? Are you a father?'
No response. Make him talk.
Shove, shove. I am sliding backwards.

He is winning.

'*Wewe, baba mzuri.*' You are a good father.

Whispering to calm him.

He takes the bait.

'*Mimi, baba mzuri.* Me good father.'

'*Wewe mama mbaya.* You bad white mother'

'*Wewe Takataka!* just rubbish!'

One hand off me

to clutch his genitals,

Grossly as he leers,

'*Mama wazungu wanataka mimi.*

White women like to have me.'

'I do not! I am not free.

I am married.

A mother of three.'

He grabs me again in anger.

Back and forth in a macabre dance,

kicking up the sand about us.

'*Hapana mzuri.* No, this is not good,'

I wheedle as if I know him.

A tattoo of a scorpion on his skinny arm.

Less pressure from his grip on my arm.

'Ali, come on now, you do not want me.

I know you are a good man'

He flings down my wrists.

'*Sawa, kwenda!* All right, go!'

He turns away in a sulk.

'*Mzungu takataka.* white rubbish.'

I back off, amazed, expecting a trick.

'*Kwenda,* Go, go! *Takataka.* You rubbish.'

My heart pounds against my breasts.

I grab my *kanga,* trampled into the sand.

'Okay, *Asante sana, Bwana,* thank you Sir.'

'*Wewe mutu mzuri,* Ali. You are a good man.'

I back off in the direction of home.

He leaps to life again angry,

Like a small flame catching light.
'*Hapana, hapana.* No, No.'
'*Rudi.* Come back.'
'*Nenda chini.* You go that way.'
He pushes me roughly to go right,
Two hours down a deserted beach,
No way I go that way.
'Are you crazy? *Samahani, hapana.*'
Taunted every few feet
Like a cat playing with a mouse,
before you rape me you bastard.
A short life with full-blown AIDS.
'*Hapana, mimi ni mgonjwa.* No, you make me sick.'
'*Sasa nina rudi nyumba.* Now I am going home.'
He pushes me up the deserted beach,
where only ghost crabs will witness his deed.

Appeal to his honour:
Muslims keep their word.
'Ali, you made a deal. You said I could go.
You are a good Muslim. Keep your promise.'
A mother ticking off a petulant child
He is simple. He relents again.
'*Wewe, kwenda! Kwa heri, takataka.*'
You, just go. Goodbye, rubbish.'

I turn to go back to the village.
Then hear '*Nataka hizi.* I want that.'
He has come away with nothing.
He deserves a peace offering
My bottle of special water?
The lunch I carry still hanging from my wrist:
He snarls like a yellow street dog.
'*Nipa embe.* Give me.'
I chuck him the mango,
Like a dog he catches it.

I slide sideways past him.
Just walk. Slowly. Don't run.
Swim slowly backwards from a shark.
Don't bring out the predator.
With dread, one footstep at a time,
I inch back up the endless beach.
Hugging the lapping sea
I will swim if I must.
He is moving away from the water
Like a furtive crab, he vanishes into a hole
in the vast stretch of sand.
I walk faster. I see the hotel and I run.
A couple entwined on the beach look up.
Naked. Adam and Eve. No shame.
He wants the same.
All infidels are depraved
Believes simple Ali.
I point, I mimic the fight.
They smile and shrug.
No English. No Swahili.
They return to fondling.
I leave them in rage.
I sympathise with Ali.

Another couple of naked Italians are enjoying the first rays of the sun unabashed at being in a public thoroughfare. When I see them, I come apart, about to crack from the delayed shock.

'Do you know what has just happened to me?' I shout at them. They stare at me as if I am deranged.

'I have just been attacked by a man further along the beach.'

185

'Oh yes, we know. It is very dangerous up the beach, so we stay here near the hotel,' a gorgeous bimbo intones in a delightful Italian accent, pushing both her lips and breasts forward.

'I have just escaped being raped,' I repeat more clearly.

'You fine, you okay? No problem?' says the man, understanding a little English.

'Yes, I am fine, thank you.'

They don't get what I'm trying to convey.

'What I mean is, can you please put some clothes on. This is a very Muslim Island.' I reply, ice cold, 'If you weren't sunbathing naked in the path of sex starved wandering males, people like me going up the beach for a walk might not get victimised by mindless men who imagine that all white women want their clothes taken off.'

My complicated stream of English is lost on them, but they guess I am upset by their nudity.

Her thickly blackened lashes bat up and down heavily.

'Oh yes, you are right. *Dobbiamo indossare i nostri vestiti, amore,*' she says to her boyfriend. The girl wriggles into her minute bikini making herself look even more seductive.

I head home, fuming that they have so little sense of propriety on this Muslim Island. I can understand how confusing it is for Ali.

When I get back, I find the family in a state of euphoria, having got back from their dive.

'Guess what Mum, we saw a whale shark.'

'It was incredible,' says Anthony, giving me a big hug. 'You won't believe it. It came right up close to the boat to inspect us and, as it went past, the diving instructor just jumped in after it and caught hold of its dorsal fin, and shouted for us to come in. So, I jumped in after him and we literally got pulled along by the whale shark for a bit. It was utterly amazing. The best thing that has ever happened to me.'

'Wow, fantastic, what an adventure ... I also had rather a ... one-off experience.'

They look up, waiting to hear. 'I only got a few kilometres up the beach when I was attacked by a lunatic.'

'Oh my God, are you alright? What happened'

Anthony looks at me alarmed.

I can see him noting: no blood, no obvious damage.

If I had something to show, a panga wound or a torn *kanga*.

But nothing. A missed rape is as good as no rape.

I am calm and unhurt. He gives me a cursory hug.

I don't want to alarm the children unnecessarily with the drama, so I play down the danger. The children shrug it off. It hardly seems to compare to their excitement about the whale shark.

I go to Rosie's room and sit on her bed. I recount the full story and she hugs me like a mother, saying nothing, just holding me. I feel her strength, and shudder in long breathes as the pent-up fear leaves my body in waves. Suddenly I am a child, and she is a rock of strength. Silent tears flow on and on. She just starts to hum a church song and rock me slowly. No words are necessary. I keep feeling the sensation of that alien hand grasping at my bosom, but it could have been worse.

I am surprised how quickly the police come to Jasmine House. They want to catch the miscreant before the tourists get wind of the attack. A story like this can ruin livelihoods in this little village.

'Can you identify anything about the man? Does he have yellow skin?'

'Yes, in fact, he is quite light-skinned.'

'Somali?'

'I don't know, maybe. He is smaller than me and has a tattoo of a scorpion on his left forearm.'

'Ah, we know him. We will get him. We know where he lives.'

The advantage of an island community. They go to his house, I hear later. He sees them and runs to hide in his latrine, but they corner him and bring him into custody.

I have to go to the seedy police depot on the hill above Lamu Town for an identity parade the very next day. Anthony has another diving trip planned.

'Don't worry, I'll be fine. I can go on my own.' He nods sympathetically, gives me a hug and wishes me luck. I wish he would not take me at my word.

Rosie says simply, 'I will come with you, Mum.'

There are ten men standing before me. Many I know by sight. I have seen them grow up into young men. They are intrigued to see if I can identify the culprit. I spot him immediately and ask that he remove his dark glasses. I look into the void of his eyes.

'You are required to identify the man who attacked you by touch,' I am told by the policeman in charge. Shrinking inwardly with repulsion I reach out and touch his shoulder. The line of suspects breaks out in whoops of delight. They break out of the line and slap my hand in turn, to congratulate me, as Ali is hauled off to a cell.

Rosie hugs me and says, 'Mum, you did so well. You are a strong woman.'

The police tell me he has just been released after a year in jail for his last offence: the rape of a 70-year-old white women on the beach. He is a Somali from the mainland and a well-known miscreant, despised by the islanders. The day before he accosted me, he tried unsuccessfully to ambush another tourist up the beach. She had escaped and had left the island immediately, terrified by her experience. As a foreigner, she was unwilling to report the incident, nervous to get involved with the local police, but I had no such qualms. I want this man behind bars if I am ever to walk down the long beach again.

The District Magistrate, by happy coincidence, is in Lamu Town on his circuit of these remote islands. This time Anthony does come. We wait in an ancient foetid corridor that goes back to the days of the slave trade. I line up with other plaintiffs in the oppressive heat outside the courtroom. I am squashed between two large women, wedged against their weighty thighs on the narrow wooden bench. After a few steamy hours, I am summoned into a tiny, cluttered office. Behind a desk, piled high with untidy files and dead flies, sits the magistrate, looking hot and bored. Not a promising scenario. I am made to swear as solemnly as in any supreme court. We sweat together through the tedious process all morning.

Ali is pushed onto the bench behind me, and I learn that 'Ali' is not in fact his name. He starts railing abuse at me when he sees me. I guess he feels cheated to be charged when he let me go. The courtroom bursts into laughter when they hear that all he got from me was the mango. What a loser, their laughter implies. Can't even rob successfully, let alone rape. He is sent back to jail, just for a year. I feel almost guilty for getting him arrested. I have only a bruise on my arm to show for all the aggression he intended. I was not physically injured. I escaped rape. I have escaped a life of HIV/AIDS. In fact, it was empowering.

'What doesn't kill you makes you stronger,' says Anthony.

Chapter 19

Wema Martyr

'Watu kuagua ugonjwa, hawaagui jeuri'
'Sickness can be cured, but not violence.'

Virginia: February 1990.

Back in Nairobi, I am still in a state of agitation constantly reliving the details of my encounter with 'Ali': a recurring fear in my gut as I picture the man running down the sand dune towards me; the squashy feel of his hand on my bosom, the hardened foot and horny toenails hooked behind my heel. I relive the terror of falling onto my back in the sand, the glint of panga and the disgusting stench of sour coconut on his breath but most of all the emblem of his evil, the scorpion on his yellow arm is branded in my mind's eye.

But this little incident was a negligible experience compared to what I now hear from Anthony.

I hear him come in and start pouring himself a whisky.

'Come and join me,' he calls out. 'Do you want a brandy and ginger ale?'

We sit on the veranda together.

'How are things at work?' I prompt him.

'Fine.'

He sips his drink, uncharacteristically morose, his thumb nail rubs his index finger, a sign he is stressed. I sense he has something to tell me.

He looks at me for a long time and then takes my hand and holds it tightly.

'I am afraid I have had some terrible news.'

I look at him, panicking. Immediately my mind reels through the possibilities: the kids are at home, it can't be them. My mother is ill, maybe?

'What is it? Has there been an accident?'

'Yes. Something terrible.'

I jump to my feet, mind reeling. 'Oh my God, what happened? What do you mean? A car crash?'

'No, much worse, I am afraid.

'What can be worse? Has someone died?'

'Yes. Wema Mission has been attacked. The *shifta* came to the mission. They shot at the sisters when they were at their prayers.'

'What? They opened fire on the nuns completely without warning?'

'Yes. Agnes was shot dead immediately.'

'No! Not Sister Agnes. She was a saint.' My mind is reeling with the horror.

His eyes fill with tears. I have seldom seen him cry before. He buries his face in his hands, unable to continue.

'The others escaped. Thank goodness the three local nuns survived, but Sister Romana...'

'God, it is so unjust.'

'She's in total shock, in hospital under sedation. Going back to America.'

'And Father Spiro? Is he alright?'

'Well. I don't know how he is in himself, but he's determined to stay on at the mission even though he is the only white there now. It just shows.'

'What does it show?'

'That no one is safe here. Sister Agnes thought they would be protected because of the need for the hospital.'

'It's pointless trying to develop a country if there is no rule of law.'

I can't get the drama of the attack out of my mind. It reels through my mind like a horror movie. Having lived for a few days in the mission, I can imagine in detail how it could have happened.

I picture the four nuns walking down the short sandy road from the hospital to their convent. The sun is setting, casting long shadows over the dry bush scrub. Sister Romana would be walking ahead of the three novices, the three beautiful girls in their early twenties, with the long faces of the Orma. The sisters were so proud of converting them. Romana would pull the fly screen door open and hold it for the girls as they went in. They would all take off their shoes and line them up neatly outside the main door, slipping their tired feet into plastic flip flops. Sister Romana would take off her dusty black work shoes. I remember their shoes so well.

Sister Josephine, the youngest, did the cooking. She would go down the corridor to the kitchen to light the fire of the stove. I remember how she snapped the sticks over her knee so expertly, blowing the embers to life. She would fill a large black tin kettle with water from a plastic drum and put it on the hob. Then she would light a paraffin lantern and put it ready in the prayer room. The other nuns would be going into the little prayer room for evening vespers, a relentless daily routine. Sister Agnes was always the last to leave the hospital. She would hurry in at the last moment, locking the large wooden door, and putting the key in a bowl in front of the statue of Our Lady. I picture her quickly washing her hands in the sink, splashing water on her face, and straightening her wimple, as she goes in to join the other sisters on their knees on small cushions facing the crucifix.

They would make the sign of the cross intoning in unison, '*In the name of the Father, and of the Son and of the Holy Ghost, Amen.*'

I imagine a dog is barking urgently outside, persistently demanding attention, trying to warn them.

Sister Romana would go to the lectern and announce the response for the evening prayers.

'*Into your hands O Lord, I commend my spirit.*'

The novices would raise their lovely voices, pure as nightingales in the early evening.

'*Let me be glad and rejoice in love, for I trust in the Lord.*' they would be singing, swaying to the rhythmic repetition of the psalm. They would intone the response unaware of the mayhem about to ensue.

Sister Agnes would be looking over their bowed heads, to the window.

Is that a shadow of the tree moving? She stiffens listening more carefully.

The dog's bark is now sounding more urgent. A movement outside, footfalls.

Agnes sings out the psalm, in a faltering voice.

A sudden smash of heavy metal against the front door.

'*Hodi! Hodi!*' shouts a rough male voice.

The sisters would look at each other, eyes widening with fear.

Sister Agnes would go to the front door.

'Who is there? *Ni nani aliye?*' she would call out in her high American drawl.

'*Fungua mlango.* Open the door,' insists the voice in Swahili.

'What is the problem? Please go to the hospital if you want treatment.'

'*Chakula sasa. Fungua.* I want food, now.'

I can imagine her backing towards the statue, reaching for the keys to open the door.

'*Fungua sasa! Mimi risasi!*' I will shoot you.

She would be signalling the other nuns to stay back.

A volley of shots would ring out. She would crumple to the ground, instantly felled by the machine gun fire through the door. The brutes would kick the door down roughly. The statue of the Virgin Mary would topple over shattering the blue and white plaster into shards of martyrdom. The troop of dark thugs would push through, stepping over her unmoving body towards the other four women cowering against the wall.

'Apparently all they wanted was food and money,' Anthony is saying, breaking into my thoughts. 'He just shot her.'

'And the other novices?'

'They escaped and ran to the hospital to get help. Father Spiro arrived with a Maasai askari who cornered one of the terrorists against the door and was beating him over the head. It was a bloodbath.'

'Poor Sr. Agnes. I can't believe they killed her. Such mindless violence. Life here is so cheap.'

'It is absolutely sickening. Now the whole area will suffer without a doctor.'

'It is not only in the wild frontier of the Tana River that living is dangerous. Crime in Nairobi has also increased. People are being hijacked by bandits, thrown out of their cars even in Nairobi.'

'It has changed so much in the last five years.'

'Policemen get fatter every year. When we first arrived, the traffic cops were quite skinny. Now they all take bribes on the road and have beer guts. So much corruption everywhere.'

'It's just a question of time before we are robbed. It's like Russian roulette and we have been lucky so far.' The injustice done to the sisters weighs heavily on us. It saps Anthony's enthusiasm to contribute to a country where the most innocent are preyed on. The futility of our contribution is clear. We feel there is no prospect of progress whilst such lawlessness thrives.

Chapter 20

Kijabi Raid

'Nyumba ya jirani ikiungua, wewe huota moto.'
'When a neighbour's house burns, warm yourself with the fire.'

Virginia: March 1990.

It is barely a week later when it is our turn to face reality. The local dogs have set up a chain of barking. Teddy is growling softly next to the bed. There is an unfamiliar click. I am suddenly wide awake.

'What's that?' I whisper clutching Anthony in the dark.

'I don't know, I also thought I heard something.'

'It's probably just the askari.'

'I'll go and check,' says Anthony. 'For once, I can't hear him snoring.'

Anthony unlocks the so called 'rape gate', an added barrier to seal off the bedroom area upstairs in exactly this sort of raid. I have always loathed it. The idea that we have to be imprisoned against invasion is in itself a reason to leave. However, just in case, I close the gate after him to protect the children. It strikes me as incongruous that he goes to see what is happening, stark naked, looking like a neanderthal, but without a club. I hear him creep quietly down the stairs and across the sitting room.

Across the length of the French windows onto the veranda, there is an expanding trellis-grille which is secured with a weighty chain and two padlocks. I hear him yank the heavy curtains apart with a decisive crack. Then there is a blood curdling yell. His yell. Instinctively, I scream in reaction. He is belting up the stairs flashing his white butt. I open the gate for him terrified.

'What is happening? Are we being attacked? Close the gate, quick.'

The children appear wide-eyed, and I grab them. He hugs us all in relief. He pushes us into the bedroom, closes the door and leans back on it, collecting his thoughts.

'Dad, why haven't you got any clothes on?' Tristan asks, looking cheeky and ignoring the drama.

'Can't you see my clothes?' he teases them. 'I am the famous emperor in your storybook.'

Anthony bursts into the most ridiculous fit of hysterical giggles. I gape at him amazed at his strange reaction.

'What happened for God's sake?'

We stare at him confused, and the kids start to giggle as well.

Between fits of mirth, he blurts out, 'I stopped them just in the nick of time. One more moment and they would have opened the sliding doors and got inside. I would have had it!'

He thinks it is hilarious. Or is it nerves? He can't stop laughing. All the children get the giggles as well. I am not so amused.

'For God's sake Anthony, what bloody happened.'

He gets a grip on himself and explains, 'There were about five men crouching on the other side of the sliding doors with huge bolt cutters. That click we heard was when they cut the first padlock. They were trying to cut the second padlock when I ripped the curtains apart with both hands,' he says miming his actions dramatically. 'I looked down to see these men just below me at cock height on the other side of the glass. I got such a fright I let off a primordial battle cry like a soldier on a bayonet charge. They must have thought I was some sort of deranged flasher.'

I was beginning to see how funny it was.

'They looked up to see this crazy screaming white man above them, dangling his privates in their faces.'

'Crikey, what a horrible sight. They will have nightmares for the rest of their lives.'

We were all catching his infectious giggles.

'When I screamed, they also screamed, then they backed off terrified and disappeared into the night.'

'One moment later they would have cut through the chain. They had a pile of heavy rocks ready as weapons.'

'It could have been horrific if they had got inside. Terrifying.'

'A miss is as good as a mile.' He pulls on a pair of shorts hurriedly and presses the panic button beside our bed.

'Let's see how long it takes for the security guys to arrive. I am going to find the askari. You stay here with the children, and close the gate, just in case. Don't come out.'

He locks us in and disappears into the garden with a long torch, heavy enough to use as a weapon. I hug the children and try to make a joke of it. 'Why didn't Daddy have any clothes?' they keep asking.

'He always sleeps without anything on, you know that. It is so hot. Then we heard a noise, and he went off to check all the doors were locked.'

Rosie comes out of her quarters, looking frightened and we open the huge steel gate to let her in. She is wide eyed with fear. I tell her quickly what happened minus the part about nakedness.

'Those boys are very dangerous, Mum. Dad must not go out in the garden alone now. They can be waiting for him.'

'Don't worry the robbers have gone. The security guards will catch them.'

There is a commotion of hooting and flicking headlights. The landline rings. It is the security team. We open the electric gate. Fully armed, the guards fan out around the house, flashing their torches to check the doors for signs of a break-in. The askari is found hiding under a bush. He acts half asleep and confused when they question him. He has seen and heard nothing. They put him in the police vehicle.

Anthony sets off with the guards across the dark gulley below the house following the tracks of the thieves. When he comes back, he is carrying a suede shoe.

'We found this stuck in the thick mud of the gulley.'

'Do you recognise this?' It's a leather *veldskoen,* common in South Africa.

I bash off the caked red mud, 'Is it one of yours?'

'I had some like that.'

'Did you recognise any of the thieves?'

'Not really. I hardly saw their faces. It was so dark. I only saw their red rimmed eyes.'

'Will you report this to the police?' asks the security guard.

'Well ... we haven't lost anything, so there is no need to involve the police.'

'Then I advise you to change your askari. It looks like an inside job. We have taken him in for questioning.'

Rosie goes back to bed. We tuck up the children and I sing to them until they finally fall asleep.

A few hours later I am still awake, lying rigid, listening and tense.

'Are you awake?' I ask Anthony. 'Hmm. Sort of,' he groans.

'I really think it is time to go home. Back to Zimbabwe. I can't stand this lack of security.'

'Hmm. I know, you are probably right. Despite everything, Kenya is a wonderful place to bring up the children.'

'Until something happens. Like what happened at Wema. Or your attack on the beach. Then our whole lives go pear shaped.'

'I guess, we can't stay here forever. It is so sad to leave just when we have finished Jasmine House.'

'We can always come back to Lamu for a holiday each year.'

'I know, but we can never be Kenyan residents. It is just an illusion. We have to go back where we have a permanent right to live. At least I am a Zimbabwean. Here we will always be expatriates.'

'Tristan really should go to a proper high school next year back home.'

Chapter 21

Kwa Heri

'Kulia kwa samaki, machozi (yake) huenda na maji.'
'The tears of the fish are carried away by the water.'

Rosie: April 1990.

They want to go back to their home. I know that the robbery made them very scared. I wonder who would do that to them. I was very much worried I would be blamed by the police because I have keys for the house. They said it was an inside job, so it means it can be the askari, the gardener or me that is helping the robbers. I think it is the askari. He is a Masai, and I don't trust him. Also why did he go to sleep far from the house. He was told to go away so they can rob the house. I think he was very much frightened that he could be killed. So Maasai are not so brave like people say. There are so many bad people here, so I think it is a gang which knows the askari. Mum said to me not to be worried because they will not let anyone arrest me. I know the old man who is the gardener, and it is not him, for sure.

I know they can't stay here in Kenya because it is not their country. Zimbabwe is their place, where the twins are born. Tristan has to go to the senior school in Zimbabwe. There is no very good English schools here. I am so sad when they tell me they will be leaving in three months.

But I don't know what I will do when they go. These white people are my family now. Mum is worrying too much about me, but I don't want to show Mum that I am worrying, so I just say nothing and smile happy-like. I tell Mum I don't want to go back to Limuru and live there without a job. So, Mum finds me a friend of hers where I can keep on working, so it is all okay.

I wait and pray to God that He can stop the days passing quickly, so I don't have to see them going back to their place in Zimbabwe without me. But the days pass. I am showing them that I am fine, so they don't worry about me. But I am so sad when I think about what is happening and that they are leaving me. My heart is not accepting that they go to their place. I am always imagining what shall happen to me when they go, but I can't get the answer.

Now there are two weeks left and they start packing things to take to Zimbabwe. I know there is nothing I can do to stop them leaving.

The children are trying very much to make me happy in these last days. They tell me how they shall not forget me ever and how they will be writing to me. I tell them, 'You are my children, I can't forget you either,' but I know they might easily forget me when they grow up.

The house is now full of men packing everything. They put all the things in that big house into so many big boxes and take them away. When I feel sad, I must go to my room and my tears start coming without stopping. After I cry a little, I wipe my tears and go back to work. When I think of them going again, I run to my room and cry some more times. Sometimes the children call me when I am in my room and I wipe my eyes and come quickly out of my room, pretending I was doing something else. I dream of a time when I can go and see them there. I just show them that it is fine.

We go in two cars to take Rosie back to her own home. The Land Cruiser, its roof rack loaded high with a wooden bed and furniture, looks like a *matatu* as it wobbles down the muddy red lane to her house. A young woman is walking along the road towards us, carrying a bag on her head. She is young and strikingly attractive, with a flowery blouse that exposes her ample breasts, which bounce provocatively as she navigates the slippery path.

'Mum, you see that lady. She is the other wife. You see she is leaving my house now because I am coming back.'

'How are you going to manage here? Isn't it going to be difficult for you?'

'I don't know, Mum. I have to try and see. Or I can go to stay in town again at my new workplace, maybe.'

Our kids pile out of the car. No introductions are needed. Charlie and Tristan run off to climb the plum trees, excited to be back after so long. We unload the goods. Rosie calls the boys, hers and mine, to carry the boxes inside. Charlie makes a grand display of handing over his bicycle to Kariuki, who is clearly too big for it, but he happily cycles off, standing on the pedals, bumping down the rutted path, a trail of boys chasing behind.

There is some curiosity about what clothes and toys await them, but Rosie says with firm authority, 'Not now, children. Come here and help.'

Rosie's two girls are now leggy teenagers with budding breasts and demure maidenly smiles. They say in careful English, 'How are you?' and I hug them.

Kimendi comes up with a burly young man, Rosie's eldest son, his biceps smeared in grease straining the Aqua Aid T-shirt we once donated.

'Goodness, you must be Ezekiah, how you've grown, I would hardly recognise you now,' I beam happily to see him.

'Yes, Good morning, Mama Tristan.' he replies politely.

'I am now a mechanic in a garage in Limuru. Now two years I work there.' He has a deep voice and his father's charm. 'I am now in my own house,' he adds, indicating the new hut where he now lives alone, ready to take a wife.

The three men go off to unload the bed from the roof of the Land Cruiser. Anthony is shown the new corrugated iron roof, with gutters connecting a tank, to enable them to collect the rainwater. Men's talk. Details of how it was done. Cost saving. Compliments on workmanship.

Rosie takes me inside for a women's tour of domestic improvements: now the floor is concrete, and the windows have glass. In the little bedroom, there are now two beds, one for the two girls and the other shared by the three younger boys. A new parents' room has been built, ready to receive the double bed, which the men bring in. With the large cupboard against one wall, there is barely enough room to get it inside.

'At last, I have my own big bed.' Rosie hugs me and says, 'Mum, thank you. I can't believe we can be given so much. How can I thank you? I can only ask God to bless you.'

It is hard to be leaving Kenya, but I know we will always be within their family. I give her a framed photo of each of the kids. This is so you will never forget the children and the wonderful years we have had together.'

Kimendi nods and looks pleased. He treads off his gumboots outside the door, next to a pile of muddy shoes. I recognise a pair of old takkies that were once Tristan's, now completely worn through. I see an old pair of leather sandals that I brought from Italy, happily rubbing toes with Anthony's *veldskoen*, except that I see only one veldschoen. A terrible thought occurs to me. Surely, Kimendi would never take advantage of us like that, after all we have done for his family. I am being a typical memsahib, suspecting the locals of pinching everything, as bad as my mother. I decide to ignore my horrible suspicion. What does it matter now who broke into the house? We are leaving soon.

Echoing our first visit, the two girls once again come in like sacristans: one holding a jug of water, the other proffering an empty bowl with a clean towel draped across her arm. The teenagers have a quiet and delicate way of moving. Water is dribbled over my fingers into the bowl, and I take the towel to carefully dry my hands. One by one, the children wash their hands and squeeze into the space. It feels like the last rites are being performed. Anthony, Kimendi and Ezekiah sit outside in a manly way, on plastic chairs.

Rosie serves up a meal of *ugali* and chicken, a treat for her children. She and I sit on stools at the coffee table, with our children kneeling on the floor, wherever they can find space. Our children are no longer the babies they were five years ago. When all have settled down with their plates before them, and a glass of juice, she starts the thanksgiving grace.

'Father, we thank you for this food, which is before us and for bringing our mother and father to eat with us in our humble home. We ask you to carry them to their home safely in Zimbabwe and return them to us, Oh Lord, so we eat together again soon. Bring them back to us, Lord, we beseech you. Lord, have mercy on us and bring us peace for our families. Amen.'

'Amen,' we chorus, and Anthony crosses himself.

There is a heavy sadness in the air. I think of our freak encounter. Of the magic spark the first time we ate together when a shared future still lay before us. Now it is over. This is it. We are leaving. What is there to say? There is nothing more to discover. We smile and eat. Gulp and swallow.

Our children are subdued during the meal. Rosie's children are respectfully quiet. I remember the intense wonder of the first time we came to her home. Now I feel like a benefactor rather than an exotic guest. Giving has not brought us closer, but rather induced a distance. The servility of the receiver is part of the price paid for the pleasure of giving. Kimendi seems reserved, even furtive. Having finished his meal, he gets up to leave, wiping his hands on the seat of his trousers.

'I must go now. I have to get back to work,' he explains to Anthony, who wishes him well. He pulls on his boots. Anthony watches too. Surreptitiously, I scan the pile of shoes more carefully, looking for the other half of the pair. Anthony follows my gaze and nods slightly. He catches my eye, and I know he too has noticed the missing shoe, but like me he will say nothing.

My tears come down in these three days until I think the water has finished in my eyes. I can't cry anymore. On the morning of Saturday is when they come to see me at my home. We are together with my family, but it is not a happy time like the last time. It is their very heavy last goodbye to me. Mum gives me a photo of each one in a lovely frame and I tell her I can never forget my children. I hug the little girl Wendy and she cries and runs to the car. When I hug Tristan, the first born, I take out my sadness in a loud voice. I cry out very loud as we people do in Africa to show we can't bear any more pain. They can't believe I am crying because they never see me cry like that before.

I hug Charlie and he ask me, 'Rosie, are you really crying or are you just pretending?'

When Charlie ask me that I cry even louder than before. This makes me not to see when their father gets into the car, so I don't hug him to say goodbye. Mum is hugging me and then she has to go as well. I can't see Mum because of my tears. Then I feel shame for my crying. I have so many tears I have to hide my eyes in my jersey. Even I can't watch them drive off. I think Mum is also crying. We are suffering very much to part.

Virginia: May 1990.

We are all packed and the children are hugging Rosie and making me feel even worse about leaving. What are we going to do without her? When Charlie gives her a huge kiss on the cheek, she bursts into tears, and I can feel Wendy is about to start howling as well.

'Come on everyone in the car,' says Anthony, extracting himself from all the drama and switching on the engine. I hug Rosie quickly before I succumb to tears as well. She looks at me with that long quiet gaze which comes straight from her heart and says gently, 'Mum, how can I manage without you?'

'Rosie, you will be fine. Write to me and let me know how it goes in your new job. I know it won't take long before you are a second mother to their little kids as well. She is so lucky to have you.'

'I don't know Mum, if I can manage with a new person, but anyway I will try.'

We leave her waving bravely as we drive off out of her life. It is worse than saying goodbye to my own mother. I worry what will happen to her. Will the second wife move out?

'At least I have fixed her up with an excellent job. I am sure Maggie is good to her staff.'

'Well, let's hope so. Sometimes expatriate women who are newly in Africa treat their staff with complete contempt, worse than the old colonials.'

'I can't imagine Maggie would be like that. They are very liberal.'

'Well, she was the best person I could think of amongst all of our friends. I told her about how I met Rosie and that she is not just any old nanny, more like an *au paire* and that I have never treated her as a servant. I just hope Maggie doesn't nit-pick over the standard of cleanliness. My standards are low compared to most of our friends. I really don't mind a bit of dust.

'Well, you have never ever shouted at her like some of them do.'

'I was just so grateful to have any help at all after that year in England. I can't imagine getting cross with Rosie.'

'Why can't Rosie come with us to Zimbabwe, Mama?' Asks Wendy who is listening carefully to the conversation.

'She isn't allowed to work in Zimbabwe. You can't just go anywhere and live. You have to get permission from the government.'

'That's why we are leaving Kenya because they won't allow us to stay here too long,' explains Anthony.

'She could come and have a holiday with us,' suggests Tristan.

'We will see her every year because we will be coming on holiday to Lamu and she will be there waiting for you, so don't worry. She will be fine.'

'When I grow up, I am going to come and live in Kenya.'

'Good idea, Tristan. But meanwhile, we have to go back to our own country. It will be much better because the friends you make in Zimbabwe will always live there. Remember you were saying how your friends here keep leaving the school? It's because they are all ex-patriate kids and they are only here for a few years then they have to go back to their own countries.'

'Also, Rosie can go back to her own children now,' adds Anthony, 'imagine how pleased her children will be to have their own Mum at home.'

'Let's hope that works out for her, I say quietly to him, 'what with Kimendi's new lady edging in.'

For the last time, we jostle with the traffic through Nairobi on Uhuru highway. This is the final trip to the airport, past the parks on the right, leading to Government House, past the conference centre and the lavish hotels. We turn off into the industrial area, down a rutted road lined with small factories, to a corrugated iron enclosure where the organisation perches in an unused government building. We park next to the ugly corrugated iron fence on which I painted a mural when I first arrived. It looks so amateurish to me now. The fence is rusty and covered in crow droppings. The raucous black and white scavengers nest each evening in the tall gum trees above the office. I wonder why I got so excited about decorating a government car park. The children jump out and run ahead.

This is to be a final parting with all the Women for Water staff. Mama Gola's secretary leads us into her simple office, no pretension. She rises to meet us, hugging the children.

We sit down next to her, and she grabs Charlie playfully and puts him on her lap.

Then turning to Anthony, she addresses him formally, 'We are very sorry you are both leaving. We have made great progress at Women for Water with your help. We don't know what we are going to do without you.'

Mama Gola presents us with a great copper wall plaque of animals and gives us all T shirts with the logo that I designed. We hug her tearfully.

'Don't worry, we'll be back,' Anthony promises, 'Every year, we'll come back to Lamu. We've learnt so much from you and the years we have spent in Kenya that we will always value. Thank you, Mama Gola, thank you all.'

'Goodbye, young man,' she says to Tristan, shaking his hand. 'You work hard at school and come back to work in Kenya, like your father, when you are big.'

Then she bends down to Charlie, who she loves for his cheekiness, 'And Bwana Charlie, one day you will be MP for Lamu, I am sure.'

Wendy gives her a loving hug round her large stomach, and Mama Gola strokes her long hair.

'Wendy, I will never forget you at the wedding, looking so beautiful. Please don't forget us here when you are big. Come and do some drawing for us like your mother has done. Virginia, go well, back to Zimbabwe, and tell them there that our loss is their gain. If they don't treat you well, you must come back to your family in Women for Water.'

PART 3

The Mosque of Shela Village. Watercolour. 1997.

KANGA IN THE BREEZE

Chapter 22

Panga Attack

'*Shoka husahu, mti hausahau*'
'The axe forgets but the tree does not forget.'

Virginia: Zimbabwe, November 1991.

I am sitting at our special look-out spot, as I do every evening, sipping a brandy and ginger ale enjoying the tranquil view to the blue hills in the distance. Anthony drives up with the children, back from school and they disappear to do their homework. He has just managed to get home before the sun sets over the hidden valley below. He passes me an envelope with a stamp from Kenya.

'Looks like a letter from Rosie,' he says handing over the mail addressed in a careful script with blue ink.

'I am really missing having her around. It just isn't the same having a man in the house. In fact, I really find it quite embarrassing having Joshua cleaning up after me. It is not really a man's job.'

Anthony sips his beer thoughtfully trying to think of a response. He is an old-fashioned husband who doesn't concern himself with housework, nor attempt to interfere. Whoever does the cleaning does not really affect his life.

'I don't think I have had a single conversation with Joshua. He is busy around me and keeps quiet. If I try and start a conversation, he just gives a monosyllabic answer, 'Yes, Madam; No Madam.' Never opens up about anything.

'He is the old type I guess: probably learnt the hard way not to be chatty with the Madam.'

'I wish we had looked for a woman to work in the house, but we couldn't very well refuse him with such a glowing reference.'

I open the letter looking forward to hearing from Rosie.

'It's only been three months since we left,' I scan the letter.

'Oh no! Listen to this. She has left her job and gone home. Shall I read it to you? Bloody hell, can you believe it? Maggie turned out to be a real cow!'

Dearest Mum,

Greetings from us in Kenya to you all in Zimbabwe. How is Babushka doing and the childrens? I am wondering very much if the childrens have started school already. Also, they must be very happy to be in their home. How is the dog Teddy and Henry the cat? Here we are missing you very much because the house is still empty where you were.

Mum, I am very sorry to tell you that I did not do what you asked me because the lady was not so good. I know you thought that she was a good person because she was your friend and her daughter also is Wendy's friend but all I can tell you Mum, she is not at all like you.

The first day I was there she was not at all kind with me. I was very much surprised to see what she is like. The problem is that I did make some tea for myself in the morning, and she was very cross about that. She told me there is only one time for tea when it is lunch time. Then I was cleaning, and she went out. So when she came back she said I had been very slow and what was I doing all day. Then she looks under the carpet and said, she saw too much dirt, so I did not do that good enough for her. But I do try hard always Mum.

The room she gave me to sleep in was very cold and in that room, there is no cooker. So, I just cooked my own food in the kitchen like I used to do with you. Then another girl who works here told her what I did, and she said that is not allowed. So, I said okay. Sorry. Then she was getting more cross with me and shouting. She told me that I was very much spoiled by you, Mum and that I must be much better for her, or I can go. So, I was worrying too much because I don't like to work with someone like that.

Please don't be worried Mum, but after one week I told her I don't want to stay with her family. She told me 'Go now', and so I just left her. Anyway Mum, I am so sorry not to stay with your friend, but you know some people can be different from what you think. Her husband is a good man, but he also gets much trouble with her because she is always cross.

So, if you want to find me Mum, I am back at my home and Kimendi is there as well and my childrens all fine, but I don't know how I am going to get money now. Maybe I will go back to pick some beans at the Limuru Estate because you know now it is now the time for picking.

Please give the children so many hugs from me and also to Dad big greetings.

Love from

Rosie.

'That's a real shame' says Anthony. 'Just shows, doesn't it?'

'What?'

'Well, just because people are so called liberal, it doesn't mean they have common humanity.'

'Now what is she going to do? That other woman is probably at home.'

'She will be fine. She isn't your problem now.'

'Why do you say that? Of course, she is my 'problem' as you put it.'

'When we go back next year, we can make a plan for her.'

Virginia: January 1992.

'This isn't Rosie's writing.'

As I look at the envelope. I sense that something is not right. I tear it open and I flip to the end.

'It's from Rosie's sister-in-law,' I mutter to myself scanning the page with alarm

'Christ, Rosie has been attacked. Listen to this. God, it's already been over a month since it happened.'

Dear Mama Tristan,

I think you have already met me one time when you came to see Rosie at her home many years ago. I am married to Rosie's brother, Amosi. I am Miriam, the one who is a nurse. Greetings from our family. I am asked to greet you and your family from Rosie.

I am afraid I have to tell you that Rosie has had very bad luck. She has been beaten badly by her husband, Kimendi, who wanted to kill her. It was a very bad affair, and he was in jail.

Rosie has told me that I must not let you be worried about her, but she wants you to know that she is in hospital. She is a bit better now. She was in a bad way. Her husband attacked her two days after Christmas.

He hit her all over with a panga and she has cuts on her shoulder, face, thigh and her hand was very bad. The hand was almost severed. We took her to hospital.

I am pleased to tell you that her state of health is now better, and she is on the road to recovery. I talked to the doctor who operated on her. He told me that unless 'plates' were put on the two bones, the ulna and the radius, the limb will have to be amputated.

But thanks to God who gave us courage to see us through this trying time, I arranged with him to transfer Rosie to a private nursing home where he could operate on her to save the arm. The operation was good because, even today, Rosie is telling us she has some sensations in the arm. The doctor explained to us that in time she will have some movement in the arm, but the pinkie and the forefinger may never move again. The wrist is fixed, and she cannot move it now. Her left hand may need a skin graft at a later date to cover up the veins properly.

The other deep cuts are healing beautifully. None of them became septic. The cuts on the head also healed well and she never lost consciousness at any time and the skull x-rays showed no fracture although he beat her badly on the head.

Her face has been messed up, but it is nearly better. One tooth was removed on the lower jaw and all the upper teeth are loose because the gum was broken when he hit her in the mouth.

Yesterday, we transferred her back to Kiambu government hospital because we could not afford to keep her in the private nursing home any longer. She was in great pain after the plates were put in but now the pain is subsiding, and she is able to sit up and walk about although she is still very weak because of losing so much blood. I will send you the doctor's report as soon as I get it, but please don't worry as the worst is now over.

I don't think she will be fit for work for at least three months, but we are praying that God will heal her quickly so that she can live a

217

normal life again. She doesn't want to stay in her home anymore, and we are thinking what to do. The problem is that her husband's family are blaming Rosie because they say it is her fault she didn't look after her husband as a wife should. They have taken the children and they are making them turn against the mother. We don't know if Kimendi will stay in jail for much longer as they released him on bail, and he is at home now with the children waiting for the trial.

Everybody, especially Rosie, sends their warmest regards to you all.

Best wishes,

Miriam

I look up at Anthony dazed, 'God, it's horrific. What can we do? Shall I go up to Kenya, and help?'

'It's best not to get too involved now, Virginia.'

'Of course, I have to get involved. She's like my sister, for God's sake.'

'Best thing we can do is to send her some money for the hospital. The sister is hinting that they can't afford to get the best treatment for her. The brother is looking after her, and they are a medical family. She'll be fine. She is not our responsibility now. She has her own family.'

'Well as I see it, she absolutely is our responsibility now. Can't you see, she has no husband?'

'Poor Rosie. I never trusted that husband of hers.'

❀ ❀ ❀

Rosie: Limuru, March 1992

Dear Mum and Dad,

First is much greetings from me. After I left the hospital, I am not bad except that my left hand can't do any work at all. I don't know how long I am going to stay working with only one hand but my surgeon doctor says that it can be for about one year or two for the nerves to get back. But feelings have started and, little by little it is coming, but I can't hold anything with my fingers. There was a big hole in my arm where they put the plate with lots of pus. This made me stay long in hospital, waiting for the plate to be covered. But I'm not feeling sore anywhere else.

Mum, let me tell you that it is by luck that you and the children shall see me again, for I was so sick that all my family and relatives could not believe that I can survive or will ever get well again. Everyone was waiting for me to be buried. But God is a good God, for he saved me from danger, so I'm still praying to the Lord. My joy is that I shall see you, Dad, and the children for I am alive.

Please don't worry about my children, for it is their dad's fault. He told them not to care about me and because of that I see it is better for them not to follow me for he will hurt them surely. I can't afford to stay with them, as I have no money as I cannot do work. They will give me a hard time to look after them by myself. They can stay in their own place with their dad, so I hope he is taking care of them now because I can't. On my side, I try not to think about them. I only think of where I can stay now that I am come out of hospital.

Mum, only what I want to tell you is that I shall never go back to Kimendi's home again, after he tried to kill me. So now I have no husband from now on. I want you to know this first. Tell Dad and the children.

Mum, listen, you can't believe it. This is what happened with Kimendi. He was doing lots of things like a mad person, like I never see him do things like that before. When I was in your house last year working, he was taking my clothes to the witch doctors. He took one blouse which you had given me, and he take it to the witchdoctor. As you know they can use a person's things to make them die.

When I get home after you left, I met one of my blouses was missing but the other clothes are still in the box. So, I think to myself, 'That is funny. Who can take only one blouse and leave the others when I got lots of clothes left? It can't be a thief because they will take everything.'

I wondered a lot about that. When Kimendi came home that afternoon, I ask him, 'I can't see one of my blouses. Do you know where it is?'

He tell me, 'Look for it well.'

I told him, 'I have searched everywhere for it and I couldn't find it.'

He said, 'My spirit tells me you will get it in one or two days.'

I look at him and he starts laughing at me in a bad way with his white eyes rolling like a mad person, and he say again, 'I am serious, you will get it soon. Why are you complaining?'

Next day, Kimendi gets into the house at 6 pm and puts back the blouse in the box and then he tells me to go and look in the box. I delayed because I was seeing how he was enjoying teasing me. I didn't look at that time but only afterwards when he went away. There I found the blouse under two other clothes.

Then I get very worried that he should use my clothes to make bad magic on me for I was not thinking that he was a devil worshipper.

When I came back and he saw me and I asked him, 'Kimendi, why did you take my blouse and where was it?'

He said, 'I have taken it to pray with the *n'anga,* so that you can like me as much as you like that blouse that your madam gave you.'

I knew he was just looking for a way to start a quarrel.

Then I went home to my parents, and I tell them. I tell my brother and Miriam all the embarrassing statements he made. I told them I wanted to leave him, but my family tell me not to leave him now because the children were doing exams. So, I stayed there waiting for the children to finish exams and I was thinking what I could do. Kimendi knew that I had told my parents and he thought that I'm going to run away from him and take everything that you have given me when I go. So, he thought of killing me, so that I could leave all my things with him.

On Saturday 28th December, at 1 am in the night I was asleep and everyone else was asleep. He was ready with his panga hidden near the bed. He waited until I was in a deep sleep. When he gets into bed he couldn't sleep because he was waiting for me to sleep. When he saw I was not asleep and the time is still going on, he started smoking. I started feeling frightened and by then I have woken up. He had already locked the doors with the padlocks which we use in our doors. He started asking for his shirt.

'Where is my shirt?' he shouted at me, 'Why are you moving my shirt from here to there, woman?'

I was frightened even more, as he seemed to be going mad.

I said to him, 'Kimendi, I am going to call your mother to hear what you are talking about.'

Because it was serious, and I thought he was sick. Before I opened my bedroom door, Kimendi took the big torch and hit me with it on my lips. I started screaming when I am trying to open the other main door so that I can run outside the house. Then he was holding the big knife, which is for cutting trees, and for that short time while I was opening the door, he was hitting me everywhere with this panga.

When the children tried to help me, he wanted to attack them also with the panga, so they stopped and ran away screaming. The first born was in his own house nearby and didn't hear all the screams. Only the smallest boy, Kariuki, helped me to open the door, even though he saw I was too much cut and had lots of bleeding everywhere, he didn't mind. I saw Kariuki has followed me and ran to my neighbours who had already heard the screaming. I was trying to run to their house but falling around under the plum trees because I was in a bad way. Then they came and held me up and tried to tie up my arm where I was bleeding, part to part, as my hand was falling off completely.

One child, Tomas, ran to my brother's house and they came and took me to hospital at Kiambu. When I reached there, they found I had no blood left. They transfused six pints of blood. I became confused. I did not know where I was for three weeks. Then I find I am in a nursing home. There was a good surgeon doctor. For the second time, they tried to put the plate in my hand then from the theatre. I got more sick because I was in great dizzying pain. All the doctors and sisters who were treating me were too busy to be worrying about me.

I stayed in that good hospital for eight days only because it was too expensive, and my brother couldn't afford it. So now I am in Kiambu hospital again and I am still very ill. I can't walk or even help myself with a bedpan. Mum, this is a very bad time. But some people believe there is a God if I am alive. I know you will ask yourself, 'Why if God love me, can he do this to me?'

My children can't come to see me because their father doesn't allow it. My brother and Miriam are the only ones who take care of me. Their mind is to pay for a good lawyer, so they are trying to search for money for that. So, when the case is over, I will write to you and tell you what happened.

I want to get back all the things from Kimendi that you gave me, for you can't believe it, but that is the reason he wanted to kill me. He wants to take all my things for himself and his new wife. Can you believe that Mum, that men are so cruel and jealous and greedy?

So, I will list the things down so you can type a good letter for the lawyer, stating that you gave me those things and that they are mine.

The court can give me police to get all those things from Kimendi. He can buy his own things for his new wife who he will marry. I know that he was pretending to be mad. It is because he got another wife who told him to kill me so that she can marry him and keep the nice house and all the things you gave us.

I can stay here with my brother and Miriam until I am better but they very much like your suggestion that I go and stay at your house in Lamu Island. I can do that after I am completely healed, and the case is over. Lots of thanks for the cheque.

May God Bless you and add you more happiness.

Lots of love from,

Rosie.

Rosie: Limuru, August 1992.

Dearest Mum,

Thank you for typing the letter to get my items from Kimendi, but I didn't get my things back yet. I was waiting to see whether I can get any news from the court, that I can tell you more about it. They can see I was telling the truth. Kimendi was asked by the court if he had anything else to say and he said he has finished to show why he cut me! Anyway, the case is still on, and the judgement will be on 5th October. Mum, Kimendi could give no good reason to show the court why he did these nonsense things to me. He was just finding a story to lie to the court.

Mum, you asked me whether Kimendi was still in jail. He stayed in jail for only three months and their family take him out of jail with bond, so when I was still in hospital he was out of jail. Kimendi showed the children how to write a letter to the children officer of the court to say that he had to take care of the children. The letter made him to be out of jail with a bond.

That letter was full of lies. But they didn't think that the Children's Officer will take that letter to the court. They said they don't come to see me because I abused them and lots of other lies. It was bad luck that my daughter girl, Mabel was called by the court to testify. She is a liar like her father! She is siding with her father, because she is the same as him.

She couldn't say anything to help me because she was afraid of her father and worried he would hit her. The court saw that the children were going against their mother. But anyway Mum, God whom I pray to is a good God. Mum it is so good to tell the truth, for my case is getting on well because we are telling the truth.

Mum, feel fine, I'm not sick anywhere else except my hand. I am still attending the hospital for physio. I am still with Miriam in her house, and I will be waiting for you after Xmas. Lots of greetings from Miriam and my brother. They are still taking care of me. Lots of thanks for that cheque. May God bless you and add you more. Mum, it is very important that you ask Dad to keep on taking my good children to the church and faith shall be their blessing from God – and you too please Mum, can you try and go to church also? But Mum, I am still waiting to go to Lamu, if God wishes. You can tell me exactly what to do when you come. I pass you lots of love from Miriam. Let me stop there, hoping to see a letter from you soon.

Hoping to see you if God so wishes. I miss you so much.

Bless you all and remember him.

Yours sincerely with so much love,

Rosie.

Chapter 23

Alone in Shela

'Baada ya kovu na jeraha ndani.'
'Even after the scar is healed, the wound still hurts inside.'

Virginia: Zimbabwe, January 1992.

It takes a year for Rosie to recover from the panga attack. Once she is up and about, I fly to Kenya to take her to Lamu. She meets me at Nairobi airport outside on the pavement. As I come through the glass door onto the road where crowds are waiting to pick up their passengers, she pushes to the front and screams out, 'Mum, Mum, I am here.'

The taxi drivers watch amused as she rushes forward to embrace me. I almost dissolve into tears when I see her so changed. She has lost all her front teeth and there is a raised scar across her mouth. She smiles as if nothing is wrong exposing a row of gums where her line of lovely white teeth used to be.

She hides her mouth with her good hand and says, 'Don't worry about my face Mum, I am alive, by God's mercy.

'You look wonderful Rosie, not as bad as I thought, and we will get you a set of new teeth easily.'

'I don't care if I have no teeth. I can just drink soup.'

'Well, you will have to have teeth if you are to be the 'hostess with the moistest,' and be able to smile at all the guests you are going to entertain at Jasmine House,' I joke.

'Mum, you see my hand, it is fixed, but I can't pick up heavy things, so I am worried I won't be able to do the job.'

'You are alive, that's the main thing. Shani can continue to do all the cleaning, Rosie, so you won't be at a disadvantage with your arm. You will be like the hostess who makes sure the guests are fine.'

Her left arm is locked in a right angle and her hand is fixed in a claw with fingers bunched together permanently, but despite this she has the same radiant expression and is laughing at my horror like an old hag. Nothing dims the sparkle in her eye. I admire her sheer grit in the face of adversity. I pick up her large plastic carrier of clothes and add it to my own luggage on the trolley, wondering how she is going to cope in Lamu.

We take a taxi to Wilson Airport to get the flight to Lamu.

'Have you seen any of the children?'

'None of them, Mum. My children can't come to see me because their father doesn't allow it. My brother and Miriam are the only ones who have taken care of me.'

'That is so unfair, don't the children understand that it was Kimendi's fault? How can they blame you for what happened?'

'They blame me Mum, because they say I went away and don't care about them.'

'Don't they appreciate that you were earning money for them, and how you improved the house?'

'That is the reason he wanted to kill me. He wants to take all my things for himself and his new wife. Can you believe that Mum, that men are so cruel and jealous and greedy? He got another wife who told him to kill me so that she can marry him and keep the nice house and all the things you gave us.'

'It is so appalling; I really can't believe that someone would try to kill for those few possessions.'

'I want to get back all the things from Kimendi that you gave me. If I can get a lawyer, I will try to get those things back. The court can give me police to get all those things from Kimendi. He can buy his own things for his new wife who he will marry.'

'What are these things that they want which we gave you? It wasn't much. It was mainly building materials, the roofing sheets and cement. You can't get that back.'

'There is the double bed, two veranda chairs. You remember the curtains and carpets. The bicycles from the children.'

'Make a list. I will type a letter for the lawyer, stating that I gave you those things, if that will help. Do you really think it is worth fighting for those things, Rosie?'

'He can't have my things, Mum, which I worked for. It is not right Mum. You see I told you; the Kikuyu are very bad.'

'The main issue is to be allowed to see the children. They can't keep them from you.'

'I can't do anything about them Mum. You know in our culture the children stay with the husband in this case. I am on his land with his family, and they protect him against me.'

'I can't imagine what it can be like to lose all the children like that. Surely some of them want to see you?'

'Perhaps they will come back when they are big but for now, they have to do what the father says.'

'It is so tough. Thank goodness when you are in Lamu, you will be away from the whole mess.'

'Also, Mum, I will be safe there. I am very much afraid of meeting Kimendi or his family when I am living nearby.'

We walk across the runway and get into the aeroplane without even a comment from her about the flight.

'Remember the first time you flew with us Rosie? it was such a new experience.'

We laugh and remember those halcyon days when everything seemed to be so perfect. We settle into our seats and as the plane takes off, I take her poor claw of a hand and turn the palm upwards. She shows me how little she can move her fingers.

She tries to squeeze my hand and closes her eyes and starts to pray for a safe journey. I close my eyes and begin to weep internally at the dreadful tragedy of it all. The psychological loss of her children is far worse than the physical agony she went through.

'I am just so sorry Rosie. If you hadn't come to work for us this would not have happened.'

She looks at me and then looks out of the window and points with her poor hand. 'Mum, look what I can see.'

There is Mount Kilimanjaro soaring high above the clouds, in majestic glory. I notice how the snow around the cone has melted since we last saw it eight years ago.

'If I had not met you Mum, I would not have seen Mount Kilimanjaro from the clouds.'

Rosie: Jasmine House, Shela. June 1993.

Dear Mum,

Here I am fine and well and working with my one hand and getting to clean nicely. Even some work which I was not doing too well, like peeling potatoes and cutting things, I am learning to do. I'm not asking anyone to help me. So, I am well and fine.

You ask me about how it is for me as a woman alone in this place. You know it is good. Since I come here to Shela, there is not any men disturbing me. That is because I don't joke with the men here, so they are very respectful to me. I am very happy and safe. I have not lots of friends in Shela village because it is all Swahili women. I got some Kikuyu friends at Lamu Town from our church. Sometimes I visit them, and they visit me, but they have all got husbands. I am also friends with the wife of the pastor, and I meet my friends when I go to church. I am talking with Swahili women, but they don't like to be visited in their houses. They only say 'Hello' to you and pretend to like you, but they don't like friendship. I think it is their religion to make them stay that way, because I am Christian, but I don't mind that because they are not bad. I copy them also and just stay in the house.

Mum, I think you want to know if I got a boyfriend. I don't have any and I don't miss a boyfriend. I hate men because of their problems, you know what I mean, Mum. I am laughing when I write this because it is funny. I will tell you what. Start to find one man from Zimbabwe who is very, very old that he can't even wake up and beat me with a panga. Bring him with you to Lamu and tell him this. Rosie have no teeth, she have no hands, she have no legs, but she have a good heart. If you find one man like that, a man who doesn't mind that I have been destroyed, I will marry him. So, I will wait for a boyfriend from you. Laugh to me little, but not very much Mum. I am managing to stay alone. So, don't worry too much about me. You want to know why I was sick, Mum. I was told it was an ulcer in my stomach from thinking too much. I don't know when I was thinking, but it brings me this problem - maybe it is because I am praying too much. Praying is like thinking with God, so that maybe makes me sick.

Love from

Rosie

✿ ✿ ✿

Virginia: Zimbabwe. November 1994.

Dearest Rosie,

It is so lovely to hear from you and that you are managing so well with the guests in Jasmine House. We have some friends coming to stay with you from Zimbabwe and they will bring you a little gift for Christmas. It is so good to hear how you are managing to fit into the village and that they respect you as a Christian. I am sure it is because you wear the *bui bui* and don't make the women think you are after their men! The children all send their best hugs and say they miss you so much. You will be glad to know the twins are going to be confirmed soon.

Dad is fine and our new organisation is going really well as we have got some support to start a big project for women's groups. I can't wait to do all the things we did with the community in Kenya back here in Zimbabwe. At least here I don't have to get a work permit so we can keep going for many years and build a really good programme. I have also decided to go to university and do a proper degree as I can't run an organisation if I am not properly qualified. So, I will be a very mature student. We had a huge party for my birthday recently and Babushka did all the cooking. She is doing well, and she likes having the grandchildren here. She is teaching Tristan how to drive, as he is really growing up fast.

Tristan is still at boarding school now and is a real teenager. Charlie is Deputy Head boy at the new school, which is the same one that Dad went to when he was young. Wendy is the main part in the school play and has to dress up as a man, so it is quite funny. I wish you could see our house here. Wendy has so many animals. Teddy is getting old now, and so we have three new dogs, two cats, as well as birds, and rabbits. Also remember the bush babies that we had in Tigoni. We have two baby ones here as well. They fell out of their hole where they were living under the roof, and the dogs got them. So, we rescued them and have trained them to go back into their cage during the day but otherwise they are in the trees at night. Wendy loves all her animals. She is very excited because we are getting her a horse for her birthday. The saddle is more expensive than the horse here, and our gardener is going to look after him. I wish you were here with us. Joshua, who is our cook, is nothing like you were, as he isn't able to relax and talk to me. He treats me like a Memsahib, and you know how I hate that.

Have you managed to contact your own children yet? Do you want some time off to go to Nairobi to see them? Let me know so we don't send any guests to Jasmine House while you are away. Keep well. We will see you in a couple of months.

Lots of love,

Mum.

Virginia: Zimbabwe 1995 - 1999

We saw Rosie most years when we came to Lamu for a holiday, and she saw our children grow up, changing each year from the little kids they were when she first met them in Tigoni, through their teenage years in Zimbabwe during the eight years she was in Shela. All of us loved the fact that Rosie was always there, a little consistency in our lives that made us feel that Kenya was almost home.

For most of the year she lived quietly on her own in Jasmine house, guarding our interests with unshakable loyalty. She established a range of international friends amongst the visitors who came to stay, who found her so engaging that they would correspond with her for many years afterwards. She became a well-known part of the village, and had local friends and a good reputation, but she never got back into her family. Her children kept their distance, and she never went back home to Limuru. She heard from her brother that the two girls were married and had children, but she never met them. Kariuki remained in contact, and she helped to pay for his training in a technical college. Once when he visited Lamu to see her, we had great hopes that he would be her support. He married and had twins and for a time Rosie was able to have a role as a grandmother, but all the other children shunned her completely. We were in touch with her regularly, a non-consequential correspondence with occasional calls and the years slipped by without incident. Anthony and I were travelling continually for work and could hardly find time to visit Lamu. But for the fact she was there, we would have sold it earlier as it was becoming hard to maintain it from a distance.

✿ ✿ ✿

Rosie: Shela 1997.

Dear Mum,

There was a little problem, here as well, but I have stopped that problem by praying, so I didn't tell anyone. Shani don't like it if I tell him anything. I am here to protect your things, Mum and I get problems for everyone when I ask them to please not borrow things from our house. But I see that Swahili people, they just help each other with borrowing when they want. So, they are used to borrowing our chairs or even beds if they are short for something. So, I don't know what you can do to make that stop because it can spoil our things. You can't let them know I am telling you these things, because the Swahili people always say to me, 'Why are you being so together with these English people, when you are really more like us? But you don't help us. Instead, you help them? It is not the normal way to help the white people who have everything when we have nothing.'

So, I don't answer them, but I just say, like you are my family, so I have to be trustworthy for you. Then they don't understand why I have to be like this for white people. They don't know our proper story of how you and me came to be like this. They think I am just like other cleaning women, who don't care about the boss people. But you know Mum, you are my sister. It doesn't matter if I am black and you are white, we are the same and we both love those children of ours.

Yours sincerely, as always, Rosie.

Virginia: Zimbabwe, 1999.

Dearest Rosie,

I am writing to say we will be with you for the Millennium celebrations for New Year Eve. I can't wait to be back in Shela and see you and all our friends there. The place is going to be crowded but it is the only time we can come during the school holidays. Wendy and Charlie are going into their third year at senior school and Tristan will be leaving school soon. He is writing his A level exams now, and I think he will do well. He wants to see you before he leaves as he plans to go on from Kenya and do a lot of travelling next year.

It is becoming a bit difficult in Zimbabwe as the government is getting out of hand. Mugabe wants to be President for life, and no one wants this, so he is having a big vote and it is making people get quite heated about politics. It will be good to get out of the country for a while, I think. Remember how Mama Gola said if they don't want us whites here, we should come back to Kenya, so you never know we might have to do that.

I have finished my degree now and it feels good to have a proper qualification at last. Our organisation is doing well, but I am worried it can all fail if we don't get any more funds next year. If the government starts to make trouble for the white farmers, then the donors won't want to give them money. So far, we have started about 500 community health clubs, and it looks like women really enjoy the meetings. I am loving my work and feel so lucky to have this way of getting into villages.

Mama Gola says she is going to come and stay at Jasmine House, so please give her our greetings and look after her and Desmond very well. We are planning to do some training in Kiwayu Island when we come as the Flying Doctors organisation has asked us to do a project there. It would be great to do that so we can come to Lamu more often. Imagine if we could work from Jasmine House. Let's see how it goes. We are travelling so much now doing this training, there is not enough time in the year. Greetings to Shani and all the others in the village.

Lots of love,

Mum.

Chapter 24

Millennium

'Afrika ni ndege wa kanga, nyeusi na matangazo meupe'
'Africa is a guinea fowl, black with white spots

Virginia: 2000

The East Coast is always such a welcome change after the dry savannah land of Zimbabwe. The New Year's Eve celebration along the beach from Shela, is the most exotic party in Kenya. The same patient donkeys that once carried the panniers of sand to build our house have hauled the massive speakers, the long tent poles and the heavy canvas along the beach to a hollow, like an amphitheatre between the sand dunes where a dance floor has been made beside the abandoned lighthouse, known locally as the 'Black Dick', an apt name for the place where I once escaped rape. Now as night falls the scene looks like a Bedouin desert encampment. Around an open bonfire stands the caravan of exhausted donkeys, heads lowered as they sleep off the demands of the day, and the villagers in their white kanzu stand around waiting for the revellers to arrive.

At sunset, groups of foreigners come straggling up the beach, lugging their supply of alcohol to ensure they are able to celebrate the eve of the Millennium in a state of euphoria. Now as night falls, a seething mêlée of revellers gyrate on the sand to the throbbing pulse of strangely atmospheric sounds. Local shopkeepers, sons of fishermen, big hoteliers and homeowners all swaying to the ambient music of Ishmael Lo. Swahili beach boys jive with unknown tourists, hoping to score one way or another. Pop songs we loved in our youth have reached the remote island of Lamu.

'All you need is love, love, love…' sing the Beatles as people from every culture sing along in unison.

Our children are the generation which have been dubbed the 'born frees' because they were born after independence, growing up in a multiracial culture in Kenya and then Zimbabwe, with little concept of the sort of racialism which was the norm in Rhodesia when we were at school. As their parents, it is one of our greatest pleasures to see how completely colour blind they are, respectful of all races, but without the self-conscious political correctness that is more usual of white liberals in South Africa.

We sit on the top of a sand dune and watch the entrancing scene below, as magical as a romantic film set. The phosphorescence glitters in the soft ocean as it laps the sands of the island. On the highest sandy hillock, a voluptuous girl in a bikini swings her strings of fireballs around, against the pitch-black night, skipping and juggling in transfixed pagan ritual under the bright stars. Tristan, now aged 18, throws himself down on the dunes, dark curls shaking with laughter. He hits the sand amid a gaggle of leggy girls. Kids he has seen every year since he was eight years old, are now nubile. Wendy, a petite blond we tease calling her 'midget Bardot,' is flitting around like a firefly in the night, her long bright hair teasing the brawny Swahili boys. This year they respond to her newfound femininity. Charlie, now a handsome teenager of 15, is maniacally throwing himself around in the thick of the dancers, mesmerised by the beat, absorbed in his own antics.

The lyrics spill into the night, matching our mood:

'Brown girl in the ring, Tra la la la laaah,

'She looks like sugar in a plum.'

'Do you remember those seamy discotheques in Joburg, when I first asked you out?' Anthony recalling the memory.

'I was only about 16 then. The fuss my mum made over me wearing a mini skirt?'

'We have to dance this one,' I urge, jumping up from the sand and pulling Anthony onto the canvas dance floor.

'Look at the kids, dancing with the locals. We couldn't have done that when we were young,' I shout as we swing together in rock and roll style. Whether God is Allah or Jehovah makes no difference to anyone.

At midnight the countdown to midnight begins... It has the feeling of hope. Everyone is hugging and kissing.

'Let's hope the next century will be even better,' Anthony says, swinging me under his arm, laughing.

Fireworks shoot skywards from mega cities around the world but from this remote island, fisher folk and foreigners alike collapse in the dunes watching the shooting stars fall from the clear tropical night sky.

From the sand dunes, high above Shela we watch the dawn of the new Millennium, a sunrise of pure hope. I watch a dipping triangle of white sail into the fresh new century. We join the rest of the world under the same sun, as the century clocks over. Now in the rosy, pink morning light, the huddled bodies of the revellers sleeping in the sand dunes slowly come to life to greet the day.

As we walk back home, the Moslem village is reawakening. The odd flip-flop of lazy feet back from the mosque. The raucous belly groan of a donkey looking for a mate in the maze of shady alley ways.

Shela has changed in the eight years since we left Kenya. When we built Jasmine House, it was still a simple fishing village with a few eccentric expatriates. Now it has been discovered by the jet set of Europe and is the San Tropez of East Africa. A famous family of European aristocrats have built a small palace as a refuge, and are here with their courtiers, all well-known models and film stars. Now each new villa is more prestigious than the last.

The local fishermen are tripping over each other to syphon off the excess from their super wealthy new neighbours.

The much-respected old chief has died, and our wonderful builder, the councillor Nilah has left the island. The new young Councillor increasing his girth daily with land deals is leading the harvest.

'Shela has changed so much. The locals used to be so charming. It is so sad that all *wazungu* are now seen as easy pickings now.'

Rafiki Hotel, with its iconic balcony above the lapping sea, is the focus for a hedonistic group of beautiful people, made shallow in their wealth and boredom.

Tristan is spending as much time as he can with this set, which worries us given our modest background. Our son is hanging round with 'She,' the supermodel face of the 90's, who is flirting shamelessly with the young Adonis. A glamorous artist with a roguish gypsy allure has been flown in from Spain to paint the celebrities. The dashing Spaniard, having completed his commissions for the rich and famous, requests to paint Tristan. The portrait he produces is wild and free and shows our son looking as entitled as Lorenzo Medici in all his youthful arrogance. For the first time we see our eldest as he is seen by others. We don't want our children to have these patrician values.

'Can I have some money? 'I am meeting my friends at Rafiki?' he whines every day.

'You have had your pocket money this week. Dad and I can't even afford to drink at Rafiki, so no… you will just have to wait until next week. I'm sorry.'

'Ah, Mum.' The universal drone of teenagers.

'No, I am telling you for the last time, I am not giving you money to fritter away there.'

'OK fine. That doesn't stop me going there.'

He showers and wraps his *kikoy* provocatively around his hips and goes off in a sulk.

'I am getting pretty fed up with this,' I say to Anthony. 'We can't compete with the wealthy here now.'

'I totally agree. Tristan is getting out of hand. We didn't build a house here to be part of the effete aristocracy of Europe.

'What is worrying is how much drugs are circulating freely now,' I add, building the case.

'These aristos may be wealthy, but they are a pretty rough bunch. The other night they got into a brawl with some beach boys and had a punch-up.'

Rosie says the same thing to me in other words, 'Mum, you must not think that it is always good for the children here in Shela. There are many things that I have heard about what the children are doing now. So, you should tell them to be careful. This island is not like it was before, you know.'

Despite our principles we too are being lured into the fun. The 'Maestro' – an internationally celebrated Italian composer has organised himself an extravagant party on Manda beach, commandeering a fleet of dhows to ferry the guests across the straights in time for 'aperitivo' on the beach. Despite my inverted snobbery, it is an irresistible invitation. I put on a diaphanous kaftan of brilliant turquoise the colour of the shallows of the warm tropical sea. We sail across the channel and anchor in the shallows. I must ease myself carefully off the dhow to prevent my silk kaftan catching on the rough wooden boat. As I tiptoe up out of the waves I am presented with a flute of bubbly champagne. A host of waiters circulate elegantly offering silver platters of tuna rolls, spicy samosa, coconut crab claws, prawn nibbles, and ripe camembert from France. We are knocking back the alcohol flown in by special delivery from Nairobi, all sinking into a glorious state of inebriation.

The beach is full of long-legged beauties hibiscus flowers behind their shell-like ears, luxuriously sifting the white sands through their blood red toenails;

bronzed men with rolled up white shirts and trousers looking like pirates of the Caribbean, fawn around the women.

Local fishermen ogle the westerners torn between disdain and fascination. 'It is against our culture to drink alcohol,' they tell each other self-righteously, whilst unable to resist the business it brings.

As the sun sets over the Shela Mosque, the merry guests are sailed back like the Owl and the pussycat, 'by the light of the silvery full moon.' We disappear into our various grand abodes. Meanwhile our young are off with the other pretty young things, to get up to whatever mischief they can. The insidious undertow of the good life is sucking us and our impressionable teenage children into its clutches. When they come back in the early hours looking dazed and confused, they find the door is locked. Anthony watches them as they try to hoist Wendy over the wall so she can open the door for them, hoping to sneak back to bed before we are up. That is the moment when we realise it is time to sell Jasmine House, but it is not the only reason: Rosie has found a husband. How could we run a guest house if she was not our housekeeper?

Chapter 25

The Fall of the Twin Towers

'Nyumba ya jirani ikiungua, wewe huota moto.'
'When a neighbour's house burns, warm yourself with the fire.'

Virginia: London 11.09.2001.

I have been locked away for months in the Infectious Tropical Diseases Department at London University on the fifth floor, researching the effectiveness of our projects in Zimbabwe, trying to write the dissertation for my PhD. I feel like Rapunzel in an ivory tower as I wrestle with some statistical improbabilities that are far too difficult for me to understand. Day after day I immerse myself in my studies incarcerated in a stuffy little room with four other students, tapping away industriously at their computers. It is late afternoon, and we are all flagging. The woman next to me, a mature student like me from the Gambia, is cruising her friends on Facebook and the young man across the room is following the news. I have little interest in what is going on in the outside world as I am intent only on getting my own work done so I can get out of England, which as usual is having a depressing effect on me.

'Bloody hell. Look at this! F...ing hell!'

I look up and see him leaning back in his chair, arms out, mouth agog, eyes on stalks. He is a dour German epidemiologist, not given to expletives.

'Come and look at this, you guys!'

We gather around his computer screen just in time to see what looks like a toy plane blast into the side of the tower.

'What is happening?' I ask as it is so unlikely, I can't tell if it is for real or some mad computer game.

'Some arse hole has flown smack into one of the twin towers. The Trade Centre in New York,' he has to explain to me as I have never heard of the famous towers. We watch the horror unfold, as the second tower is attacked, and people start jumping out of windows. It is so surreal I do not at that moment realise that it is the starting gun of a series of events that will pit Muslims against the non-Muslim world.

Over the next year as the American rhetoric ramps up against the 'Axis of Evil,' I find myself wondering if this western backlash will affect our own investment in one of the staunchest centres of Orthodox Muslims in East Africa.

Lamu 2002

Westerners are reeling from the realisation that there is a serious collision of cultures. As suicide bombers launch themselves against targets in European cities, ordinary people begin to realise that Muslim fundamentalism is something which can threaten their personal safety. First Afghanistan and then Iraq are invaded. Saddam is on the run. Then I get a letter from Rosie clearly needing our support. Across the other side of the world the ripples from the fall of the twin towers are beginning to reach the remote little island in the Indian Ocean.

> 'There is a problem for us now, because many of these Moslems in Lamu think Saddam is a very great man. Bin Laden is the new prophet, they love him here. So now they think all the Americans are bad and so are

the English. So, you and Dad are like the English, and they tell me that I work for the enemy of the Moslem people. I don't know what to say to them because I don't understand the whole story about Mr. Saddam. Can you tell me what the problem is so I can answer them properly, so they also understand better?'

The dhow sails into the familiar little jetty outside Rafiki Hotel and we hop ashore and make our way to Jasmine House. We immediately sense a different mood as we are not being greeted by the locals as we pass. They seem to be closing their doors in our faces as we walk along the narrow alleyways to our house. On the door of our local *duka* is a poster of Bin Laden's prophetic face. We see a crowd of locals gathered around the antique black and white television set in a tea shop next to the *duka* which is broadcasting from the Middle East in Arabic.

Rosie greets us but she is tense and clearly worried for her safety.

'Mum, at church our pastor has told us to be careful because some Christians have been beaten up. If they call us infidel, we must not say anything. He has told us we have to turn the other cheek like Jesus.'

'Has anyone you know been hurt yet?'

'Some Kikuyu houses have been set on fire, Mum. It is very dangerous now. When I walked to Lamu last week, a young man shouted to me 'go home, Christian woman.' Even my friend next door, she won't talk to me now when I go past her door.'

We take a drink up to our roof top for our customary sundowner, but what used to be a view of the sea is now blocked by our neighbours' ugly three-story house.

'God, look at this, the view is completely wrecked.'

'Hm... so much for always being able to see the sea, we are completely hemmed in now.'

The Muezzin clears this throat and starts to yell at the top of his voice.

'Allahu Akbar ašhadu 'anla ilāha illal-Lāh, wa 'ašhadu 'anna muḥammadan rasūlul-Lāh.'

'I used to love the call to evening prayer but now it sounds like a call to arms. We haven't a clue what they are saying. They could be telling everyone to sharpen their knives and slaughter the nearest *mzungu* for all we know.'

'It's really uncomfortable being here this time,' Anthony adds thoughtfully.

I take a sip of my drink and try to put the feeling into words, 'Almost as if by being a foreigner, they blame us for the invasion of Iraq.'

'I saw Nilah today and I asked him what he thought about the war, but he just looked away and wouldn't comment. Then when I asked him to drop by this evening, he made an excuse and said he was very busy. It is not like him to refuse an invitation.'

'There is a sense of being in the camp of the enemy.'

'Exactly, no one says anything to us, but it is a sort of passive aggression.'

We listen to a long vehement sermon in Arabic broadcast at top volume over the village. We sip our drinks and watch the sun go down. We are like frogs being slowly heated in water. When is the danger sufficient to be alarmed?

'You know there are active jihadists establishing bases of resistance on the mainland across the narrow strait from Lamu, according to BBC. Christians who for years have lived in harmony with their Muslim neighbours are being harassed by youth all along the Swahili coast and it's being encouraged by the extremist mullahs.'

'It's going to affect tourism. People just won't come here for holidays if it is anti-west. It seems many actively support Al Shabab.

'And if anything happens anywhere near Lamu we won't be able to rent out Jasmine House, we are going to be in a fix.

'I hate to say this, but It might be better to sell the house before the situation gets any worse.'

There is a long silence while we watch the stars appear and think of the many times, we have enjoyed such an evening.

'The main reason I loved being here was the sense of community with the locals, but if that is gone, it completely loses its appeal.'

'It's that horrible feeling once again, of being damned by default.'

'Exactly, in South Africa it was for being white, here it is for being non-Muslin, or in my case being a complete infidel.'

'We don't even have the time to keep coming here, what with you studying in London, all the kids in England. Now with me working in Sierra Leone, it is really hard to keep it going.'

Anthony turns on the BBC news on the radio. The Western world is bracing itself for evermore suicide attacks in the great capitals of Europe. All things considered, we bow to the inevitable and spread the word that Jasmine House is for sale. Within a surprisingly short time, we have a serious buyer. When we tell George he advises us to take it, 'Things are not going to get better here. That is a good offer, and it is a good time to sell,' he urges us. So, with great sadness we accept the offer.

Chapter 26

Rosie's Shamba

'Nyumba ya jirani ikiungua, wewe huota moto.'
'When a neighbour's house burns, warm yourself with the fire.'

Lamu 2003

Rosie says, 'Mum, I don't want to work for the family who have brought the house. I am getting old now and want to get some land and start a small farm where I can retire.'

'You are not even fifty yet, Rosie, same as me, that is not so old. What will you do if you are not here?'

'I have found a good man, like you said, and he is very old, I think about sixty. He wants to marry me. He wants me to live with him where he has a *shamba*.'

'That is such good news, Rosie. That is definitely the best for you, so you are not by yourself anymore. What is he like? I hope he is good enough for you,' I say hugging her.

'The man is a pastor and is very religious. Because he is a good Christian, I think he is honest. Sometimes when I pray, I am told that this is what I should be doing. Other times I am doubting because you know, Mum, men can change when you are the wife. Can you give me advice Mum? Do you want to meet him?'

'Of course, I want to meet him. Shall we go and see the land together before I go, then I won't be so worried about you. I don't want to lose track of you.'

'The plot is behind the sand dunes in the middle of the island. I have been to see it and it is okay but not very good. The best thing is that it is very cheap.'

A range of high sand dunes runs down the length of Lamu island like a backbone. On the land side is a vast desert that is seldom visited by tourists. I follow her down the sandy path which passes through coconut plantations providing some welcome relief from the baking heat. On the other side we come out to a flat area of farmland where plots are divided by barbed wire fences. There are no trees, and the place looks deserted.

'Are you sure you want to live here Rosie; it is very isolated.'

'This is the plot that is for sale. It is very cheap Mum, and I can grow vegetables.'

She points to a mud hut next to a small one room house with a tin roof in the distance.

'That is the pastor's house over there.'

We walk to his house, which looks abandoned. Clearly, he is not much of a farmer. There is no one on the land and the few lines of maize are stunted and pale in colour. I have my doubts that this place will suit her.

'He must be in town, I think,' says Rosie, looking apologetic on his behalf. 'He wants me to help him with his land, as he is not able to do it alone. The pastor says I can stay in Lamu with him. There are many Kikuyu people, and we all go to his church.'

'Is there any water here? It looks so dry.'

'Every plot has a well, so the water is there under the ground. I think the soil is good, if it is watered properly. I can grow my vegetables here.'

She is adamant this is the perfect retirement plan, and although I am not impressed by her choice of land, I don't want to discourage her, as there is no alternative now that we have sold the house. If this is her decision, we must support her where we can, so we purchase the plot for her. I am relieved that she is still open to the idea of a husband as it will take care of her future. Shani wants to stay on as housekeeper for the new owners.

We now have the painful task of emptying the house of all our precious belongings: the carved wooden furniture we had made in the little workshops of Lamu and the enormous Lamu beds are dismantled, the Kanga bedspreads are folded into baskets, the tiles that I painted with colourful tropical fish are prised off the walls and stacked in a box, our books mouldy with salty air will all go with us by car. The goods are carried by the noble donkeys, onto the dhow to Matondoni port where they are transported by truck, in a convoy with others to avoid being attacked by the *Shifta*. We load up the boxes which will travel by boat to Cape Town, where we have found a retirement house. Once our material goods have gone, the soul of the house seems to evaporate.

Learning from our mistake when we left Kenya originally and showered her with gifts, we give Rosie nothing material when we leave. She must have no smart goods in the house to tempt her neighbours, nothing which could make her a target for thieves. We are even nervous of showing our white faces on her land, lest some green-eyed monster assumes she has something of value. We have learnt that just by association we can cause harm to her.

We left Rosie happy in the thought that she would be safely married to the pastor. She would move to the land once the new owners move into Jasmine House.

'I am with my Kikuyu people, and the Muslim people know I am good. I don't fear them. I wear their *bui bui* when I go out. They know I am fine.'

'Can't you get any of your children to come and live here with you?' I suggest.

'You know, Mum, I am in touch with Tomas, and he has just got married. He said maybe he can come and help me, with his new wife. He is the only one who likes to farm, and they have not enough land for them in Limuru.'

'That would be the perfect solution,' I say, hugging her tightly. 'You will continue to write to me, won't you?'

'Of course. I am fine Mum. Don't worry about me. It is good here. I am very happy now.'

She stands in front of her hut, waving bravely.

'You go off now and God bless you on your travels. Give the children a big hug from their Rosie.'

We board the dhow for Lamu and watch the skyline of Shela recede into the distance, the red bougainvillaea of Jasmine House dimming to a tiny dot between the palms.

❀ ❀ ❀

Within a few months I get a letter from Rosie, and once again her life has unravelled.

> Dear Mum,
>
> I found out that the pastor is really a crazy man. He is a pastor pretender. When he said I can stay with him, I brought a sheep to keep in his shamba. One day a big snake came, and it was bitten in the leg. That crazy man did not help me, he was just laughing too much. I see he could be as bad as Kimendi, and I could be killed by him. I think I just stay alone now I don't want any husband. They are all bad. I have found a better shamba on the mainland. This piece of land is good for farming. It is a Christian community of Kikuyu farmers. They grow vegetables for Lamu.
>
> The land is not far south of Matondoni. If you come you can easily find me because the main road passes through the Kikuyu settlement. I have made a house

249

and I am living by myself. I don't want another husband. I have five acres of good soil and an old man to help me with growing the cassava, beans, maize and tomatoes.

Please don't worry Mum, this is a very good place for me to retire. Pass many greetings to everyone, to Tristan, Charlie and Wendy and say to study hard. Also to Dad and to you, many blessings.

Love from your sister,

Rosie.

Rosie's shamba. Watercolour.

Chapter 27

Al Shabab

'Tembo wakigombana, nyasi ndizo huumia'
'When elephants fight, it is the grass which suffers.'

A decade later: 2014.

With Rosie happily settled on her land, I feel I can close the chapter of our life in Kenya. We exchange the occasional letter but both Anthony and I are travelling so much it becomes hard to stay in touch. The years pass without incident until a decade later when Anthony is watching the BBC news.

He recognises the familiar Matondoni ferry crossing to Lamu and calls to me to watch. On the edge of the sea, we see an oil-encrusted landing with a jetty for the dhows. Long-distance buses are parked on the quay, waiting for the passengers to trundle back to Mombasa. Beside the bus shelter are high stacks of mangrove poles, collected from the islands, waiting to be sold. Bare-chested scrawny labourers shift this cargo tirelessly on and off the dhows. The sun is setting and the vendors at the stalls are covering their wares and packing their bags away. Women are wandering past, carrying loads of produce home on their heads.

We listen, horror-struck.

'On 15 June 2014, masked gunmen hijacked a van and raided a police station in the predominantly Christian town of Mpeketoni, Kenya.'

'Oh my God! That's only a few kilometres from Rosie's farm.'

The camera on the television pans to the little village we know so well: a collection of seedy government buildings, a police station, a hotel and a few *dukas*. The shoulder of the muddy main road is fringed with vegetable stalls. Lively gaggles of women vendors and street kids hang around, while touts swerve past shouting from *matatus* looking for customers to take to Mombasa.

Along the road comes a skinny Orma herder, wielding his stick, goading his Zebu cattle home. He wanders along in his scruffy toga, looking mediaeval compared to the young men wearing T-shirts and baseball caps who are streaming into the local hotel. This is the only place to watch the World Cup football. France is playing Côte d'Ivoire.

The camera swings round and catches a wobbly picture of a battered Land Rover hurtling down the muddy highway, which screeches to a halt before an old man. He looks up.

A band of masked men pour out of the back, wielding guns and screaming, '*Akbar Allahu! Akbar Allahu!*' A volley of gunfire rains down on the police station. No one is there. The men whirl around madly unleashing bullets on anyone who moves. The old man crumples to the ground. Women shriek and scatter, *kangas* flapping as they too hit the ground. One girl with a baby on her back is shot dead. A boy runs for cover, behind a car. The gunmen pour shots into the car, which bursts into flame.

'*The assailants also burn hotels, restaurants, and government offices.*' the reporter intones without any emotion, just another crazy African civil war.

We see the police running out of the hotel firing at the attackers, who push past them and fire into terrified football fans. France scores the third goal. No one cheers. They are running for their lives.

'*At least 53 people were reportedly killed during the attack on a hotel, and eight others are unaccounted for. Most of the dead Kenyans are Kikuyu.*'

'Oh my God, I hope Rosie is okay.'

We try to phone her but there is no answer. Another day passes and brings more horrific news. The gangs of al-Shabaab are terrorising local villages in the vicinity of her farm. Anyone who can't recite the Qur'an is shot. Still, we can't get hold of her.

'I think she recited the *Shahada*. She will be wearing her *bui bui* at least,' I say to Anthony, trying to convince myself that she has escaped.

The phone rings. It is Wendy, distraught. She has also seen the news and her first thought is for Rosie.

'We have no idea where she is,' I admit.

'Can't you phone her?'

'We have tried. Her number just rings. Maybe she has lost her phone.'

Is Tomas and his wife with her now?'

'No, they never came in the end. She has an old man as a labourer minding the farm.'

'What about Kariuki? Can you try him?'

'I have no idea where he is either. Rosie hasn't seen him for months.'

'I'll try and track him down. He might be on social media.'

An hour later she calls back, bursting with excitement:

'Guess what? It is amazing. I found Kariuki on Facebook. He is a safari guide in Rwanda. I have already got a message back from him. He doesn't know where Rosie is and hasn't heard the news. Apparently, they have completely lost touch. He is phoning around the family to find out if anyone knows. Even Rosie's brother doesn't know what has happened.'

'Kariuki is a safari guide. That's fantastic. I always thought he would make something of himself. Let's hope he can track her down.'

We wait for a week. Nothing comes back. Her family has no idea where she is. She did not come back to Limuru. If she is still alive, she will be in Lamu. After two more weeks of searching, Wendy decides there is only one way to find out. She herself will go and find her. It doesn't take much to persuade us to meet her in Lamu.

Chapter 28

Market Woman

'Nyumba njema si mlango'
A good home isn't judged by the door

Virginia: Lamu, 2014.

We have not been back to Lamu since we sold the house. The years we have been away just vanish. but it feels so different being here now Rosie has disappeared. The little plane bumps down on Manda Island, and we see that the runway has been patched up and is no longer a dirt strip ending in a couple of shacks. As the plane taxis to a halt, there is a glow inside me, the sense of a familiar homecoming. The little door is opened, and the fold-up stairs are dropped onto the scalding runway shimmering in the heat. The suffocating humidity blasts into the small cabin. I extricate myself from the seat thinking how often we had done this before. Wendy grabs my hand luggage and helps me down the wobbly steps, as I nurse my unreliable knees. Anthony is enthusing and glowing with the excitement of our return after so long.

Gone is the scrabble of men rudely grabbing one's baggage from the runway. Now all luggage is delivered by official porters to the waiting area, where it is checked carefully before being allowed onto the island. Gone are the sacks of fresh *miraa* being off-loaded surreptitiously, secreted away before the authorities confiscate the narcotic leaves.

Where once stood a little *makuti* thatched shelter, there is now a proper reception hall: the building has no walls but is cooled by large overhead fans. We find our bags easily and make for the quayside. No more picking our way over the dilapidated remains of a barnacled jetty to get to the boat. Instead, a gleaming white sandy road leads to the quayside, with smart carts pulled by uniformed porters delivering baggage to the waiting taxi *dhows*. The light is so intense, I can hardly open my eyes. Sweat pours down my back. I take my new *kanga* and wind it into a turban round my head, to fend off the intense heat.

Captain Tufani is waiting for us, and I see how he too has aged.

'Hey, *habari siku nyingi*?' he hails us warmly.

'*Karibu sana*. Where you stay now? No Jasmine House now, eh?' jokes the captain, with his attractive pirate grin.

'You *mzee* now.' He nods to Anthony, who strokes his greying beard like an elder and smiles.

'And you, still strong, Tufani. You don't get old.'

'I am *mzee* also. I don't work now. My son, he is the captain on the boat now. This time I come to airport so I can greet you, my friend. Wendy, you are a woman now, I see. Are you married? If not, I have a very good son for you to marry. *Hakuna matata*.'

Wendy laughs and says she has been married for five years already. She is glowing with the anticipation of finding Rosie.

The sails fill and the dhow speeds off across the channel to Shela.

'Captain, do you remember our *ayah*, Rosie, who lived so many years at Jasmine House?'

'*Ndiyo*, I remember her well. A good woman.'

'We don't know where she is. We have come to find her. Have you seen her around Lamu?'

He looks into the distance to avoid our eyes, searching for a tactful answer.

'Big problem here now for Kikuyu. Many people have died. Ask at her church, they will know if she is here. I have not seen her for a long time'

'That's a good idea,' says Wendy, 'She was living near Mpeketoni before the massacre.'

The captain shades his eyes from the sun, and I sense he is hiding his fears.

'Maybe you won't find her. It was bad on the mainland, but here also in Lamu Town, there are problems for the Kikuyu. *Mbaya Sana.* Very bad. The young men have gone crazy here.'

Landing on the familiar jetty is disconcerting. Instead of weaving our way into the heart of the village, we take a left turn past the prestigious Rafiki Hotel and walk through the clean alleys of the smart end of the village. It makes me nostalgic and sad that Jasmine House no longer belongs to us and we're not going home. Instead, we make our way to Minyarani house which was built at the same time as ours. The lane is deserted and absolutely quiet - no tourists, no guests, no rich homeowners on holiday. The huge palaces are empty, like hollow skulls.

As we arrive, the muezzin clears his phlegmy throat over a microphone. The minaret is hard up against the balcony of our room and the familiar call that I used to love so much I now find abrasive as well as invasive. The Muslim culture that once fascinated me, now gives me a chill, as like most westerners I have become prejudiced by the shock of the recent attacks aimed specifically at Christians. '*Akbar Allah*' has become a jihadist war cry.

We settle into our luxurious rooms, but all have the same urge to see our own house as soon as we can. As we pad down the familiar lanes in single file, past the little dhow port, past the Flying Doctor's old house, past Palm Tree House and through the backstreets to Jasmine House, there is a melancholic silence between us. The bougainvillaea almost covers the roof with brilliant vermillion flowers, vivid against the cobalt blue sky. The palm trees we planted twenty years ago now tower above our walls two storeys high.

I knock on the old Lamu door we had brought from Pâté Island, calling, '*Hodi hodi*. Anyone at home?'

No response. We go around to the kitchen door and bang hard. Shani, our old housekeeper, opens the door. He steps back in complete surprise to see us standing there. He too has aged. No longer a lively young father but a middle-aged man, quiet and restrained, almost servile. He falls on us, close to tears.

'You have come. Memsahib, Bwana, Wendy. *Karibu sana*.' He ushers us inside remembering his position.

'Shani, you look well. How are your family?'

He tells us his children have grown up and married and he has three grandchildren.

The central courtyard has been paved over and the iconic Jasmine bush is no more. The curious little splash pool that we designed, taking the shape from the famous Alhambra fountain in Granada, is as perfect as ever, but there is no water in the pond. The house is almost the same as when we left, with no real alterations, but unused. It has been sold twice over and now stands empty most of the year, a house of ghosts. We don't even know who owns it.

'Don't the owners like to come here now?'

'No, they don't come now because it is dangerous in Lamu. Al-Shabab is making tourists afraid. These men come by boat from Somalia and kill people. No visitors now.'

'We are looking for Rosie. Have you seen her recently? Since the al-Shabab attack in Mpeketoni?'

He immediately looks agitated. 'No. She was on her farm. I don't know what has happened. The Kikuyu had to run away from Al-Shabab. Maybe she went to Nairobi. Maybe Lamu. I haven't seen her. You can go to her church and ask there. Many Kikuyu have been buried.'

The next day we sail to Lamu Town, with the captain's son. He pulls up alongside a row of *dhows* clunking against the high oily jetty that serves the ancient customs building. To get ashore, we must clamber over the decks of the wooden boats. The town still feels mediaeval, still the same as it was when we first came to the island twenty-five years ago. Even now, there is still not one car on the whole island. Men are still pushing wooden barrows of goods back and forth from the shore to the *dukas*. Donkeys are still ambling about, looking for scraps to eat. More skinny cats than ever lurk around the dirty alleyways. In the workshops, craftsmen still carve Swahili doors and elegant bedheads. But now the coffee shops, even the few with internet, are empty of tourists. Instead, they are filled with idle touts, fingering their cell phones, chewing *miraa*.

We go straight to the little Catholic church, its entrance hidden beneath an overgrown canopy of bougainvillaea and tamarind. The Maltese priest we once knew has long since gone home, leaving soon after the massacre at Wema Mission. We explain our quest to the young black priest, and he asks us to come in and sit down.

'Can I give you some water?' He shows us into his office, where an ancient fan is swinging noisily overhead.

'Now let's see,' he says brightly. 'You are looking for a Kikuyu woman who was working for you many years ago but retired in Mpeketoni. You do, of course, know what happened in Mpeketoni last month, do you not?' He crosses himself and says sorrowfully, 'So you must prepare yourselves for bad news. I buried 45 Kikuyu last month. Can you write her name please? I will consult my records of the dead.'

He pushes a notepad and biro towards me and smiles unctuously. Crossing to an ancient filing cabinet, rusting in the next room, he pulls out the squeaky drawer of hanging files. Wendy takes my hand and squeezes it. Although she is a grown woman, she has a tiny hand and I feel the fear of a child. The fan clunks round and round over our heads. I start to count the rotations, waiting for the axe to fall. The priest comes out with a blue folder and scans it once again. He puts his hand on his heart as if about to start a sermon and smiles.

'I am happy to say that Ndongu Rosie is not on my list of the dead.'

We hug each other with tears of relief.

'The bad news is, I have no record of where she is. She does not attend Mass here. I would advise you to ask in the marketplace for her. That is the place you will find Kikuyu traders. She may be there with them if she is still in the Lamu District.'

We cross the great piazza, shaded by the almighty tamarind tree in front of the old fortress. To the side is a narrow street of little stalls, where market women offer carefully stacked pyramids of tomatoes, lush red money makers. As most of the women are shrouded in black *bui bui* they all look similar from a distance, and it is difficult to see if any of them are Rosie. We go up and down the little passages between the stalls trying to see their faces.

'You want tomato or potato, Mama? A young woman asks.

'Do you know someone called Rosie?' I ask her.

She shakes her head. '*Sijui*, I don't know her.'

'Karibu mama?' says another, offering us ripe mangoes and pawpaws.

'We are not here to buy. I am looking for a friend called Rosie, do you know her?' Wendy asks smiling, but they too shake their heads.

'*Pole sana, sijui*. So sorry but I don't know her.'

Finally, I ask a middle-aged woman loading up the scales with onions. 'Do you know a Kikuyu woman called Rosie Ndongu?'

She looks up at me and pauses, then smiles knowingly. She yells over her shoulder, 'Mama Ndongu, *kuja hapa. Nini wageni.* Come here. Your friends are here.'

Through the torn sacking of the little stall, I see the shadow of a large woman budge. She stands and stretches, flipping her *kanga* around her head. She pokes her head around the stall and our eyes meet. Brown, soft, soulful eyes. Wendy has also seen her and leaps forward shrieking.

Rosie rushes to us in a wild display of delight, knocking over her piles of tomatoes. I hug her on and on, my chest heaving with relief.

'Praise God you have come at last, Mum.'

'Thank God, we have found you.' I tell her with tears welling in my eyes.

'See Wendy, this is your Rosie. I am a market mama now. She envelops Wendy in the folds of her black gown and drags her behind the canvas curtain of the stall to meet her friends. She shouts to the whole group of market women with huge pride: 'See my daughter has come at last.'

'*Jambo, jumbo, habari gani?*' we say, smiling like embarrassed gentry.

They all shout greetings. Rosie issues a string of instructions to the woman in the stall to mind her produce. She grabs her *bui bui,* which is falling off her, draping it over her head, and gives Wendy a big hug.

'You see, Wendy, your mother is a poor woman now.' She scoops up a stack of tomatoes and empties them into her basket.

'I can only give you tomatoes. Can you still love me now?' Rosie always did laugh in the face of adversity.

'Did you grow these tomatoes?' I ask.

'No, I just sell them for my Kikuyu friends near Mpeketoni.'

'Are they from your farm? Is your land okay?' Wendy asks hopefully.

'No, my friends are using my land, what is left. I will tell you later how it was.'

'Where are you living?'

'I have a room nearby. Mum, it is so good you are here. Come and see my place. My prayers have been heard.'

She leads us down a confusion of alleyways to the poorest side of the town, where the stone houses give way to humble brick huts on the outskirts, against the dunes. She pushes open the front door of a dilapidated building into the central courtyard. Taking out her keys, she unlocks a door to what looks like a bicycle shed.

'I just rent this one room now.'

There is no furniture, just a woven grass mat on the floor of damp earth. All the room contains is a chair, a light bulb suspended from the tin roof and a plastic carry-bag of clothes. She switches on the light.

'Kitty, kitty, kitty,' she calls. A tiny cat unfolds itself from a broken plastic chair in the yard and comes meowing to Rosie.

'See, Wendy, I have my kitty like before. Do you still love cats?'

She takes out a few dried *kapenta* from a packet and feeds her kitten.

We say nothing. What is there to say? I am so ashamed she is having to live like this. At least we can give her a few nights in a comfortable bed while we are here.

'Will you come and stay with us for a few days in Shela. We are staying at Minyarani house.'

'I can come with you Mum. But I must take this bag, because there are too much thieves here.'

Wendy picks up her bag and Rosie carefully locks up her empty room with a small padlock.

'Do you have to lock, Rosie?' I ask. 'What is there to take?'

'Yes, I must lock it. Otherwise, the landlady will get another person to take my place and I will lose this room. It is hard to find a cheap place here.'

We stay up all evening, talking. There is so much news to share. I love to see how Rosie talks to Wendy like a mother. I remember how Wendy used to confide in Rosie about her most private worries when she was too nervous to come to me. She was like the traditional auntie in many African cultures, the eldest brother's sister who has a special duty to help counsel her nieces on women's issues.

'What happened in Mpeketoni? We saw it all on the TV.' I ask again.

Finally, we hear her story.

'I was saved by Jesus. I left on the bus to go to Lamu Town on the same day it happened. Two hours before they came.'

'What a bloody miracle.'

'Yes, you see, Mum, it is God's work I am alive. I was almost to be dead this day, but I am saved, by the grace of God.'

I look at her imagining the horror of that massacre. 'Did they come to your place?'

'So many people were killed, Mum. Yes, they came there, Mum. You know the old man on my farm? He is dead with many others.'

'Oh, I am so sorry.'

'They asked him to say the Muslim prayers and he could not. He is a Christian man. He does not know the Muslim prayers. I wish I could have been there to save him because I could tell them about their Qur'an. But Mum, they just hit him on the head with the gun and kicked him till he died. They are very bad, those young boys.'

'And your house?'

'It is gone, Mum, they burnt it down. I can't go back there. It is too dangerous.

'Why did you come back to Lamu, Rosie? Surely, it is much safer with your own people. The coast is dangerous. Can't you go back to Limuru now?'

'I want to go back to Limuru but it's only I can't get enough money for the bus fare. So, I am selling tomatoes to raise that money to go there.'

'How many tomatoes does it take to get a bus fare?'

Rosie laughs. 'Too many, Mum. I don't know. I can make about five shillings for each kilogram. But it can take a lot of time to get enough for the bus fare.'

'How much is the bus fare?'

'It is about 1000 shillings.'

'So at least 200 kilograms of tomatoes to be sold to get you from here to Nairobi.'

'It is a very, very, long journey, Mum. But also, you know, I am fearing to go because the people are being taken off the bus on the way to Mombasa and tortured or even killed. It is those young Muslim boys who hate the Christians. Also, if they find out I am carrying photos of my white family, they can kill me for that.'

'What do you mean?'

Rosie opens her bag, 'Look what I have got here.'

She pulls out the three large, framed photos of the children that I gave here when we left Kenya. These photos are the only possessions that she still carries with her apart from a few clothes. I realise she is our responsibility. With no support from her own children, we are her family.

I have carried the guilt of her attack for years, in the realisation that it was our presents that provoked her husband's greed. Imagine if by being found with photos of our family, she could be assaulted, perhaps even killed. Unintended consequences. Naivety in a merciless world. I want to get her away from the treachery of this island, back where she belongs, in Limuru.

'Don't worry. Come back on the plane with us now and we will get you back to your own family.'

'Mum, my children don't care about me. Only if they see you give me money, then they come to see how they can profit.'

'Can't you stay with your brother and sister-in-law?'

Let me phone him. There is a long conversation in Kikuyu that I don't understand and at the end, '*Sawa Sawa*. Okay.

'They can accept having me to stay as long as I can pay the rent.'

A few days later we leave Lamu, and she flies back with us.

As we fly past Mount Kilimanjaro Wendy points it out to Rosie.

'Remember the first time you saw it from the air, Rosie? Do you see how it has changed in the last thirty years?

'I don't see any snow now, 'Rosie frowns, 'What has happened to the snow?'

It's all melted because of the change in the climate. The world is getting warmer and that is the proof.' Wendy explains.

'And in the same period of time the number of people in Kenya has increased by three times … so much has changed in this short time.' Anthony adds which depresses us further.

'The first time I came with you on a plane, I was so afraid. You were so kind to me Wendy, when you were only a very little girl. You were so clever. Now you are a woman, and you are even kinder and more clever. You are my real daughter.'

Chapter 29

Student of the World

'Waendao wawili hukumbushana.'
'Two people walking together help each other remember.'

We climb up the winding road to Banana Hill, past the coffee plantations to the tea estates of Tigoni. It is thirty years since my flirtation with Kenya began as a young, naïve development worker, enjoying the novelty of 'real' Africa. I thought with a glow of those days of hope when Rosie first came to work for me, when our children were young and happy. Before it all went wrong, and she lost her family.

We park next to a large iron gate, and Miriam, her sister in law, a kindly educated woman, welcomes us inside. Curious neighbours stop work in lush gardens to watch the unusual sight of *wazungu* visiting their neighbourhood. We go into a smart sitting room, with a big comfortable brown sofa, a dining room with good quality furniture, and a large orderly kitchen. Very soon we are being served tea like royalty, in china cups as delicate as those used by Mrs. Hunter-Price. Rosie is with her own Kikuyu people at last, away from the volatile Swahili coast.

We go into her room and sit on the bed as she arranges her belongings in a comfortable room at last. She props the photos of the children on a table against the wall and sits down contentedly.

'Mum, do you recognise this bed? It is the one you gave me. I got it from Kimendi in the end, after you typed that letter. My brother helped me to get it.'

'You have to take it easy now Rosie. If you can stay here safely, we will send you money, don't worry.'

'Mum, I am just wondering how I can make some money here. I am too old to work for a *mzungu*, because I have many problems with my health now.'

Wendy is looking from me to Rosie, smiling excitedly. 'I have had an idea. Why don't you two write your story?'

'What story?'

'This whole story. How you two met, walking in the tea estates. It's a good story. Two people, so different, but you have managed to remain sisters over such a long time. It's really unusual for an ordinary black woman and a posh white woman to have such a bond.'

Rosie is laughing at the thought. 'Is it a good story? Can people read about our story, Mum?'

'I guess so. We could try. We used to write so much to each other.'

'I remember, Mum, I was always writing too, too much, to you. I liked to write to you.'

'I know. I have got all your old letters. I also loved your letters. You were really good at writing.'

'Rosie, this will keep you busy.' Wendy has planned it all. She puts a school exercise book on the table in front of her, and hands Rosie a pen. 'There you go, your homework begins.'

Rosie looks at Wendy and then at me and laughs delightedly, 'What will I write about? I am just an ordinary person, so I don't think my story is very interesting.'

'Just write what you can remember about those times we had together, and I will do the same.'

'I can write many things, Mum.' She turns her eyes up to heaven as if drawing inspiration from above, 'like when I went to the sea. The first time I went on an aeroplane. You will read it one day.'

Like a pupil on the first day of school, she writes her name on the front, 'Rosie Ndongu.'

'Class: ...' She pauses. 'Shall I write Standard 7 on the front? That is my last year at school?'

'Rosie, don't worry that you only had primary school. It's not how long you were at school that is important. Everybody has a story and if you are willing to try and write about your experience of the world it is as valuable as any professional writer. You are a mature student; it doesn't matter what class you reached in school.' Wendy gives her a hug.

Rosie lifts the pen again and writes giggling to herself at the joke, 'Mature Student of the World.'

She opens the dull beige cover, flattens the cheap paper with its faded green lines and looks up at the ceiling again and pushes her lips forward in concentration. Then she sighs and puts down her pen, 'I will have to think a lot Mum.'

She reaches across and opens her bag, then hands me a paper packet. 'I have a little present for you, Mum.'

I pull a *kanga* out of the wrapping and thank her with a hug. I know it will contain a special message for me. It's like opening a birthday card. Along the side I read, '*Waendao wawili hukumbushana*. What does it mean, Rosie?'

'It says that 'Two people walking together help each other remember."

269

'Very appropriate,' I laugh, 'I think we will help each other to remember the good times we had and share our story, so people realise how special our friendship is.'

'We had a good time, Mum. I am happy we met.'

As we leave, I hug her and say gently, 'Rosie, you can't rely on us indefinitely. You have to patch things up with your own children because they must look after you. Surely one of your six children will come back to you.'

'I will try to find them, Mum, but you know they blame me for what happened in our family.'

'Let's write our story then they will understand what really happened. I can imagine they must have felt abandoned when you came to work for us. You left them to look after my children. I feel so bad about that.'

'Don't be sad about that Mum, we will write our story and when I am a famous writer, I will have money and they will come back to me,' she jokes.

Chapter 30

Rosie

Mwishoni, kila kitu ita kuwa sawa na, Kama kila kitu siwe sawa, sio mwishoni.
'Everything will be alright in the end. If it's not all right, it isn't yet the end.'
– Deborah Moggach, *The Best Exotic Marigold Hotel* (2004)

Cape Town, 2022

This year both Rosie and I turn seventy. We are two old women, post-family, forging our own way as individual women once again. It has taken us five years to get our simple story down on paper, physically sending letters and redrafted manuscripts back and forth with friends between South Africa and Kenya. Now I have stalled at the last chapter: I cannot finish it because the story has not ended: our lives are still unfolding.

For a few years after we met up in Lamu and took her back to Limuru, she stayed with her brother and sister-in-law. When he died, she moved into a rented room, and made a living selling second hand clothes.

She is now living alone in a tiny room in the poorer part of Limuru. I wonder if she managed to hang onto the fateful bed. I worry about her health since she is large and unfit. Her blood pressure is an issue, she has arthritis in her joints due to the damp climate of the highlands, and her eyesight is failing like mine. When the Covid pandemic struck last year, she was confined to her tiny room with people dying all around her. Somehow, she survived that dreadful period, and life is returning to normal in Kenya but with rampant inflation everyone is short of money. Even though we are devoted to her, it does not make sense to take her out of her own culture and bring her here where xenophobia against the foreigners from other parts of Africa is rife.

I keep hoping her own family will reclaim her. For a few years it seemed that Kariuki would be Rosie's salvation but for some unexplained reason he dropped her. He divorced his wife and vanished into the dark heart of Africa, working in Rwanda and she gave up hope ever to have his support.

When she is desperate, when she gets sick or when she just wants to talk, she sends me a text message on an ancient cell phone, and I call her on skype. If she doesn't hear from me, she gets just as worried about us as we are about her survival. We chat for hours, mainly about my children as she has no news of hers. Although we are still hoping that somehow our children will come back into our lives, Rosie and I both understand that they have their individual paths to follow, and it does not include us at this stage. Her analogy is so wise: 'children are like the seeds of a tree. They must get from under the shade of the mother tree, or they cannot grow tall. They need their own sun.'

I have been hoping to hear if Rosie is alright. There is a blip of a WhatsApp call. By coincidence, it is Rosie on her new smart phone, calling me for the first time ever on video. I haven't seen her face for five years and I wonder how she has aged.

There is a confusion of blurred images as the camera lurches around the small shop where a kind young girl is trying to help her get connected to me. Across Africa grandparents are being connected to their children and grandchildren they have never seen by this wonderful technology.

'Mum, can you hear me? she is shouting at the top of her voice. With the background noise of numerous clients in the little *duka*, it is difficult to hear her.

'Yes, yes. Hi Rosie. Are you managing with your new phone? Is everything okay, after the election?'

'Mum, I can see you,' she squeals in delight. She is fumbling with the device trying to see me more clearly.

'Can you see me, Mum? It's me, Rosie. I can see you so well,' she is giving me closeups of various bits of her face, laughing in excitement.

'Hey Rosie, Amazing. I can see you. Brilliant. Just hold the camera steady.' I see she is no longer bothering with her false teeth and has a rakish gap where her teeth were knocked out by her husband. Her cheek bone looks bruised as if she has been hit below her eye. The pupil looks bluish as if she has a cataract.

'What's the matter with your right eye? Has there been violence?'

'It's fine Mum, don't worry, there was no violence in our area. It was fine. I moved to a safe place, but this time there was no fighting.'

'But what is the matter with your eye?'

'It is something else Mum. I don't know what it is, but I have been to the hospital, and they have given me some *dawa*.'

'You are wearing glasses now, like me. Have you checked for having a cataract?' She can't hear as she is talking at the same time.

'Don't worry Mum, my eye is not serious. How is Dad? Wendy told me he had some cancer on his skin. I have been so worried it made my blood pressure go up high.'

'Dad is all okay now. Totally recovered. You mustn't worry about him. It is so great to be able to see each other on video at last.'

'Mum, you know that I saw Tristan at the airport in Nairobi. He gave me his old phone so now he sends me photos of his children. I saw Tristan's childrens Mum, they are so good. The wife is very nice, like you when you were her age. The little boy was so happy to see me just like when Tristan was small. I ask the girl, 'Can you remember my name, and she says, 'I know you are Tristan's granny. You are Rosie.' I ask her, 'Have you got a nanny in England?' She tell me 'Yes, she is very big and beautiful and always fun.'

I said to the wife of Tristan, 'Can you give me one child to look after for my grandchildren to play with?' The wife saw I was joking and said, 'With pleasure, which one do you want? I said, 'Can I have that little boy, because he is just like his father used to be.'

Tristan laughed and said, 'Don't try that trick again, Rosie.' I laughed with him that he remembered the first time in the Tea Estate when he met me walking with my donkey grass on my head. I said to Tristan, 'Remember, I told you when you are big you have to come and get me in an aeroplane? Now you have come at last.'

I would love to have seen her with our grandchildren, to see history repeating itself. There is something deeply poetic about the repetition of one's own life through a child, a reaffirmation of the past transformed into the present.

Rosie burst into my thoughts, 'Mum, I have even bigger news.'

'My goodness! What can that be?'

'It is so so good Mum. How can I tell you? I met my one daughter at last after so many years. You remember the oldest girl, Faith? She is so large now; I can't believe it is her. She is so fat, she can't even move properly. But she is so kind, Mum.'

'Wow. Amazing, Rosie.' My heart swells in happiness for her. 'How fantastic. How did you find her?'

'She came to find me, Mum. You know my two sisters have died very quickly, one after the other. Maybe it was this Covid thing. I don't know what happened to them.'

'Oh dear, I'm so sorry, Rosie. I didn't even know you had sisters, as they never helped you.'

'It is true, Mum. I never told you about my sisters as they were like dead to me. When they died, then the family all needed me to go to the funeral because now I am the oldest in the family that is still alive. I have to attend the funeral, or the ancestors will be offended. If I don't come, the family are very scared they will be cursed and that I can cause trouble for them all with the ancestors. So, when Faith told me this, I went with her to the funeral of my sister. I saw everyone. Even they welcomed me. Some of my children were there. You can't believe it, Mum. It was so good to be with my people again after 40 years.'

'I'm so happy for you Rosie.' I was almost sobbing with relief for her, imagining her joy. 'Do tell me about everyone. How is Kariuki, and how old are his twins now?'

'Kariuki is happier. I think he got a new wife. For five years he has not talked to me, but I think maybe it is better now. You know he even sent me a little money. I think I will see him soon.'

'What about your other daughter, Mabel?'

'Well, she is still a problem to me. She was not there at the funeral because he has taken the side of my husband and still doesn't care about me. Also, the oldest boy, Ezekiah, he also didn't come to pay his respects to my family. They can't talk to me because they are close to their father. So, I don't worry about them.

'What about the smallest boy, Tomas? I have heard nothing about him.'

'Mum, everyone says that he's a very nice kind man, but Tomas is very, very poor. You remember, he didn't get any training when he left school. I had left the family by then and could not pay for him to have some training. Ezekiah and Joseph were trained as *fundis*, and Kariuki did that course for tourism. But poor Tomas, he has no skills, so he is there just farming.'

'At least he has the farmland, Rosie. I am so happy for you, what a wonderful reunion. Now you are the matriarch of the family, they have some respect for you at last. Perhaps the family will look after you now.'

'I am happy to meet Faith after all this time. You know, Mum, the best thing? Her first born is a daughter, who is now 20 years old. Faith named her after me, she is called Rosie. She is very, very clever. So smart, you can't believe it. She is learning to be a teacher. The first person in our family to go to university.'

'Wow, that is so great! A granddaughter with your name and your brains.'

'Little Rosie wants to help her mother and she wants to meet me. My daughter even said, 'Maybe we can get a place together. She can't live alone as she has diabetes.'

I fell into a reverie and forgot to answer her. At last, out of her six children and numerous grandchildren, one person has succeeded in breaking through the spiral of poverty and family dysfunction.

The fact that Faith named her first daughter after her mother shows how hurt she was by the breakup of their family. She must have missed her mother dreadfully. Faith had to be the mother to her other siblings in Rosie's absence. Now history has gone full circle and she wants her mother back to care for her.

'Mum are you there? Can you hear me still?'

'I am here, Rosie. I'm just thinking about the good news. I'm so happy for you.'

'And also, Mum, there is more good news. I think I will get together with my son Joseph soon. Faith told me he is having big problems, and she is so worried about him. He is becoming a drunkard like his father. You know he is a carpenter now and he lives near Tigoni. He has five children, all in school. The oldest boy is also very bright like little Rosie, but he had to leave school early, because Joseph can't afford the school fees for him to continue. So, Faith says he is drinking because he is so depressed. Like Kimendi did. That is what our men do when they have problems. Faith says I must go and talk to him.'

'Rosie, I'm sure that you will be able to help him a lot.'

'Mum, you know that both Wendy and Tristan have sent me some money. So, I can give him this money for the school fees, and it will help him to stop worrying. He will stop drinking if I tell him that I have some money to help. You know in our culture, if you have money, the family always welcomes you. It's just when you have nothing to give them, they leave you because you can't help.'

I remember how charming her husband was in the beginning when she had our support, and she was the main breadwinner. Then how powerless she became when we left Kenya, and none of her children cared about her. I thought of Mrs. H-P's words so long ago when I was so naïvely impressed by traditional ways. Sadly, and I hate to have to admit it, but Rosie's story has proved her characterisation of the Kikuyu correct. By ignoring her warning and employing Rosie, I had been the unwitting instrument in her destruction.

'Rosie, there is one thing you must do.'

'What is that Mum?'

'Get rid of the photos of Wendy, Charlie and Tristan. Please, Rosie, just burn those pictures. You don't need them now. At last, you have a chance to get back with your own family. Forget about my kids. Your grandchildren don't want to see the pictures of the little white kids on their grandmother's wall. Don't tell them you and I are still in touch. It was our friendship that led to all the problems in your family. We took you away from them.'

There was a long silence. I saw Rosie on the screen of the cell phone, thinking hard, pursing her lips forward as she always does when she concentrates.

Then she said softly, 'You are right, Mum. I will burn the photos. The photos of your children made me happy for many years when my own children did not want me. I wanted to believe Tristan, Charlie and Wendy were my only children, but I don't need the photos now because Tristan has sent me lots of pictures of his children on my phone.'

'You know what, Rosie? Now that you have at least one loyal daughter, and a clever granddaughter. We can end our story.'

'I have my own children, and a granddaughter called Rosie. I am alright.'

> **'Everything will be alright in the end.**
> **If it's not all right, then it isn't yet the end.'**

Epilogue

White Africans

I am sitting on our rooftop balcony in the morning sun, looking out over False Bay to the distant mountains on the other side of the sea. I take a sip of my coffee and revel in the sight of a flock of sugar birds swooping from one giant protea bush to another with their long tails blowing in the wind. Orange-breasted sunbirds flash their brilliant colours between the crimson aloes along the path that leads directly onto the mountain, towering above us. Breakfast outside is the finest hour of the day, I think to myself, as I warm my face in the winter sun.

After the harsh environments we have encountered in our working life, Simon's Town, at the very tip of Africa, on a peninsula that dangles provocatively between the Indian and the Atlantic Ocean, is a constant delight, a paradise rich with natural beauty. Below me, the sea crashes on the little beach where penguins breed in their thousands all year round. The waters are some of the most pristine on earth, with an underwater forest of kelp which is home to sharks, seals and dolphins. Southern Right whales come to give birth in our tranquil bay, and Sunfish bask in the naval port. Living near the Cape Point Nature Reserve, we are visited by all manner of wild animals: porcupines and mongoose are common, with the occasional caracal. The worst problem in our retirement is the troop of urbanised baboons who invade our homes regularly. Snakes are a constant danger but as our grandson reminded me, 'There are good snakes and bad snakes.' That also applies to people.

Around the iconic Table Mountain, a thin band of green suburbs houses people like me. The beauty and sophistication of these properties do not represent the reality of the bulk of the population who live on the margins of society in the shack lands of the informal settlements which stretch forever on the flat coastal plain between the Indian and the Atlantic Ocean. Across the bay from where we live, a heavy blanket of smoke hangs over the Cape Flats, where thousands of women just like Rosie still live in a shack eking out an existence, living hand to mouth taking whatever employment they can find. The Xhosa stream in from the Eastern Cape, Zulus from KwaZulu Natal, Twana and Venda from the north, and beyond the border, refugees from Zimbabwe coming to find a job. There are Nigerians and Somalis, Kenyans and Ugandans, French speakers from the Congo and North Africa. So many people both black and white have landed up here to find a better life. But so many get no further than the shack-land on the other side of the bay.

When I was a young mother, the close relationship that I established with Rosie was unusual given the disparity of power that existed between the two races in that era. Now when I see our own children trying to find this same bond with those that care for their children, I understand at last that the sisterhood we shared was not in fact unique at all. It is a universal story as long as the society condones it. Raising children alone is difficult. Given the opportunity, women often share the maternal joys of their children which can transcend the barriers of culture, class, education and race. It is perhaps one of the most positive instincts in our wondrous female nature that through an instinctive love of children, mothers across very different strata develop the deepest bonds of sisterhood. This silent sharing is not often acknowledged and seldom documented but it is there.

When Anthony and I married in 1978 we left our parents in South Africa, where the races could not meet, and went to explore the dark continent to the north of us way out of their reach. We left the country where we were brought up, because we did not want our own children to grow up in an apartheid system of separate development of the races and the consequent oppression of the majority who were black, by a privileged minority of whites. At that time South Africa was the pariah of the world, ruled by an authoritarian right-wing government of nationalists and Nelson Mandela and other freedom fighters trying to challenge the system were in jail. Many of us were consumed by the guilt of our forefathers.

Before 1994, when Mandela became the first black President, we were ashamed of calling ourselves South African. To get a work permit in the rest of Africa we had to hide our true identity and white South Africans were presumed to be racist and ostracised by the rest of Africa. Now I look at my younger self and realise how my effort to help Rosie was a naïve effort to compensate for the historical injustices of our tribe, to prove to myself, if no one else, that women across the great racial divide could care for each other. There is no shame in being South African now.

Today, in 2022, the government is representative of the people, our elections are free and fair, and despite endemic corruption which resulted in state capture by an elite, we have a constitution which is the envy of Africa with regard to women's rights. Our country is one of the most progressive of the emerging middle-income states in Africa, with a better growth rate than so-called first world countries in Europe. We have a free press which allows all shades of political rhetoric. Systemic racial discrimination against blacks has not been experienced by the 'born free' generation who are now taking over the country from the first generation who struggled for such a freedom. Although corruption and mismanagement are endemic in South Africa, ours is the most sophisticated country in the continent the economic powerhouse of sub-Saharan Africa. When we are frustrated by present day politics, we should look back to where we have come from in order to feel more positive about the future.

Kenya too, is slowly shedding the tribalism that has undermined its development. There has just been an election in Kenya and for the first time it seems that it has been free, and perhaps fair - at last democracy is beginning to get beyond traditional tribal divisions. The new President, William Rutu, has beaten the elderly Luo candidate, Raila Odinga who was trying for the seventh time to get into power supported by the previous President Uhuru Kenyatta son of the first Kikuyu President of Kenya. Ruto convinced the voters by his platform of non-tribalism, saying "I may be the son of a nobody, but I promise to make Kenya the country of everybody." If the new generation has broken with the traditional default of voting across tribal lines, there is hope for the country. People like Rosie may finally be primarily Kenyan rather than be defined as Kikuyu more than anything else.

In Lamu, the more virulent strain of religious fundamentalism has subsided and almost two decades after the terror of Al Shebab, the little fishing village of Shela is booming again, and tourists are back on the elegant balcony of the hotel. The old order based on elites holding onto power on the basis of tribe, race or religion appears to be changing. The breeze of democracy is slowly blowing across Africa, as the generation rolls over.

Much of what I have written in our story may not seem particularly ground-breaking to the Born Free generation and those that followed them the Millennials. Today thousands of South Africans work north of the 'great, grey, green, greasy Limpopo River', as Kipling once described the boundary between white and black Africa. In the fast-modernising independent states of Africa, there is infinite demand for technical expertise and many South Africans have made their fortunes there, providing luxuries from 'down south' for a fast-growing African middle class. People like me, brought up in Africa, can now claim without shame to be what we are: white South Africans.

Glossary

Unless otherwise stated all words in this Glossary are Kiswahili, the official language of Kenya.

abaya black over coat worn by Orthodox Muslim women in the Middle East
Allahu Akbar God is greater - an expression of gratitude (Arabic)
'Allahu Akbar ašhadu ʾanla ilāha illal-Lāh, wa ʾašhadu ʾanna muḥammadan rasūlul-Lāh' is the Shahada, the testimony of faith for a Muslim meaning 'I bear witness that there is no deity (none truly to be worshipped) but, Allah, and I bear witness that Muhammad is the messenger of Allah.'
asante thank you
asante sana thank you very much
askari watchman
ayah name for a nanny (Indian)
banda small hut
barraza the entrance porch
bei gani? How much?
boers farmers (Afrikaans)
bon good (French)
bui bui A large flowing black overgarment
bwana boss / man of the house
chai tea (Indian)
chakula food
chevda a spicy snack (Indian)
chumvi salt
dawa medicine
dhow fishermen's wooden boats on the Kenyan coast
duka corner shop

fundi skilled artisan

fungua open

Giriama the name of a tribe living north of Mombasa

habari garni? How are you?

habari siku nyingi long time no see

hakuna matata no problem

hapana no

hapana mzuri not good

harambee 'Let's pull together' - a community fundraising event

Hodi! Hodi! 'knock! knock!' called out by visitors before entering

inshallah God (Allah) willing

imam: Muslim priest/teacher

jambo! hello!

Jino lako nani? What is your name?

kali hot / spicy

kapenta *a* type of small fish

kanga/s 2-metre length printed cotton sarong used by women

kanzu white kaftan worn by Muslim men

karibu sana most welcome

kofia embroidered white hat worn by Muslim men

Kikoy Two metre length of women cotton used as a sarong usually by men

Kikuyu the name of the largest tribe in Kenya (and name of a type of grass)

Kili an abbreviation of Mt. Kilimanjaro

Kiswahili the main language of Kenya

konyagi Kenyan clear alcohol like gin

Koobi Fora the name of an archaeological site

Kusii the name of the south wind on East African coast

Kuja hapa! Come here!

kwa heri goodbye

Luo the name of a large tribe in western Kenya

Luya the name of a small offshoot of the Luo tribe

madafu green coconut juice

madaka entrance porch

mama a mother

Maasai a tribe of pastoralists in northern Kenya

Maasai Mara the name of a game reserve in Kenya

mbaya sana very bad

maji safi clean water

maji mbaya bad water

makuti palm thatch

matatu / matatus privately owned minibuses

Mau Mau the name of the Kikuyu uprising of 1952-1956

mbu mosquitoes, also a euphemism for prostitutes

Memsahib 'Madam' (formal way used to address the lady of the house)

mlango a door

miraa a narcotic twig that is chewed as a stimulant

moran or il-murran age set of boys 12 and 25 years initiated together

moto fire / hot

mpishi cook

muezzin singer of the Islamic call to prayer

Mungu God

mzee grandfather/ old man

mzuri good

mzuri sana very good

mzungu/ wazungu white person/s (man or woman)

mzuri sana very good.

nyama choma roast meat

ndiyo yes

n'anga traditional healer, derogatory term 'witch doctors'

oeuvre work of art (French)

Orma the name of a Nilotic tribe in Northeast Kenya

Oroma the name of a tribe in southern Somalia

panga machete or hatchet

papai the name of a fruit sometimes known as pawpaw

pole sana apologies / I am very sorry

Qur'an Muslim Holy Book (Arabic)

sana very

sasa immediately

siafu army or safari ants

sikumi wiki wild spinach

Shahada Muslim testimony see above 'Allahu Akbar ašhadu...'

shamba/s cultivated fields

shifta bandits from Oroma tribe in Somali terrorizing Northeast Kenya

soda all fizzy drinks (coke, fanta, sprite, tonic, cream soda)

Swahili name of the coastal people of Kenya

tafadhali please

toto/watoto child / children

tutaonana see you soon

Turkana the name of a pastoralist tribe living in northwest Kenya

ugali stiff maize porridge, the staple diet of most Kenyans

veldskoen (Afrikaans) suede safari boot commonly used in South Africa

wageni guests / visitors

watu indigenous or common people

watoto children

wazungu white people

Acknowledgements

As this story is based on actual events, we would like to acknowledge those who have unwittingly been part of this drama, including all the people of Kenya with whom we have interacted, and who have supported us over the years. We would like to thank especially the wonderful people of Lamu for giving us the chance to live on their island, and to both my own and Rosie's children and grandchildren. May they forgive any omissions or misrepresentations we have may have made.

Unless they have specifically asked to use their real names, all living characters appearing in this story have been given fictitious names, to protect their privacy, and any similarity to them is coincidental. Organisations and enterprises have also been given fictitious names.

To honour the memory of the deceased characters depicted in the book, we have kept their real names for posterity to remember them:

Missionaries and Development Professionals for their selfless dedication to African communities

- Sr. Agnes, the Doctor of Wema Mission in Lower Tana, murdered in 1989.
- Father Tieland of Mbita Mission on Lake Victoria.
- Margaret Mwangola, (Mama Gola) Founder/Executive Director of Kenya Water for Health Organisation, our mentor who taught us so much about community development, and who died in 2016.

Doctors both buried in Shela, Lamu Island:

- Dr. Anne Spoerry, the famous Flying Doctor of AMREF, who 'probably saved more lives than any other individual in East Africa – if not the whole continent,' according to the anthropologist Dr. Richard Leakey, who is also mentioned in the story.
- Dr. George Feegan, famous for his revolutionary treatment of varicose veins, who died in 2007.

Our mothers, both of them strong and inspirational matriarchs who encouraged me to write:

- Virginia's mother, Wendy (Babushka) who died on the 2nd August 2016,
- Anthony's mother Angela who died on 19th December 2020.

All place names are realistic, the events are based on real situations, although some of the dates have been tweaked to enable a better flow of the storyline.

On a professional level, my gratitude to Richard Beynon and Jo-Anne Richards of 'All About Writing' for guiding me through the tricks of non-academic writing and for their professional editing of our story.

Grateful thanks to my family who have helped to encourage and advise me as I struggled to deliver this story: my dear husband Anthony who has given me the emotional support to complete this process, and the three children for agreeing to allow their lives to go public. A special recognition of Wendy who cared for Rosie when we almost lost her, and as recounted in this book seeded the idea of this project.

Also hugely appreciated are my dear friends, firstly my honorary sister Miranda Forshaw who gave me her honest assessment which has led to a much better product, and then to my two stalwarts who have given so much of their time to help me finalise the manuscript: Diana Leighton Morris for editing of the numerous drafts, and Susan Abraham who perfected the photos. Also of course, thanks to Anthony for invaluable proof reading over and over again with such patience and for his informed advice. Thank you for this adventure.

My thanks most of all to Rosie for her private letters to me which she bravely allowing to be published.

I quote the words of Kathryn Stockett whose protagonist's mother in 'The Help' said of her nanny:

'They say it's like true love, good help. You only get one in a lifetime.'

Printed in the United States
by Baker & Taylor Publisher Services